DASH DIET
COOKBOOK

1000-DAYS HEALTHY HEART RECIPES

to Naturally Reduce Blood Pressure and Improve

Your Health Without Sacrificing Taste

SAMANTHA DAVIS

TABLE OF CONTENTS

164. Chicken Squash Soup
165. Veggie and Beef Soup
166. Collard, Sweet Potato and Pea Soup
167. Bean Soup
168. Brown Rice and Chicken Soup
169. Broccoli Soup
170. Hearty Ginger Soup
171. Tasty Tofu and Mushroom Soup
172. Ingenious Eggplant Soup
173. Loving Cauliflower Soup
174. Garlic and Lemon Soup
175. Cucumber Soup
176. Vegetable Pasta Soup
177. Easy Black-Bean Soup
178. Curried Carrot Soup
179. Chicken Noodle Soup
180. Chicken and Veggie Soup
181. Sweet Potato & Lentil Soup
182. Curried Squash, Lentil & Coconut Soup
183. Courgette, Pea & Pesto Soup
184. Cauliflower Carrot Soup
185. Mom's Bean Soup
186. Chicken And Spring Vegetable Soup
187. Sweet Potato, Collard, And Black-Eyed Pea Soup
188. Green Beans Soup
189. Turkey Soup
190. Potato and Carrot "Impeccable" Soup
191. Meticulous Butternut Squash Soup
192. Omnipotent Organic Chicken Thigh Soup
193. Very Low Carb Ham and Cabbage Bowl
194. Cabbage and Leek Soup
195. Moroccan Sweet Potato Soup
196. Potato Soup
197. Split Pea Cream Soup
198. Italian Veggie Soup
199. Carrot Ginger Soup with Spinach and Chicken
200. Taco Soup
201. Ground Beef Soup with Tomatoes
202. Chipotle Squash Soup
203. Kale Verde
204. Escarole with Bean Soup
205. Roasted Garlic Soup
206. Roasted Carrot Soup
207. Golden Mushroom Soup
208. Butternut Squash Soup
209. Black Bean Soup
210. Chicken & Rice Soup
211. Tom Kha Gai
212. Chicken Corn Chowder
213. Turkey Ginger Soup

POULTRY
214. Parmesan and Chicken Spaghetti Squash
215. Apricot Chicken
216. Oven-Fried Chicken Breasts
217. Rosemary Roasted Chicken
218. Artichoke and Spinach Chicken
219. Pumpkin and Black Beans Chicken
220. Chicken Thighs and Apples Mix
221. Thai Chicken Thighs
222. Falling "Off" The Bone Chicken
223. Feisty Chicken Porridge
224. The Ultimate Faux-Tisserie Chicken
225. Oregano Chicken Thighs
226. Pesto Chicken Breasts with Summer Squash
227. Chicken, Tomato and Green Beans
228. Chicken Tortillas
229. Chicken Tikka
230. Honey Spiced Cajun Chicken
231. Italian Chicken
232. Lemon-Parsley Chicken Breast
233. Chicken Rolls with Pesto
234. Epic Mango Chicken
235. Chicken and Cabbage Platter
236. Hearty Chicken Liver Stew
237. Chicken Quesadilla
238. Mustard Chicken
239. Chicken and Carrot Stew
240. The Delish Turkey Wrap
241. Zucchini Zoodles with Chicken and Basil
242. Duck with Cucumber and Carrots
243. Parmesan Baked Chicken
244. Buffalo Chicken Lettuce Wraps
245. Thai Chicken Pasta
246. Paprika Baked Chicken Breasts
247. Chicken Lettuce Wraps
248. White Wine Garlic Chicken
249. Turkey Medallions
250. Walnut Pesto Chicken Penne
251. Green Chicken and Rice Bowl
252. Creamy Turkey Mix
253. Turkey and Onion Mix
254. Balsamic Chicken
255. Coconut Chicken and Olives
256. Turkey and Peach
257. Paprika Chicken and Spinach
258. Chicken and Tomatoes Mix

INTRODUCTION

What is the DASH Diet?
There are now so many diets that you can hardly count them anymore. You have probably already lost track and are wondering which diet is the best for achieving your goals. You have probably already tried one or the other method to get to grips with your hip gold. They should all be promising, from the cabbage soup diet to the pineapple diet. They aren't always due of their one-sidedness. Many individuals quit up after only a few days since they can't see the specific meal they're meant to eat in large quantities. Who would want to eat pea soup every day!?

The pounds do drop swiftly on these 'crash diets.' However, you merely lose water at first. If your usual eating habits are resumed after diet, the yo-yo effect starts, and you acquire again weight. You went to such lengths. You rationed your diet and only ate the approved foods after that. You've gained even more weight! Isn't that inequitable?

On the contrary, the DASH diet is straightforward since it is diverse, it enables you to fast lose weight and enhances your health. It is, in essence, a method of eating rather than another trendy diet.

The DASH diet is still relatively unfamiliar in the United States. It won the 'Best Diet' title for the first time in 2013. In the interim, it has already been named the greatest diet or nutritional technique seven times. In 2018, DASH was awarded this honor once more.

The diet has been re-ranked by US News & World Report. A group of dietitians, doctors, and nutritionists evaluated and ranked 40 various nutritional approaches, and the DASH diet was named the 'best general diet' once again. Weight-loss programs like Weight Watchers and the Dukan Diet were also investigated.

DASH was created to treat high blood pressure, or hypertension, but it turns out that many other health issues, such as being overweight, developing diabetes, and many of the other difficulties we've already talked about, are all linked. They share a same cause, at least in part, at their core.

Exercise is essential for lowering blood pressure since it aids in weight loss and maintains a healthy heart. Muscle strength can aid in the regulation of blood pressure and the maintenance of a healthy weight. The more you work out, the better. You must make a daily commitment to increase your physical activity.

The food you eat is also a matter to be considered, as it impacts your health significantly. If you change your dietary habits, you'll see a difference in your overall health, including your risk of heart disease. Blood pressure can be controlled with the use of healthy diets. That is why the DASH Diet is extensively promoted in the United States, as it has been shown to minimize the majority of metabolic risks in both men and women. The DASH diet is an effective method for preventing and treating hypertension in a wide range of people, particularly those who are at risk of developing hypertension and its complications.

You will achieve your goal if you persevere and trust in yourself. Prepare to welcome the new you. I have faith in you. So, get started today and DASH your way to a healthier life.

WHY DASH DIET?

What Exactly Does DASH Stand For?

Dietary Approach to Stop Hypertension,' or DASH, is a German term that translates as "nutritional model against excessive blood pressure" .The diet is not only good for controlling high blood pressure, but it can also help you lose weight. Although slender people can have high blood pressure, being overweight is the most common cause. This diet is recommended by the German Hypertension League, a society for patients with high blood pressure. However, it also aids in the maintenance of a healthy body weight.

DASH Was Created by Who?

A group of professionals came up with the DASH approach. The National Heart, Lung, and Blood Institute of the United States was part in the research. Originally, the approach was not intended to be used for weight loss, but rather to treat excessive blood pressure. The Weight Loss is just a bonus that appear when someone follow the diet properly, eating the right quality and quantity of food having

What is the DASH Diet and How Does It Work?

You will be instructed to consume meals that are particularly low in calories as part of the diet modification. You will lose weight more quickly as a result of this. Simultaneously, you will consume extremely little salt. Even though you can't believe it right now, the foods are still spicy and tasty.

You're probably asking why you should eliminate salt from your diet. Quite simply. In the body, salt binds water. As a result, it causes water retention, which raises blood pressure. Herbs and onions are utilized as salt substitutes, and they add a kick to many meals. Furthermore, you will never be permitted to go hungry and will be required to eat a substantial amount of food. Despite the fact that salt is listed as an ingredient in the following recipes, make an effort to gradually minimize the amount of salt used.

Do you have a strong need for sweet, salty, fatty, or rapid food? With the feeding strategy, this will go gone. Cravings are always triggered by a shortage of something in the body. The diet provides everything the body requires. This is an example of a nutrition plan:

- Whole grain products: 5-8 servings daily. One serving corresponds to a slice of bread or a small bowl of muesli.
- Vegetables: 4-5 servings per day. There is half a cup of cooked vegetables Nutrition.
- Fruit: 2-4 servings daily. One medium-sized apple is equivalent to one serving.
- Low-fat dairy products: 2-3 servings per day. One cup of yoghurt or 250 ml of milk equals one serving.
- Lean meat: up to 2-3 servings daily. One portion corresponds to a maximum of 100 g.
- Nuts and legumes: 4-5 servings per week. For nuts, one serving corresponds to 40 g, seeds 1 tbsp, beans to half a cup of uncooked beans.
- Fats and oils: 1-3 servings daily. One teaspoon of oil, one teaspoon of margarine or two tablespoons of salad dressing correspond to one serving.
- Sweets and sugary drinks: 5 servings per week. 250 ml lemonade or a tablespoon of sugar correspond to one serving.

What Are the Benefits of this Diet?

High blood pressure is caused by many different factors like dietary intake, arteriosclerosis, atherosclerosis, kidney disease, but also genetic predisposition. People with blood pressure readings exceeding 140/90 mmHg are more likely to have a heart attack or stroke, as well as develop vascular disease. Blood pressure can be reduced without medication by following the diet. Of course, this is a far healthier way for you to manage your high blood pressure. Drugs, after all, usually have side effects.

Within 8 weeks, blood pressure can be decreased by roughly 10/5 mmHg with this nutritious strategy. This is consistent with the effects of several antihypertensive medications. Furthermore, the diet lowers blood lipid levels. Too high blood lipid levels raise the risk of heart attack and stroke, as well as cardiovascular and vascular illnesses. The DASH Diet can both prevent and cure certain disorders. At the same time, because the quantity of salt in the daily diet is lowered, the risk of developing diabetes is reduced, and kidney function improves.

This diet has earned the title of best general diet. There are no inadequacies with this diet, which is not always the case with crash diets. The diet is well-balanced and beneficial to one's health. A healthy diet, such as DASH, is a must if you want to feel healthy and live well.

BENEFITS OF DASH DIET

We now understand what the DASH diet is and some of the advantages that make it worthwhile to incorporate into your daily routine, but let's dig a little deeper.

High Blood Pressure Prevention and Treatment

Thousands of people in the United States are using blood pressure medication that may be avoided with a healthy diet modification. The DASH diet allows you to make that transition in a healthy way. Lower blood pressure reduces the risk of developing ailments such as heart disease, strokes, kidney disease, and heart attacks. According to the National Institutes of Health, "if adults with high blood pressure followed the DASH diet exactly for ten years, they could avert roughly 400,000 deaths from cardiovascular disease." The DASH diet has the potential to significantly enhance our population's health and safety.

Assist in the Treatment and Prevention of Metabolic Syndrome

Blood pressure, blood sugar, triglycerides, bad cholesterol, and insulin resistance are all reduced by the DASH diet. For people suffering from metabolic syndrome, obesity, or type 2 diabetes, this is a dream come true. For people with metabolic syndrome, you'll notice changes in your blood pressure points and systolic pressure in just a few weeks. In addition, the DASH diet has been shown to lower the risk of colorectal cancer. This diet has been shown to be a life-saving remedy for a variety of health issues that people face on a daily basis.

Getting in Shape

Starting the DASH diet doesn't have to be about losing weight. If you're wanting to lose weight, though, the diet may be beneficial. Because the diet already avoids things that cause weight gain, such as sweets and red meat, you may notice that you lose weight when you first start it. Reduce the quantity of poultry and fish in your diet and increase the number of vegetables in your diet if you want to lose weight in a healthy way. Moreover, despite being taught that three meals a day is the golden rule, eating a variety of meals throughout the day allows your metabolism to work smarter, not harder, to help you lose weight.

Immune System Strengthening

Foods high in antioxidants is included in the DASH diet. These dietary groups assist your body in producing antioxidants to protect your cells from free radicals. Antioxidants can help you avoid cancer, heart disease, and other serious diseases by boosting your immune system and keeping you safe. This is especially crucial now that flu season is approaching.

WHAT TO EAT AND WHAT TO AVOID?

Let's look at which items you can eat on the diet and which you should avoid. Throughout the day, we'll look at portion sizes for healthy DASH diet meals. Remember that the DASH diet is a lifestyle adjustment, so don't make drastic changes to your diet.

Foods to Consume

To begin, grains are an important part of the DASH diet. Pasta, rice, cereal, and bread are examples. Grains should make up the majority of your diet, with 6-8 servings recommended. This varies by individual, but for a 2,000-calorie diet, this is a reasonable number of servings. A slice of whole wheat bread, half a cup of cooked pasta or rice, or one ounce of dry cereal can all be counted as one serving.

Vegetables are the next largest food group. 4-5 servings of veggies should be consumed throughout the day for a 2,000-calorie diet. Vegetables high in fiber and Vitamins are beneficial to the DASH diet. Combining different colored vegetables on your plate will ensure that your plate is as colorful as possible. Make sure to incorporate leafy greens in your diet for a boost of iron and protein. One serving of cooked or raw vegetables is half a cup, while one serving of leafy greens is an entire cup.

Fruits are next, and they should be consumed in the same quantity as vegetables. This equates to 4-5 servings of delectable fruit. Fruits are beneficial to the DASH diet because they include fiber, potassium, magnesium, and other essential Vitamins and minerals. Eat a broad variety of fruits, and don't peel the skin off some of your favorite fruits, such as apples, to increase your fiber intake. Fiber nutrients are abundant in the skin.

In addition to fruits and vegetables, nuts, seeds, and legumes should be ingested. Attempt to consume 4-5 servings of these nutrient-dense meals every day. Protein, potassium, magnesium, fiber, phytochemicals, and other nutrients are all found in them. To meet these serving requirements, include a variety of beans, seeds, and nuts in your diet.

Low-fat or fat-free dairy products should account for only two to three servings of your daily diet. Milk, cheese, and yogurt are all examples of this. When purchasing these items, we emphasize that they should be low in fat or fat-free. Dairy is included in the DASH diet to increase calcium, protein, and Vitamin D levels, not to increase calories or fat.

On the DASH diet, you can have up to 6 one-ounce servings of poultry or fish each day. However, you should attempt to consume mostly vegetables and to substitute vegetables for meat in your meals. If you must eat meat, season it lightly with salt and remove the skin before eating. Choose fish that are high in omega-3 fatty acids while eating fish. This can include fish such as salmon, which are high in omega-3 fatty acids and are good for your heart.

Foods to Avoid

Let's look at what foods should be avoided on the DASH diet now that we know what foods are good to eat on the DASH diet and how many servings of each food group we should consume. Avoid foods that are heavy in sugar, fat, or salt in general.

The DASH diet does not include sweets. It is suggested that you consume no more than 5 servings of sweets per week. Again, the DASH diet is not about eliminating items you enjoy, but rather about consuming them in moderation. Therefore, the DASH diet allows you to indulge in these "cheat" items in tiny doses throughout the week.

It has been proved that alcohol raises blood pressure. It is suggested that ladies consume no more than one drink per day, while males consume no more than two per day. The best option is to fully abstain from alcohol, although we recognize that a drink now and again is OK. Keep alcohol outside the house if you find yourself drinking a bit more than you should each night. This way, you can enjoy it on a night out without having to get it out of the fridge.

With the DASH diet, red meat should be avoided or consumed in moderation. Red meat is heavy in fat and sodium, both of which are detrimental to the DASH diet. If you want to consume meat, choose for chicken or lean pork.

Heavy whipping cream and 2 percent milk are full-fat dairy products that should be avoided. This increases the number of fat servings you consume every day, and in order to stick to the DASH diet, you must count your servings carefully.

Be cautious of various beverages. Many beverages, such as soda, contain a lot of sugar and artificial sweeteners. Instead of drinking them, obtain your sugar servings from full foods. Rather than drinking your calories, eat them.

Fast food should be avoided since the manufacturing of the meal typically results in high salt levels. Chips, pizza, and other unhealthy treats fall under this category. They can also cover hidden sugars added to improve the taste of the dish, but the essential nutrients are lost.

The DASH diet emphasizes mindful eating. You are in charge of selecting foods that will nourish and energize you rather than deplete you.

THE DASH DIET LIFESTYLE

ith a long-term approach to eating, moving, and living, we can reach health and wellness. Consider the DASH diet to be a way of life; it is a simple, practical eating plan that may be followed for a long time. Fiber-rich fruits and vegetables, healthy fats, and lean protein will keep you full and content, while regular physical exercise and enough sleep will keep you awake and energetic, all of which contribute to a healthy mind and body.

Habits of Eating

It is not necessary to make severe lifestyle or dietary modifications to follow the DASH diet. Consider your long-term objectives and begin with tiny, attainable adjustments that work for you. Try:

- Going vegan for a meal or two every week
- Snacking on a handful of nuts instead of chips and crackers
- Filling at least half your plate with plant-based foods
- Experimenting with herbs and spices
- Having fruit for dessert
- Eating seasonally and locally, especially if you have access to a farmers' market

Exercise

"Assume the vertical," or, in other words, get up, is one of my favorite sayings. Physical activity is essential for good health and wellness, and it is an integral part of the Mediterranean way of life. Walking, climbing stairs, and performing yoga are all examples of physical activity. To reduce weight, you don't have to run a marathon or take tough spinning classes. Rather, strive for consistency by engaging in at least an hour of physical exercise five days a week. Consider standing up for 5 to 10 minutes every 45 minutes if you spend a lot of time sitting due to work or other responsibilities. Are you looking for extra motivation to exercise? Consider the following

- Exercise fights disease
- Exercise relieves chronic pain
- Exercise aids weight loss
- Exercise improves mood
- Exercise increases energy
- Exercise increases sex desire
- Exercise improves sleep

Whatever form of exercise you select, the main line is that being as active as possible throughout the week promotes physical and mental well-being.

Sleep

I adore sleeping! Many of us place sleep low on our priority list because of today's fast-paced lives and excessive responsibilities, yet sleep is critical for general health and wellness. Sleep deprivation causes a host of physical concerns, including heart disease, obesity, depression, chronic stress, and cognitive impairments, in addition to making you weary and grumpy.

The number of hours you sleep as well as the quality of your sleep are both critical. Aim for seven to nine hours of sleep each night and adopt excellent sleeping habits, such as:

- Having a regular bedtime
- Exercising frequently
- Avoiding stimulants such as caffeine around night
- Avoiding alcohol before bedtime

Following the DASH diet can also help you get a good night's sleep. Seafood, dairy, almonds, beans, and dark leafy greens are some of the items that might help you sleep better. These foods offer minerals including tryptophan, calcium, folate, and magnesium, which assist to raise serotonin and melatonin levels and promote improved sleep quality. Getting your sleep also contributes to a healthy lifestyle!

BREAKFAST AND SMOOTHIES

1. Apple and Spice Oatmeal

Preparation: 5 minutes   **Cooking: 9 minutes**   **Servings: 1**

Ingredients

- *1 sweet apple, such as Gala, peeled, cored, and cut into ½ -inch dice*
- *2/3 cup water*
- *1/3 cup old-fashioned (rolled) oats*
- *Pinch of ground cinnamon*
- *Pinch of freshly grated nutmeg*
- *A few grains of kosher salt*
- *½ cup fat-free milk, for serving*

Directions

1. In a small saucepan, mix the water, apple, oatmeal, nutmeg, cinnamon, and salt. Bring to a boil over medium heat, reduce heat to low, and cover.
2. Cook over low heat until oats are tender, about 4 minutes.
3. Microwave: In a 1-liter microwave-safe bowl, combine the apple, water, oatmeal, cinnamon, nutmeg, and salt. You should cover it and microwave on high power until oats are tender, about 4 minutes.
4. Uncover carefully, mix, and let stand 1 minute.
5. Transfer the oatmeal to a bowl, pour in the milk, and serve.

Nutrition: Calories 190, Carbohydrates 39g, Protein 5g, Fat 2g, Sodium 52 mg

2. Apple Oats

Preparation: 10 minutes   **Cooking: 7 minutes**   **Servings: 2**

Ingredients

- *2 apples, cored, peeled, and cubed*
- *1 cup gluten-free oats*
- *1 ½ cups of water*
- *1 ½ cups of almond milk*
- *2 tbsp. swerve*
- *2 tbsp. almond butter*
- *½ tsp. cinnamon powder*
- *1 tbsp flax seed, ground*
- *Cooking spray*

Directions

1. With cooking spray, grease a slow cooker and toss the oat with the water and other ingredients inside. Stir a little and simmer for 7 minutes.
2. Divide into bowls and serve for breakfast.

Nutrition: Calories 140, Carbohydrates 28g, Protein 5g, Fat 4g, Sodium 44mg

3. Apple-Cinnamon Baked Oatmeal

Preparation: 10 minutes   **Servings: 2**

Ingredients

- *2 cups steel-cut oats*
- *8 cups of water*
- *1 tsp. cinnamon*
- *1/2 tsp. allspice*
- *1/2 tsp. nutmeg*
- *1/4 cup brown sugar*
- *1 tsp. vanilla extract*
- *2 apples, diced*
- *1 cup raisins*
- *1/2 cup unsalted, roasted walnuts, chopped*

Directions

1. Spray the cooker with non-stick cooking spray.
2. Add all the ingredients to the cooker except the nuts. Mix well to combine.
3. Put the cooker on low heat for 30 minutes. Serve garnished with chopped walnuts.

Nutrition: Calories 312, Carbohydrates 60g, Protein 9g, Fat 7g, Sodium 84mg

4. Apples and Cinnamon Oatmeal

Preparation: 5 minutes   **Cooking: 15 minutes**   **Servings: 2**

Ingredients

- *1 ½ cups unsweetened plain almond milk*
- *1 cup old-fashioned oats*
- *1 unpeeled Granny Smith apple, cubed*
- *¼ tsp. ground cinnamon*
- *2 tbsp. toasted walnut pieces*

Directions

1. Bring the milk to warm over medium heat and add the oatmeal and apple.
2. Beat until almost all the liquid is absorbed, about 4 minutes. Add the cinnamon.
3. Pour the oat mixture into two bowls and garnish with walnuts.

Nutrition: Calories 377, Carbohydrates 73g, Protein 13g, Fat 16g, Sodium 77mg

5. At-Home Cappuccino

Preparation: 5 minutes   **Cooking: 5 minutes**   **Servings: 2**

Ingredients

- *1 cup low-fat (1%) or fat-free milk*
- *3 tbsp. ground espresso beans*

Directions

1. Heat the milk in a medium-hot saucepan until steamed. (Or microwave over high heat for about 1 minute.) Meanwhile, add cold water to the bottom of the coffee pot until the steam has evacuated.
2. Add the coffee beans to the basket and screw them on. Bring to a boil over high heat and cook until coffee stops splashing from the vertical flow under the lid. Remove from the heat.
3. Transfer the hot milk into a blender and mix until frothy.
4. Divide the coffee between two cups.
5. Pour in an equal amount of milk from the blender to cover the coffee, then pour in the remaining milk. Serve hot.

Nutrition: Calories 135, Carbohydrates 17g, Protein 10g, Fat 2g, Sodium 112mg

6. Banana Almond Yogurt

Preparation: 5 minutes   **Cooking: 15 seconds**   **Servings: 1**

Ingredients

- *1 tbsp. raw, crunchy, unsalted almond butter*
- *3/4 cup low-fat plain Greek yogurt*
- *1/4 cup uncooked old-fashioned oats*
- *1/2 large banana, sliced*
- *1/8 tsp. ground cinnamon*

Directions

1. Use the microwave to soften the almond for 15 seconds.
2. Transfer the yogurt into a medium bowl and whisk in the almond butter, oatmeal, and banana.
3. Sprinkle with cinnamon.

Nutrition: Calories 337, Carbohydrates 48g, Protein 25g, Fat 12g, Sodium 65mg

7. Banana Cookies

Preparation: 10 minutes   **Cooking: 15 minutes**   **Servings: 4**

Ingredients

- *1 cup almond butter*
- *1/4 cup stevia*
- *1 tsp. vanilla extract*
- *2 bananas, peeled and mashed*
- *1cups gluten-free oats*
- *1 tsp. cinnamon powder*
- *1 cup almonds, chopped*
- *1/2 cup raisins*

Directions

1. In a bowl, combine the butter with the stevia and the other ingredients and mix well with a hand mixer.

2. Pour medium molds of this mixture onto a baking sheet lined with parchment paper and flatten slightly.
3. Bake them at 325°F for 15 minutes and serve them for breakfast.

Nutrition: Calories 280, Carbohydrates 29g, Protein 8g, Fat 16g, Sodium 20mg

8. Banana Steel Oats

Preparation: 10 minutes   **Cooking: 15 minutes**   **Servings: 3**

Ingredients

- *1 small banana*
- *1 cup almond milk*
- *1/4 tsp. cinnamon, ground*
- *1/2 cup rolled oats*
- *1 tbsp. honey*

Directions

1. Take a saucepan and add half the banana, mix the almond milk, ground cinnamon. Season with the sunflower seeds. Stir until the banana is well mashed, bring the mixture to a boil, and add the oats.
2. Simmer for 5-7 minutes and reduce the heat to medium-low until the oatmeal is tender.
3. Cut the remaining half of the banana into cubes and place it on the oats.

Nutrition: Calories 385, Carbohydrates 76g, Protein 7g, Fat 6g, Sodium 48mg

9. Banana-Berry Smoothie

Preparation: 10 minutes   **Servings: 1**

Ingredients

- *1/2 ripe banana, preferably frozen*
- *1/2 cup fresh or frozen blueberries*
- *1/2 cup low-fat (1/%) milk*
- *1/2 cup plain low-fat yogurt*
- *1/4 tsp. vanilla extract*
- *1 tbsp. amber agave nectar (optional)*

Directions

1. Peel and cut the banana into pieces.
2. Combine all ingredients, including sweetener (if using), in a blender until smooth.
3. Transfer into a tall glass and serve immediately.

Nutrition: Calories 180, Carbohydrates 33g, Protein 8g, Fat 2g, Sodium 95mg

10. Barley Porridge

Preparation: 5 minutes   **Cooking: 25 minutes**   **Servings: 4**

Ingredients

- *1 cup barley*
- *1 cup of wheat berries*
- *2 cups unsweetened almond milk*
- *2 cups of water*
- *1 cup Toppings, such as hazelnuts, honey, berry, etc.*

Directions

1. Take a portable saucepan and put it on medium-high heat. Add barley, almond milk, wheat berries, water, and bring to a boil.
2. Reduce the heat and allow it to simmer for 25 minutes.
3. Divide into bowls and garnish with desired toppings. Serve and enjoy!

Nutrition: Calories 295, Carbohydrates 56g, Protein 6g, Fat 8g, Sodium 110mg

11. Basil and Tomato Baked Eggs

Preparation: 10 minutes   **Cooking: 15 minutes**   **Servings: 2**

Ingredients

- *1/2 garlic clove, minced*
- *1/2 cup canned tomatoes*
- *1/4 cup fresh basil leaves, roughly chopped*
- *1/4 tsp. chili powder*
- *1/2 tbsp. olive oil*
- *2 whole eggs*
- *Pepper to taste*

Directions

1. Preheat the oven to 375°F. Take a small baking dish and grease it with olive oil. Add the garlic, basil, tomatoes, chili, olive oil to a plate and mix.
2. Break the eggs into a plate, leaving a space in between. Sprinkle the entire plate with sunflower seeds and pepper.
3. Place in the oven and bake for 12 minutes until the eggs have solidified, and the tomatoes are foamy.
4. Serve with the basil on top. Enjoy!

Nutrition: Calories 235, Carbohydrates 7g, Protein 14g, Fat 16g, Sodium 126mg

12. Berries Deluxe Oatmeal

Preparation: 10 minutes   **Cooking: 10 minutes**   **Servings: 2**

Ingredients

- 1 ½ cups unsweetened plain almond milk
- 1/8 tsp. vanilla extract
- 1 cup old-fashioned oats
- 3/4 cup mix of blueberries, blackberries, and coarsely chopped
- 3 strawberries, sliced
- 2 tbsp. toasted pecan

Directions

1. Heat the vanilla and almond milk in a saucepan over medium heat.
2. The moment the mixture starts to simmer, add the oatmeal and stir for about 4 minutes, or until most of the liquid is absorbed. Add the berries.
3. Pour the mixture into two bowls and garnish with a toasted pecan.

Nutrition: Calories 261, Carbohydrates 63g, Protein 7g, Fat 10g, Sodium 115mg

13. Blueberry Breakfast Quinoa

Preparation: 10 minutes   **Cooking: 30 minutes**   **Servings: 4**

Ingredients

- 2 cups low-fat/nonfat milk
- 1 cup quinoa, uncooked
- 1/4 cup honey
- 1/2 tsp. cinnamon
- 1/4 cup chopped almonds, pecans, or walnuts
- 1/2 cup fresh blueberries

Directions

1. In a portable saucepan, bring the milk to a boil.
2. Add the quinoa and bring to a boil. Cover, reduce heat and cook until most of the liquid is absorbed about 12 to 15 minutes. Keep away from heat.
3. Add the rest of the ingredients to the quinoa, cover, and let it stand for another 10 minutes before serving.
4. For a finer consistency, add more milk.

Nutrition: Calories 302, Carbohydrates 59g, Protein 12g, Fat 5g, Sodium 70mg

14. Blueberry Muffins

Preparation: 10 minutes   **Cooking: 25 minutes**   **Servings: 12**

Ingredients

- 2 bananas, peeled and mashed
- 1 cup almond milk
- 1 tsp. vanilla extract
- 1/4 cup pure maple syrup
- 1 tsp. apple cider vinegar
- 1/4 cup coconut oil, melted
- 2 cups almond flour
- 4 tbsp. coconut sugar
- 2 tsp. cinnamon powder
- 2 tsp. baking powder
- 2 cups blueberries
- 1/2 tsp. baking soda
- 1/2 cup walnuts, chopped

Directions

1. In a bowl, combine the bananas with the almond milk, vanilla, and other ingredients and mix well.
2. Divide the dough into 12 muffin cups and bake at 350 degrees F for 25 minutes.
3. Serve the muffins for breakfast.

Nutrition: Calories 180, Carbohydrates 31g, Protein 4g, Fat 5g, Sodium 222mg

15. Blueberry Pancakes

Preparation: 7 minutes   **Cooking: 10 minutes**   **Servings: 4**

Ingredients

- 2 eggs, whisked
- 4 tbsp. almond milk
- 1 cup full-fat yogurt
- 3 tbsp. coconut butter, melted
- 1/2 tsp. vanilla extract
- 1 ½ cups almond flour
- 2 tbsp. stevia
- 1 cup blueberries
- 1 tbsp. avocado oil

Directions

1. In a bowl, combine the eggs with the almond milk and the other ingredients except for the oil and mix well.
2. Warm a pan with oil over medium heat, add 1/4 cup of the batter, spread into the pan, cook 4 minutes, turn, cook another 3 minutes and transfer to a plate.
3. Repeat with the rest of the batter and serve the pancakes for breakfast.

Nutrition: Calories 164, Carbohydrates 5g, Protein 2g, Fat 4g, Sodium 152mg

16. Blueberry-Maple Oatmeal

Preparation: 30 minutes   **Servings: 1**

Ingredients

- 1/2 cup rolled oats
- 1/2 cup water or nonfat milk
- 1/8 tsp. of sea salt
- 1 tbsp. chia seeds (optional)
- 1-2 tsp. maple syrup
- 2 cups fresh blueberries

Directions

1. In a bowl or jar, combine oats, water or milk, and salt.
2. Cover and place in refrigerator overnight.
3. Before serving, top with chia seeds, maple syrup, and blueberries.

Nutrition: Calories 260, Carbohydrates 49g, Protein 9g, Fat 3g, Sodium 160mg

17. Chocolate Smoothie

Preparation: 5 minutes   **Servings: 2**

Ingredients

- 1 ripe banana, frozen at least overnight
- 2/3 cup low-fat (1%) milk
- 2/3 cup plain low-fat yogurt
- 2 tbsp. chunky peanut butter
- 2 tbsp. unsweetened cocoa powder
- 1 tbsp. amber agave nectar (optional)
- 4 ice cubes

Directions

1. Peel and cut the banana into pieces. In a blender, combine the banana with the milk, yogurt, peanut butter, cocoa powder, sweetener (if using), and ice cubes.
2. Pour into two tall glasses and serve immediately.

Nutrition: Calories 250, Carbohydrates 31g, Protein 13g, Fat 11g, Sodium 134mg

18. Cantaloupe Dash Smoothie

Preparation: 5 minutes   **Servings: 2**

Ingredients:

- 2 ½ cups Frozen cantaloupe
- 1/2 cup Nonfat or low-fat milk
- 1 sliced Frozen banana
- 160 g carton - Nonfat vanilla Greek yogurt
- 1/2 cup Ice
- 1 tsp. Honey

Directions:

1. Peel, cube, and freeze the cantaloupe.
2. Place the milk, banana, yogurt, ice, and honey in a blender.
3. Work and mix the fixings till incorporated and creamy.
4. Toss in the cantaloupe pieces - process until incorporated and creamy smooth and serve.

Nutrition: Calories 214, Carbohydrates 46g, Protein 11g, Fat 1g, Sodium 64mg

19. Chocolate Berry Dash Smoothie

Preparation: 5 minutes   **Servings: 1**

Ingredients:

- 2 tbsp Cashews
- 1 cup Water - cold
- 1/4 cup Frozen blueberries
- ½ of Avocado
- 2 tbsp Organic cocoa powder
- 1/2 tsp Vanilla extract
- Agave nectar/sub honey (as desired)

Directions:

1. Toss each of the fixings into a blender.
2. Set the function to high and mix for 40 to 60 seconds.
3. Pour and serve.

Nutrition: Calories 250, Carbohydrates 17g, Protein 6g, Fat 17g, Sodium 105mg

20. Chocolate Smoothie with Banana & Avocado

Preparation: 5 minutes   **Servings: 2**

Ingredients:

- 2 cups Vanilla soy milk
- 1 Medium banana
- half of 1 Avocado
- (2 individual packets) Splenda
- 1/4 cup Unsweetened cocoa powder

Directions:

1. Peel the banana and remove the avocado peel and pit.
2. Toss each of the fixings into the blender - process them till they're creamy smooth and serve.

Nutrition: Calories 252, Carbohydrates 33g, Protein 11g, Fat 12g, Sodium 102mg

21. Fresh Fruit Smoothie

Preparation: 15 minutes   **Servings: 4**

Ingredients:

- 1 cup Fresh pineapple chunks
- 1/2 cup Cantaloupe or other melon chunks
- 1 cup Fresh strawberries
- Juice (from 2 oranges)
- 1 cup – cold Water
- 1 tbsp Agave nectar/sub honey

Directions:

1. Discard the rind from the pineapple and melon - slice them into pieces.
2. Remove the stems from strawberries.
3. Toss each of the fixings into a blender. Mix them till they're incorporated and creamy smooth. Serve the smoothies cold.

Nutrition: Calories 172, Carbohydrates 17g, Protein 1g, Fat 3g, Sodium 87mg

22. Ginger Carrot & Turmeric Smoothie

Preparation: 10 minutes   **Servings: 2**

Ingredients:

- *(2 cups) Carrots*
- *(1 ½ cups) Filtered water*
- *The Smoothie:*
- *(1 large + more for sweetness as desired) Ripe banana*
- *(1 cup) Frozen or fresh pineapple (1 cup)*
- *(1/2 tbsp.) Fresh ginger*
- *(1/2 cup) Carrot juice*
- *(1/4 tsp.) Ground turmeric*
- *(1/2 tsp.) Cinnamon*
- *(1 tbsp.) Lime juice*
- *Unsweetened almond milk (1 cup)*

Directions:

1. Add the water and carrots to the blender. Mix till it's incorporated and smooth.
2. Add more water as needed, scraping down its sides. Keep the juice in the refrigerator.
3. Toss the rest of the fixings into the blender for the smoothie and mix thoroughly.
4. Serve in two chilled glasses.

Nutrition: Calories 114, Carbohydrates 32g, Protein 4g, Fat 3g, Sodium 112mg

23. Healthy Smoothie

Preparation: 6 minutes   **Servings: 4**

Ingredients:

- *1 Banana*
- *(1 lemon/about 4 tbsp.) Juice*
- *(1/2 cup) Strawberries*
- *(1 cup) Ice or cold water*
- *(1/2 cup) Berries - such as blueberries or blackberries*
- *(2 cups) Baby spinach*
- *Fresh mint (as desired)*

Directions:

1. Toss each of the fixings into a blender or juicer.
2. Puree and serve in chilled mugs.

Nutrition: Calories 64, Carbohydrates 12g, Protein 4g, Fat 1g, Sodium 55mg

24. High-Protein Strawberry Smoothie

Preparation: 10 minutes   **Servings: 1**

Ingredients:

- *(1/2 cup) Low-fat cottage cheese -low-salt*
- *(3/4 cup) 1% milk*
- *(1 cup) Fresh/frozen strawberries*

Directions:

1. Toss each of the fixings into the mixing container dish
2. Blend each of the fixings till creamy.
3. Pour it into a tall-chilled glass to serve.

Nutrition: Protein: 22g Carbohydrates: 26g Fat: 2.8g Sodium: 141mg Calories: 215

25. Orange Juice Smoothie

Preparation: 5 minutes   **Servings: 2**

Ingredients:

- *(1 cup) Vanilla frozen yogurt - no sugar*
- *(3/4 cup) Milk - fat-free*
- *(1/4 cup) Frozen orange juice concentrate - no-sugar*

Directions:

1. Toss each of the fixings into your blender - mixing till creamy.
2. Serve in a cold mug and enjoy them right away.

Nutrition: Calories 220, Carbohydrates 41g, Protein 12g, Fat 1g, Sodium 177mg

26. Orange- Tofu Lover's Smoothies

Preparation: 6 minutes   **Servings: 4**
Ingredients:
- *(1 tbsp.) Dark honey*
- *(1 cup) Chilled light vanilla soy milk*
- *(1/2 tsp.) Vanilla extract*
- *(1 ½ cups) Chilled orange juice*
- *(1/3 cup) Soft/silken tofu*
- *(1 tsp.) Orange zest*

Directions:
1. Grate the orange for zest and prepare the juice.
2. Pour the milk, orange juice, honey, vanilla, orange zest, tofu, and ice into a blender.
3. Mix till the smoothie is as desired (30 sec.).
4. Pour the smoothies into cold glasses. Garnish each glass with an orange segment.

Nutrition: Calories 110, Carbohydrates 20g, Protein 3g, Fat 1g, Sodium 40mg

27. Spinach & Avocado Smoothie

Preparation: 5 minutes   **Servings: 1**
Ingredients:
- *(1 cup) Plain yogurt*
- *1 Frozen banana*
- *(1/4) Avocado*
- *(1 cup) Fresh spinach*
- *(1 tsp.) Honey*
- *(2 tbsp.) Water*

Directions:
1. Toss the yogurt with avocado, honey, banana, water, and spinach in a blender.
2. Let the mixture work and puree till it's creamy smooth.
3. Serve in a chilled mug.

Nutrition: Calories 357, Carbohydrates 57g, Protein 17g, Fat 8g, Sodium 237mg

28. Apple Corn Muffins

Preparation: 10 minutes   **Cooking: 30 minutes**   **Servings: 6**
Ingredients:
- *(1) Apple*
- *(1/2 cup) Corn kernels*
- *(2 cups) A. P. flour*
- *(1/2 cup) Yellow cornmeal*
- *(1/4 cup - packed tight) Brown sugar*
- *(1/4 tsp.) Salt*
- *(1 tbsp.) Baking powder*
- *(2) Egg whites*
- *(3/4 cup) Fat-free milk*
- *Also Needed: 12-count muffin tin*

Directions:
1. Line the containers with foil or paper liners.
2. Preheat the oven to reach 425° Fahrenheit/218° Celsius.
3. Peel and coarsely chop the apple.
4. Whisk the brown sugar with the cornmeal, salt, baking powder, and flour in a big mixing container.
5. Prepare another container and beat the eggs with the milk. Blend in the corn kernels and apple bits.
6. Whisk and combine all of the fixings till they are slightly moistened.
7. Scoop the batter into the cups (leaving 1/3 of the top open).
8. Set a timer to bake for 1/2 hour.
9. Test the muffins for doneness by gently pressing the center. They should spring back.

Nutrition: Calories 120, Carbohydrates 26g, Protein 4g, Fat 1g, Sodium 127mg

29. Blueberry & Lemon Scones

Preparation: 15 minutes   **Cooking: 40 minutes**   **Servings: 6**
Ingredients:
- *(2 cups) A. P. flour*
- *(1/4 cup) Granulated sugar*
- *(1 tbsp.) No-sodium baking powder - your choice*
- *(6 tbsp.) Cold unsalted butter*

- *(2 large) Eggs*
- *(1 tbsp.) Lemon: Zest + juice*
- *(1/2 cup) Half & Half*
- *(1 cup) Fresh blueberries*

Directions:
1. Warm the oven temperature setting to reach 400° Fahrenheit/204° Celsius.
2. Cover a baking tray using a layer of parchment baking paper. Sprinkle it lightly using a tiny bit of flour.
3. Rinse, remove the stems, and dry the blueberries using a few paper towels. Prepare the lemon and set it aside for now.
4. Whisk the flour with butter, sugar, lemon zest, and baking powder into a big mixing container - mixing till it's crumbly.
5. Break and whisk two eggs into a smaller container. Whisk in the Half & Half and lemon juice - beating till it's thoroughly blended.
6. Toss the egg mix into the dry fixings - stir till blended.
7. Gently mix in the berries. Scoop the batter onto a floured surface - such as a chopping block.
8. Work the dough into a disc/ball - arrange it in the center of the parchment-lined baking tray - as you flatten it into a one-inch circular disc. Use a floured knife to portion it into six wedges.
9. Put the baking tray in the fridge to chill and harden the dough's butter (15 min.).
10. When chilled, pop it into the oven to bake till it's nicely browned (20 min.).
11. Put the tray onto a wire rack to cool. Recut the scones while still warm.
12. Serve with a mix of honey and butter or plain unsalted butter.

Nutrition: Calories 328, Carbohydrates 57g, Protein 45g, Fat 19g, Sodium 35mg

30. Asparagus Omelet Tortilla Wrap

Preparation: 10 minutes   **Cooking: 10 minutes**   **Servings: 1**

Ingredients:
- *(2 tsp.) Parmesan cheese - grated*
- *(1/8 tsp.) Black pepper*
- *4 Fresh asparagus spears*
- *(1 whole large) Egg*
- *(1 tbsp.) Fat-free milk*
- *(2 large) Egg whites*
- *(1 tsp.) Butter*
- *1 Green onion*
- *(1 small warmed) Whole wheat tortilla*

Directions:
1. Beat the eggs with the pepper, parmesan, and milk till it's incorporated.
2. Spritz a skillet using a tiny portion of cooking oil spray. Warm it using the medium temperature setting.
3. Add and sauté the asparagus (3-4 min.). Scoop the asparagus from the pan.
4. Use the same pan to warm the butter using med-high heat.
5. Add and cook the eggs, pushing them to the center until it's one layer and thickened.
6. Trim and slice the asparagus and chop the onion.
7. When eggs are thickened, spoon the green onion and asparagus on one side. Fold the omelet in half and serve in a tortilla.

Nutrition: Calories 319, Carbohydrates 39g, Protein 21g, Fat 13g, Sodium 444mg

31. Baked Banana-Nut Oatmeal Cups

Preparation: 15 minutes   **Cooking: 35 minutes**   **Servings: 12**

Ingredients:
- *(3 cups) Rolled oats*
- *(1/3 cup) Brown sugar - tightly packed*
- *(1 ½ cups) Milk low-fat*
- *(3/4 cup) Ripe bananas*
- *(2) Large eggs*
- *(1/2 tsp.) Salt*
- *(1 tsp.) Baking powder*
- *(1 tsp.) Cinnamon*
- *(1 tsp.) Vanilla extract*
- *(1/2 cup) Toasted chopped pecans*

Directions:
1. Set the oven temperature to 375° Fahrenheit/191° Celsius.
2. Lightly spritz the cups of the muffin tin using a cooking oil spray.
3. Mash the bananas. Lightly whisk the eggs and mix with the oats, milk, bananas, baking powder, salt, brown sugar, cinnamon, and vanilla in a big mixing container.
4. Fold in pecans. Scoop the batter into the muffin cups (.33 or 1/3 cup).
5. Bake till they're nicely browned (25 min.). Allow cooling in the pan (10 min.).
6. Transfer the oatmeal cups onto a cooling rack to thoroughly cool before storing.
7. Serve as desired - either cooled or warm.
8. Meal Prep Tip: Wrap tightly in foil or place in a container in the refrigerator to enjoy for a day or two. They are a wonderful freezer option to prepare and save for up to three months.

Nutrition: Calories 176, Carbohydrates 26g, Protein 5g, Fat g, Sodium 165mg

32. Blueberry Low-Sodium Pancakes

Preparation: 5 minutes　　　**Cooking: 10 minutes**　　　**Servings: 8**

Ingredients:
- *(2 cups) A. P. flour*
- *(4 tbsp.) Brown sugar*
- *(2 tbsp.) Reduced sodium baking powder*
- *(1 tbsp.) Vinegar - apple cider*
- *(1 tsp.) Vanilla extract*
- *(1 cup) Oat milk*

Directions:
1. Toss all the dry fixings (flour, brown sugar, baking powder & salt) into a mixing container. Whisk till it's all combined.
2. In another mixing container or liquid measuring cup, add the wet fixings (oat milk, apple cider vinegar & vanilla), whisking till incorporated.
3. Combine all of the components till creamy. Wait while it rests (5 min.).
4. Pour the batter (65 grams or 1/2 cup) into a griddle or skillet using a medium-temperature setting.
5. When the top begins to bubble, flip the pancake and continue cooking till they're nicely browned.
6. Serve warm with honey or syrup.

Nutrition: Calories 177, Carbohydrates 16g, Protein 2g, Fat 6g, Sodium 113mg

33. Breakfast Scrambled Egg Burrito

Preparation: 10 minutes　　　**Cooking: 15 minutes**　　　**Servings: 1**

Ingredients:
- *Tortilla (1 homemade - low or zero sodium - 6-8 inch/15-20-cm tortilla)*
- *Small sweet pepper (1-2 tbsp. diced)*
- *Egg (1)*
- *Shredded Swiss & Gruyere cheese (1 tbsp.)*
- *Low/no sodium pasta sauce or salsa (1 tsp.)*

Directions:
1. Lightly spritz a skillet using a bit of cooking oil spray.
2. Whisk the egg and mix in the peppers and salsa.
3. Warm the skillet on the stovetop using a medium-temperature setting. When it's heated, stir in the egg mixture - folding the egg over itself until large curds begin to form. Move the skillet to a cool spot and set it aside.
4. Plate the tortilla flat and pop it into the microwave to heat for ten seconds.
5. Sprinkle a tablespoon of cheese down its center.
6. Add the scrambled egg and roll the tortilla - burrito-style.
7. Plate it again - seam side down and reheat it in the microwave to melt the cheese (5 sec.).
8. Cut the burrito on a diagonal across the middle and serve promptly with extra salsa as desired.

Nutrition: Calories 273, Carbohydrates 27g, Protein 2g, Fat 15g, Sodium 116mg

34. Cinnamon Oatmeal

Preparation: 10 minutes   **Cooking: 4 minutes**   **Servings: 1**

Ingredients:
- 2 cups Low-fat milk
- 1 ½ tsp. Vanilla extract
- 1 ½ cups quick oats
- 1/4 cup Light brown sugar
- 1/2 tsp. Ground cinnamon

Directions:
1. Add milk and vanilla to a saucepan and bring to a boil.
2. Then reduce heat, stir in oats, brown sugar, and cinnamon, and cook and stir for 3 minutes and serve.

Nutrition: Calories 208, Carbohydrates 59g, Protein 8g, Fat 3g, Sodium 58mg

35. Egg White and Vegetable Omelet

Preparation: 10 minutes   **Cooking: 20 minutes**   **Servings: 1**

Ingredients:
- 6 Egg whites
- 1 Tbsp. Water
- 2 tsp. Olive oil
- 1/2, Yellow onion chopped
- 1 Tomato diced
- 2 asparagus stalks cut into small pieces
- 3 to 4 Mushrooms sliced

Directions
1. Whisk egg whites in a bowl. Add 1 tbsp. water, and whisk until well blended.
2. Heat 1 tsp. oil in a skillet. Add tomato, onion, asparagus, mushrooms, and sauté until vegetables are tender for about 3 to 4 minutes. Remove from pan and set aside.
3. Add another tsp. of oil and heat for 2 minutes.
4. Add beaten eggs to the pan, tilting the pan to cover the entire pan.
5. Cook until eggs are almost finished but still soft in the middle.
6. Add vegetable mixture to the middle of the omelet. Fold and serve.

Nutrition: Calories 145, Carbohydrates 19g, Protein 28g, Fat 4g, Sodium 77mg

36. Fruity Green Smoothie

Preparation: 5 minutes   **Servings: 1**

Ingredients:
- 2 cups Fresh spinach leaves –
- 1 peeled medium banana –,
- Strawberries – 8, trimmed
- Orange juice - 1/2 cup
- Crushed ice – 1 cup

Directions:
1. Blend everything in a blender.
2. Serve.

Nutrition: Calories 235, Carbohydrates 56g, Protein 5g, Fat 1g, Sodium 64mg

37. Fruit and Yogurt Breakfast Salad

Preparation: 10 minutes   **Cooking: 15 minutes**   **Servings: 6**

Ingredients:
- 2 cups Water
- 1/4 tsp Salt
- 3/4 cup Quick-cooking brown rice
- 3/4 cup Bulgur
- 1 cored and chopped large apple
- 1 cored and chopped large pear
- 1 peeled and cut Orange
- 1 cup dried cranberries
- 8 ounces low-fat or nonfat Greek-style yogurt, plain

Directions:
1. Heat water in a large pot.
2. Add salt, rice, and bulgur to boiling water. Lower heat to low.

3. Cover, and simmer for 10 minutes. Remove from heat.
4. Transfer grains to a large bowl and keep in the refrigerator until chilled.
5. Remove chilled grains from the refrigerator.
6. Add apple, pear, oranges, and dried cranberries.
7. Fold in the yogurt and mix gently until grains and fruit are mixed well and serve.

Nutrition: Calories 190, Carbohydrates 40g, Protein 4g, Fat 1g, Sodium 118mg

38. Lemon Zucchini Muffins

Preparation: 10 minutes   **Cooking: 7 minutes**   **Servings: 1**

Ingredients:

- *2 cups all-purpose flour*
- *1/2 cup Sugar*
- *1 Tbsp. Baking powder*
- *1/4 tsp. Salt*
- *1/4 tsp. Cinnamon*
- *1/4 tsp. Nutmeg*
- *1 cup shredded zucchini*
- *3/4 cup Nonfat milk*
- *2 Tbsp. Olive oil*
- *2 Tbsp. Lemon juice*
- *1 Egg*
- *Nonstick cooking spray*

Directions:

1. Preheat the oven to 400F. Grease the muffin tins.
2. Combine sugar, flour, baking powder, salt, cinnamon, and nutmeg in a bowl.
3. In another bowl, combine zucchini, milk, oil, lemon juice, and egg. Stir well.
4. Add zucchini mixture to flour mixture. Stir until just combined.
5. Pour batter into prepared muffin cups.
6. Bake for 20 minutes and serve.

Nutrition: Calories 145 Carbohydrates 25g, Protein 3g, Fat 4g, Sodium 62mg

39. Greek-Style Breakfast Scramble

Preparation: 10 minutes   **Cooking: 8 minutes**   **Servings: 1**

Ingredients:

- *Nonstick cooking spray*
- *1 cup fresh spinach*
- *1/2 cup Mushrooms*
- *¼ Onion*
- *1 Whole egg*
- *2 Tbsp. Feta cheese*
- *Freshly ground black pepper to taste*

Directions:

1. Heat a skillet over medium heat.
2. Spray with cooking spray and add spinach, mushrooms, and onion.
3. Sauté for 2 to 3 minutes or until onions turn translucent and spinach has wilted
4. Meanwhile, whisk egg and egg whites together in a bowl. Add feta cheese and pepper.
5. Pour egg mixture over vegetables.
6. Cook eggs, stirring with a spatula, for 3 to 4 minutes, or until eggs are cooked and serve.

Nutrition: Calories 150, Carbohydrates 6g, Protein 17g, Fat 7g, Sodium 440mg

40. Blueberry Green Smoothie

Preparation: 10 minutes   **Servings: 2**

Ingredients:

- *2 cups Chopped mixed greens*
- *1/4 cup Water*
- *1/3 cup Chopped carrot*
- *1/2 cup Frozen blueberries*
- *1/2 cup Chopped unpeeled cucumber*
- *1/4 cup Unsweetened almond milk*
- *4 Ice cubes*

Directions

1. Place the greens and water in a blender. Blend until smooth.
2. Add the remaining ingredients and blend until desired consistency is achieved and serve.

Nutrition: Calories 82, Carbohydrates 17g, Protein 4g, Fat 1g, Sodium 66mg

41. Green Smoothie

Preparation: 5 minutes   **Servings: 2**
Ingredients:
- 2 cups Spinach
- 2 chopped large kale leaves
- 3/4 cup Water
- 1 large, chopped Frozen banana
- 1/2 cup Frozen mango
- 1/2 cup Frozen peach
- 1 Tbsp. Ground flaxseeds
- 1 Tbsp. Almond butter

Directions:
1. Place the spinach, kale, and water in the blender.
2. Blend until smooth.
3. Then add fruit, flaxseeds, and nut butter and blend until smooth and serve.

Nutrition: Calories 157, Carbohydrates 35g, Protein 5g, Fat 2g, Sodium 48mg

42. Cheesy Baked Eggs

Preparation: 5 minutes   **Cooking: 15 minutes**   **Servings: 4**
Ingredients:
- 4 large eggs
- 75g (3oz) cheese, grated
- 25g (1oz) fresh rocket (arugula) leaves, finely chopped
- 1 tablespoon parsley
- 1/2 teaspoon ground turmeric
- 1 tablespoon olive oil

Directions:
1. Grease each ramekin dish with a little olive oil.
2. Divide the rocket (arugula) between the ramekin dishes, then break an egg into each one.
3. Sprinkle a little parsley and turmeric on top, then sprinkle on the cheese.
4. Place the ramekins in a preheated oven at 220C/425F for 15 minutes, until the eggs are set, and the cheese is bubbling.

Nutrition: Calories 198, Carbohydrates 2g, Protein 13g, Fat 9g, Sodium 45mg

43. Green Egg Scramble

Preparation: 10 minutes   **Cooking: 5 minutes**   **Servings: 1**
Ingredients:
- 2 eggs, whisked
- 25g (1oz) rocket (arugula) leaves
- 1 teaspoon chives, chopped
- 1 teaspoon fresh basil, chopped
- 1 teaspoon fresh parsley, chopped
- 1 tablespoon olive oil

Directions:
1. Mix the eggs with the rocket (arugula) and herbs.
2. Heat the oil in a frying pan and pour it into the egg mixture.
3. Gently stir until it's lightly scrambled. Season and serve.

Nutrition: Calories 250, Carbohydrates 8g, Protein 11g, Fat 7g, Sodium 70mg

44. Spiced Scramble

Preparation: 10 minutes   **Cooking: 5 minutes**   **Servings: 1**
Ingredients:
- 25g (1oz) kale, finely chopped
- 2 eggs
- 1 spring onion (scallion) finely chopped
- 1 teaspoon turmeric
- 1 tablespoon olive oil
- Sea salt
- Freshly ground black pepper

Directions:
1. Crack the eggs into a bowl.

2. Add the turmeric and whisk them. Season with salt and pepper.
3. Heat the oil in a frying pan, add the kale and spring onions (scallions) and cook until it has wilted.
4. Pour in the beaten eggs and stir until eggs have scrambled together with the kale.

Nutrition: Calories 259, Carbohydrates 3g, Protein 9g, Fat 3g, Sodium 30mg

45. Strawberry Buckwheat Pancakes

Preparation: 20 minutes   **Cooking: 5 minutes**   **Servings: 4**

Ingredients:
- *100g strawberries, chopped*
- *100g buckwheat flour*
- *1 egg*
- *250mls milk*
- *1 teaspoon olive oil*
- *1 teaspoon olive oil for frying*
- *Freshly squeezed juice of 1 orange*
- *175 calories Nutrition*

Directions:
1. Pour the milk into a bowl and mix in the egg and a teaspoon of olive oil.
2. Sift in the flour to the liquid mixture until smooth and creamy.
3. Allow it to rest for 15 minutes. Heat a little oil in a pan and pour in a quarter of the mixture (or the size you prefer.)
4. Sprinkle in a quarter of the strawberries into the batter.
5. Cook for around 2 minutes on each side.
6. Serve hot with a drizzle of orange juice.
7. You could try experimenting with other berries such as blueberries and blackberries

Nutrition: Calories 106, Carbohydrates 7g, Protein 8g, Fat 2g, Sodium 79mg

46. Hash Brown Mix

Preparation: 10 minutes   **Cooking: 30 minutes**   **Servings: 6**

Ingredients:
- *Cooking spray*
- *6 eggs*
- *2 cups hash browns*
- *1/4 cup non-fat milk*
- *1/2 cup fat-free cheddar cheese, shredded*
- *1 small yellow onion, chopped*
- *A pinch of black pepper*
- *1/2 green bell pepper, chopped*
- *1/2 red bell pepper, chopped*

Directions:
1. Heat up a pan greased with cooking spray over medium-high heat, add onions, green and red bell pepper, stir and cook for 4-5 minutes.
2. Add hash browns and black pepper, stir and cook for 5 minutes more.
3. In a bowl, combine the eggs with milk and cheese, whisk well, pour over the mix from the pan, introduce in the oven and bake at 380 degrees F for twenty or so minutes.
4. Slice, divide between plates and serve.

Nutrition: Calories 221, Carbohydrates 3g, Protein 32g, Fat 4g, Sodium 435mg

47. Cheddar Baked Eggs

Preparation: 10 minutes   **Cooking: 15 minutes**   **Servings: 4**

Ingredients:
- *4 eggs*
- *4 slices low-fat cheddar*
- *2 spring onions, chopped*
- *1 tablespoon extra-virgin olive oil*
- *A pinch of black pepper*
- *1 tablespoon cilantro, chopped*

Directions:
1. Grease 4 ramekins while using oil, sprinkle green onions in each, crack an egg in each ramekin and top with cilantro and cheddar cheese.
2. Introduce inside oven and bake at 375 degrees F for quarter-hour and enjoy every morning!

Nutrition: Calories 198, Carbohydrates 3g, Protein 30g, Fat 10g, Sodium 165mg

48.   Banana and Walnuts Bowls

Preparation: 10 minutes   **Cooking: 15 minutes**   **Servings: 4**

Ingredients:

- *2 cups water*
- *1 cup steel cut oats*
- *1 cup almond milk*
- *1/4 cup walnuts, chopped*
- *2 tablespoons chia seeds*
- *2 bananas, peeled and mashed*
- *1 teaspoon vanilla flavoring*

Directions:

1. In a reduced pot, combine water while using the oats, milk, walnuts, chia seeds, bananas and vanilla, toss, bring using a simmer over medium heat, cook for fifteen minutes, divide into bowls and serve.

Nutrition: Calories 162, Carbohydrates 30g, Protein 12g, Fat 4g, Sodium 345mg

49.   Cream Basmati Rice Pudding

Preparation: 10 minutes   **Cooking: 25 minutes**   **Servings: 6**

Ingredients:

- *2 cups coconut milk*
- *1 and 1/4 cups water*
- *1 cup basmati rice*
- *2 tablespoons coconut sugar*
- *3/4 cup coconut cream*
- *1 teaspoon vanilla flavoring*

Directions:

1. In a pot, combine the coconut milk with all the water, rice, sugar, cream and vanilla, toss, bring having a simmer over medium heat, cook for 25 minutes, stirring often, divide into bowls and serve.

Nutrition: Calories 265, Carbohydrates 29g, Protein 2g, Fat 5g, Sodium 90mg

50.   Eggs, Sausage and Veggies Salad

Preparation: 10 minutes   **Cooking: 10 minutes**   **Servings: 6**

Ingredients:

- *9 eggs, hardboiled, peeled and cut into small wedges*
- *1 pound breakfast pork sausage, casings removed*
- *3 cups cherry tomatoes, halved*
- *2 avocados, chopped*
- *1/4 cup onion, chopped*
- *1/2 cup cilantro, chopped*
- *A pinch of black pepper*
- *Juice of 2 lemon*

Directions:

1. Shape sausages mix into small meatballs.
2. Heat up a pan over medium-high heat, add meatballs, brown for 3-4 minutes to them, transfer with a plate leave them to cool down the down.
3. In a salad bowl, combine the meatballs with eggs, onion, tomatoes, avocado, pepper, cilantro and freshly squeezed lemon juice, toss and serve each morning.

Nutrition: Calories 319, Carbohydrates 21g, Protein 20g, Fat 11g, Sodium 214mg

51.   Sweet Potatoes and Apples Mix

Preparation: 10 minutes   **Cooking time: 1 hour**   **Servings: 1**

Ingredients:

- *2 pounds sweet potatoes*
- *2 tablespoons water*
- *1/2-pound apples, cored and chopped*
- *1 tablespoon low-fat butter*

Directions:

1. Arrange the potatoes around the lined baking sheet, bake inside oven at 400 degrees F for an hour, peel them and mash them in the meat processor.
2. Put apples in the very pot, add the river, bring using a boil over medium heat, reduce temperature, cook for ten mins, transfer to your bowl, add mashed potatoes, stir well, and serve every day.

Nutrition: Calories 324, Carbohydrates 21g, Protein 20g, Fat 8g, Sodium 200mg

52. Chickpeas Breakfast Salad

Preparation: 10 minutes   **Servings: 2**
Ingredients:

- *16 ounces canned chickpeas, no-salt-added, drained and rinsed*
- *1 handful baby spinach leaves*
- *1/2 tablespoon freshly squeezed lemon juice*
- *4 tablespoons essential olive oil*
- *1 teaspoon cumin, ground*
- *Black pepper to the taste*
- *1/2 teaspoon chili flakes*

Directions:

1. In a bowl, mix freshly squeezed freshly squeezed lemon juice, oil, cumin, black pepper and chili flakes and whisk well.
2. In a salad bowl, mix chickpeas with spinach, add salad dressing, toss to coat and serve for breakfast.

Nutrition: Calories 158, Carbohydrates 20g, Protein 12g, Fat 4g, Sodium 196mg

53. Orange Delight

Preparation: 5 minutes   **Servings: 2**
Ingredients:

- *1 cup low fat milk*
- *1 cup orange juice*
- *6 ounces low-fat yogurt*
- *20 ounces strawberries, frozen and thawed*

Directions:

1. In your blender mix orange juice with milk, yogurt and strawberries and whisk well.
2. Divide into 2 glasses and serve.

Nutrition: Calories 200; Fat 10g; Carbohydrates 10g; Protein 20g Sodium 246mg

54. Spinach Omelet

Preparation: 10 minutes   **Cooking: 5 minutes**   **Servings: 4**
Ingredients:

- *8 eggs, whisked*
- *Cooking spray*
- *Salt and black pepper to the taste*
- *2 tablespoons chives, chopped*
- *A pinch of cayenne pepper*
- *2 ounces low-fat cheddar cheese, grated*
- *2 cups spinach, torn*
- *For the red pepper relish:*
- *2 tablespoons green onion, chopped*
- *2/3 cup red pepper, chopped*
- *1 tablespoon vinegar*

Directions:

1. In a bowl, mix eggs with salt, pepper, cayenne and chives and stir well.
2. Heat up a pan over medium high heat, spray it with cooking spray, add eggs, spread into the pan, stir and cook for 1 minute.
3. Add cheese and the spinach and fold your omelet.
4. Continue cooking until cheese melts and divide it into plates.
5. In a bowl, mix red pepper with green onions, black pepper to the taste and the vinegar and stir well.
6. Top your omelet with the relish and serve.

Nutrition: Calories: 189; Fat: 2g; Carbohydrates: 5g; Protein: 6g Sodium: 246mg

55. Breakfast Crunch

Preparation: 10 minutes   **Servings: 6**
Ingredients:

- *4 cups mixed orange, apple, grapes and pineapple pieces*
- *2 tablespoons honey*
- *1/2 cup whole wheat and barley cereals*
- *12 ounces low fat vanilla yogurt*
- *1/4 cup coconut, toasted and shredded*

Directions:

1. Divide mixed fruits in 6 breakfast bowl, add yogurt and stir gently.
2. Sprinkle cereals and toasted coconut on top and serve right away.

Nutrition: Calories: 387; Fat:10g; Carbohydrates:14g; Protein: 11g Sodium: 266mg

56. Stuffed Yogurt Peaches

Preparation: 10 minutes   **Cooking: 40 minutes**   **Servings: 4**

Ingredients:

- *1/2 cup dried fruits*
- *1/4 cup almonds, toasted*
- *4 peaches, pitted and halved*
- *2 tablespoons graham crackers, crumbled*
- *1/4 teaspoon allspice, ground*
- *2 tablespoons brown sugar*
- *1/2 cup fat free vanilla yogurt*
- *12 ounces canned peach nectar*

Directions:

1. Scoop each peach half, chop pulp and put into a bowl.
2. Add dried fruits to this bowl and mix.
3. Also add almonds, crackers, sugar and allspice and stir everything.
4. Stuff each peach with this mix, place them on a baking sheet, add nectar all over, introduce in the oven at 350 degrees F and bake for 40 minutes.
5. Divide peaches on plates, drizzle pan juices, top with yogurt and serve.

Nutrition: Calories: 245; Fat: 12g; Carbohydrates: 8g; Protein: 4g; Sodium: 221mg

57. Papaya Breakfast Parfait

Preparation : 10 minutes   **Servings: 4**

Ingredients:

- *3 tablespoons honey*
- *1 cup fat free yogurt*
- *2 and 1/4 teaspoons vanilla extract*
- *1 and 1/2 cups papaya, chopped*
- *6 tablespoons granola*
- *1 and 1/2 cups pineapple, cut into medium pieces*
- *1 and 1/2 cups strawberries, cut into medium pieces*

Directions:

1. In a bowl, mix honey with yogurt and vanilla extract and stir.
2. Divide papaya, strawberries and pineapple pieces into tall glasses, add yogurt mixture and stir gently.
3. Top with granola and serve.

Nutrition: Calories:267 Fat: 10g; Carbohydrates: 29g; Protein: 6g Sodium: 176mg

58. Banana and Peanut Butter Breakfast Smoothie

Preparation: 5 minutes   **Cooking: 5 minutes**   **Servings: 2**

Ingredients:

- *1 c. non-fat milk*
- *1 T. all-natural peanut butter*
- *1 medium banana*

Directions:

1. Prepare all ingredients in a blender and mix until smooth.
2. Serve and enjoy!

Nutrition: Calories: 230 Fat: 9g Carbohydrates: 30g; Protein: 10g Sodium: 76mg

59. Apple-Spice Baked Oatmeal

Preparation: 10 minutes   **Cooking: 30 minutes**   **Servings: 2**

Ingredients:

- *1 egg, beaten*
- *1/2 c. sweetened applesauce*
- *1/2 c. non-fat or 1% milk*
- *1 tsp. vanilla*
- *2 T. oil*
- *1 apple, chopped*
- *2 c. rolled oats*
- *1 tsp. baking powder*
- *1/4 tsp. salt*
- *1 tsp. cinnamon*
- *2 T. brown sugar*
- *2 T. chopped nuts*

Directions:

1. Prepare and warm the oven to 375° F. Lightly oil an 8 x 8-inch baking pan.
2. Mix applesauce, egg, milk, vanilla, and oil in a bowl, then add in the apple.
3. In another bowl, combine baking powder, rolled oats, cinnamon, and salt, and add this to the liquid mixture. Mix well.
4. Get the mixture and pour it into the prepared baking dish. Bake for about 25 minutes.
5. Remove from the oven when done and sprinkle with brown sugar and nuts. Allow broiling in the oven for an additional 3-4 minutes until the top is brown and sugar bubbles start to appear.
6. Cut into squares and serve warm.

Nutrition: Calories: 160 Fat: 6g Carbohydrates: 22g; Protein: 6g Sodium: 96mg

60. Banana-Nut Pancakes

Preparation: 10 minutes   **Cooking: 20 minutes**   **Servings: 2**

Ingredients:

- *1 c. whole-wheat flour*
- *2 tsps. baking powder*
- *1/4 tsp. Salt*
- *1/4 tsp. cinnamon*
- *1 large banana, mashed*
- *1 c. 1% milk*
- *3 large egg whites*
- *2 tsps. oil*
- *1 tsp. vanilla*
- *2 T. walnuts, chopped*

Directions:

1. Put and mix well all dry ingredients in a large bowl.
2. In a different bowl, mix oil, milk, egg whites, mashed bananas, and vanilla until smooth.
3. Add now the wet ingredients with the dry, but DO NOT over mix.
4. Heat a large skillet over medium heat and lightly spray with cooking oil. Pour around 1/4 cup of the pancake batter on the hot skillet.
5. When the batter starts to set and bubble, flip it over. Repeat with the remaining batter.

Nutrition: Calories: 114 Fat: 5g Carbohydrates: 16g; Protein: 20g Sodium: 116mg

61. Cheese and Broccoli Mini Egg Omelets

Preparation: 10 minutes   **Cooking: 30 minutes**   **Servings: 2**

Ingredients:

- *2 c. broccoli florets*
- *4 eggs*
- *1 c. egg whites*
- *1/4 c. reduced-fat cheddar cheese*
-
- *1/4 c. grated Romano or parmesan cheese*
- *1 tbsp. olive oil*
- *Salt and pepper to taste*
- *Cooking spray*

Directions:

1. Preheat oven to 350° F.
2. In a small saucepan, steam broccoli with water for about 6-7 minutes.
3. Once broccoli is cooked, drain well, then mash with salt, pepper, and oil.
4. Spray some cooking oil in a muffin tin, then spoon broccoli evenly into each muffin well.

5. In a separate bowl, beat egg whites, grated parmesan cheese, eggs, salt, and pepper.
6. Pour this mixture into the spooned broccoli mixture in the muffin pan.
7. Put some grated cheddar on top and bake for 20 minutes. Serve immediately.

Nutrition: Calories: 167 Fat: 8g; Carbohydrates: 5g; Protein: 18g Sodium: 189mg

62. Mushroom and Shallot Frittata

Preparation: 10 minutes   **Cooking: 30 minutes**   **Servings: 2**

Ingredients:

- *1 T. unsalted butter*
- *4 shallots, finely chopped*
- *1/2 lb. mushrooms*
- *2 T. fresh parsley, finely chopped*
- *1 tsp. dried thyme*
- *3 eggs*
- *black pepper to taste*
- *5 large egg whites*
- *1 T. milk or fat-free half-and-half*
- *1/4 c. fresh-grated parmesan cheese*

Directions:

1. Preheat oven to 350° F.
2. Warm and melt butter in a large, oven-safe skillet. Stir in shallots and sauté until golden brown.
3. Add parsley, thyme, mushrooms, and black pepper.
4. Get another bowl, then whisk eggs and egg whites together with parmesan cheese and milk.
5. Add the egg mixture to the skillet.
6. When the edges begin to set, place the entire skillet in the oven.
7. Bake until frittata is fully cooked, about 15 minutes.
8. Cut into four wedges and serve.

Nutrition: Calories: 132 Fat: 7g Carbohydrates: Sodium: 116mg; Protein: 10g

63. Green Breakfast Smoothie

Preparation: 5 minutes   **Cooking: 5 minutes**   **Servings: 2**

Ingredients:

- *1 medium banana*
- *1 c. baby spinach*
- *1/2 c. fat-free milk*
- *1/4 c. whole oats*
- *3/4 c. frozen mango*
- *1/4 c. plain non-fat yogurt*
- *1/2 tsp. vanilla*

Directions:

1. Prepare blender and put all ingredients. Mix well and serve!

Nutrition: Calories: 265 Fat:13g Carbohydrates: 25g; Protein: 13g Sodium: 109mg

64. Fruit and Grain Breakfast

Preparation: 10 minutes   **Cooking: 15 minutes**   **Servings: 2**

Ingredients:

- *3 c. water*
- *1/4 tsp. salt*
- *3/4 c. quick-cooking brown rice*
- *3/4 c. bulgur*
- *1 granny Smith apple*
- *1 red apple*
- *1 orange*
- *1 c. raisins*
- *1 (8 oz.) c. low-fat vanilla yogurt*

Directions:

1. Heat water and salt in a large pot over high heat.
2. Reduce heat to low after adding rice and bulgur, then cover and cook for 10 minutes.
3. Take it from the heat and let it stand for 2 minutes.
4. Spread the hot grains to cool on a baking sheet.
5. Prepare the fruit, then transfer the chilled grains and cut fruit into a mixing bowl.
6. Add in the yogurt. Serve.

Nutrition: Calories: 140 Fat: 2g Carbohydrates: 27g; Protein: 2g Sodium: 126mg

LUNCH

65. Curried Chicken Wrap

Preparation: 10 minutes   **Cooking: 10 minutes**   **Servings: 2**

Ingredients:

- *2 medium whole-wheat tortilla*
- *1/3 cup cooked chicken, chopped*
- *1 cup apple, chopped*
- *1 tablespoon light mayonnaise*
- *1 teaspoon curry powder*
- *1 cup, or about 15, raw baby carrots*

Directions:

1. Mix all the ingredients except tortillas.
2. Divide and place at the center of the tortillas.
3. Roll and serve.

Nutrition: Calories: 380 Fat: 9g Carbohydrates: 47g Protein: 27g Sodium: 107mg

66. Open-Faced Garden Tuna Sandwich

Preparation: 10 minutes   **Cooking: 15 minutes**   **Servings: 2**

Ingredients:

- *2 cans (5 ounces each) low sodium tuna packed in water, drained*
- *4 green onions, sliced*
- *4 slices hearty multigrain bread*
- *1 tablespoon fresh parsley, chopped*
- *1 tablespoon lemon juice*
- *1 tablespoon extra-virgin olive oil*
- *1/4 cup cherry tomatoes, sliced*
- *A handful of fresh arugulas*
- *2 tablespoons low fat whipped cream cheese - Black pepper powder to taste*

Directions:

1. Mix oil, lemon juice, parsley, green onion, and pepper.
2. Add tuna to a bowl. Add about 2/3 of the above mixture and mix well.
3. Spread a little of the remaining mixture lightly on both sides of the bread.
4. Heat a nonstick pan over high heat. Place the bread slices and cook until the bottom side is golden brown. Turn and cook the other side. Add the remaining mixture to the arugula and toss well.
5. To make sandwiches: Spread cream cheese on each of the bread slices. Divide and spread the tuna mixture over the slices. Place the arugula over the tuna mixture and finally cherry tomatoes.

Nutrition: Calories: 360 Fat: 20g Carbohydrates: 18g; Protein: 24g Sodium: 76mg

67. Baked Macaroni

Preparation: 10 minutes   **Cooking: 30 minutes**   **Servings: 2**

Ingredients:

- *1-pound extra-lean ground beef*
- *2 large onions, diced*
- *2 boxes (7 ounces each) whole-wheat elbow macaroni, cooked according to instructions on the package*
- *2 jars (15 ounces each) low sodium spaghetti sauce*
- *3/4 cup Parmesan cheese*

Directions:

1. Prepare a large nonstick pan over medium heat. Add onions and sauté for a few minutes until the onions are translucent.
2. Add beef and cook until brown. Add pasta and spaghetti sauce. Mix well and transfer into a greased baking dish.
3. Bake in a preheated oven at 350 degrees F for about 30 minutes.
4. Serve garnished with Parmesan cheese.

Nutrition: Calories: 200 Fat: 7g Carbohydrates: 25g Protein: 4g Sodium: 99mg.

68. Easy Roasted Salmon

Preparation: 5 minutes   **Cooking: 25 minutes**   **Servings: 2**

Ingredients:
- 8 oz wild salmon fillets
- 2 lemons, cut into 8 wedges
- Freshly ground black pepper to taste
- 1/2 cup fresh dill, minced
- 8 cloves garlic, peeled and minced

Directions:
1. Lay the salmon fillets in a large greased baking dish. Sprinkle lemon juice, pepper, dill, and garlic.
2. Prepare the oven at 400 degrees F then place the dish and bake for about 20-25 minutes until the salmon is opaque and serve.

Nutrition: Calories: 240 Fat: 14g Carbohydrates: 1g; Protein: 28g Sodium: 116mg

69. Shepherd's Pie

Preparation: 10 minutes   **Cooking: 30 minutes**   **Servings: 2**

Ingredients:
- 1 large baking potato, peeled, diced
- 1/4 cup low-fat milk
- 1/2-pound lean ground beef
- 1 medium onion, chopped
- 2 cloves garlic, minced
- 1 tablespoon flour
- 2 cups of frozen mixed vegetables
- 1/2 cup low sodium beef broth
- 1/2 cup cheddar cheese, sliced
- Pepper powder to taste

Directions:
1. Prepare a saucepan covered with water then put the potatoes. Cook until the potatoes are done. Drain and mash the potatoes.
2. Add milk to the mashed potatoes and mix well. Keep aside
3. Place a skillet over medium heat. Add onion, garlic, and beef. Cook until the beef is browned.
4. Add vegetables and broth. Heat thoroughly.
5. Transfer to a baking dish. Spread the potato mixture over this.
6. Sprinkle cheese on top.
7. Bake in a warm oven at 375 degrees for 25 -30 minutes or until the cheese is lightly browned.

Nutrition: Calories: 420 Fat: 21g Carbohydrates: 29g; Protein: 28g Sodium: 87mg

70. Salmon and Edamame Cakes

Preparation: 10 minutes   **Cooking: 30 minutes**   **Servings: 2**

Ingredients:
- 1 ½ cups flaked, cooked salmon
- 1 cup frozen edamame, thawed
- 4 large egg whites
- 1/2 cup whole-wheat panko breadcrumbs (Japanese breadcrumbs)
- 2 scallions, finely chopped
- 2 tablespoons fresh ginger, peeled, minced
- 2 cloves garlic, crushed
- 2 tablespoons cilantro, finely chopped
- Canola oil cooking spray
- 1 whole Lime, cut into wedges to serve

Directions:
1. Add all the Ingredients except lime wedges to a bowl and mix well.
2. Divide the mixture into 8-10 balls and shape them into cakes.
3. Arrange the cakes on a wax paper-lined plate. Refrigerate the cakes for about 30 minutes.
4. Place a nonstick skillet over medium heat. Spray with cooking spray. When the skillet is heated, place the cakes 3-4 cakes.
5. Cook until the underside is golden brown. Flip and cook the other side.
6. Serve hot with lemon wedges and a dip of your choice.

Nutrition: Calories: 637 Fat: 30g Carbohydrates: 58g Protein: 21g Sodium: 206mg

71. Flat Bread Pizza

Preparation: 5 minutes **Cooking: 20 minutes** **Servings: 2**

Ingredients:
- *1 tbsp. of olive oil, plus topping if needed*
- *1 lb. flatbread dough (use the whole-grain dough while on a DASH diet)*
- *1/2 tsp of dried herbs, red pepper flakes, or other needed spices*
- *1 bunch of fresh broccoli, cauliflower, arugula, or other leafy greens vegetables*
- *1 bell pepper, diced*

Directions:
1. Set the grill to medium heat and brush a thin oil layer.
2. Cook the flatbread dough on both sides until golden brown, about 2 minutes on either side.
3. Top flatbread with freshly sliced vegetables and green vegetables. Season to taste, using olive oil, salt, pepper, red pepper flakes, or herbs.
4. To finish cooking, relocate flatbread pizza to the oven.

Nutrition: Calories: 130 Fat: 1g Carbohydrates: 25g; Protein: 5g Sodium: 113mg

72. Spinach Salad with Walnuts and Strawberry

Preparation: 10 minutes **Cooking: 15 minutes** **Servings: 2**

Ingredients:
- *1/2 cup walnuts*
- *4 cups of fresh spinach, loosely trimmed stems*
- *3 tbsp. of honey*
- *2 tbsp. of spicy brown mustard*
- *1/4 cup of balsamic vinegar*
- *1/4 tsp of sea salt*
- *1/4 cup of crumbled feta (about 1 oz.), optional*

Directions:
1. Heat the oven until 375 ° F.
2. Arrange walnuts on a rimmed baking sheet and bake for 8 minutes, until they are fragrant and toasted. Switch to a cool plate.
3. Place the spinach in a large container. The honey, mustard, vinegar, and salt are whisked together in a small cup.
4. Drizzle the salad over 3/4 of the dressing and scatter the walnuts on top.
5. Serve sprinkled with both the cheese (if it is used) and the remaining side dressing.

Nutrition: Calories: 129 Fat: 8g Carbohydrates: 10g; Protein: 7g Sodium: 120mg

73. Chicken Vegetable Soup

Preparation: 5 minutes **Cooking: 15 minutes** **Servings: 2**

Ingredients:
- *2 tbsp. of olive oil*
- *3 garlic cloves*
- *1 onion*
- *4 cups of low sodium chicken broth*
- *1/2 cup of carrot, sliced*
- *1/2 cup of a parsnip, sliced*
- *2 cups of a green collar, minced*
- *1 can of black beans, drained*
- *1/2 cup of seaweed (optional)*

Directions:
1. Simmer in the olive oil, garlic, and onion blended.
2. Pour the broth and vegetables into the chicken and turn to a boil. Switch to a simmer when boiling.
3. Keep on simmer until the vegetables are soft.
4. Pour in the strained canned beans and optional seaweed when 5 minutes left to cook.

Nutrition: Calories: 120 Fat: 4g Carbohydrates: 11g Sodium: 102mg; Protein: 10g

74. Avocado Sandwich with Lemon and Cilantro

Preparation: 10 minutes   **Cooking: 10 minutes**   **Servings: 2**

Ingredients:

- 1 medium Hass avocado
- 2 slices of 100% whole wheat bread
- 1/2 cup spinach
- 1/4 cup cilantro
- 1/2 carrots
- 1/4 cup cucumber
- 1/4 cup blueberries
- 1/4 cup red cherries
- 1 tbsp. lemon juice
- 1 cup skim milk

Directions:

1. Toast the bread.
2. Slice the avocado (or as desired) into thin strips and put on toast.
3. Slice the vegetables, then put them on toast.
4. Sprinkle with a splash of salt and lemon juice.
5. Prepare the fruit and enjoy a bowl of mixed fruit on the side with skim milk.

Nutrition: Calories 580, Carbohydrates 50g, Protein 9g, Fat 31g, Sodium 120mg

75. Veggie Sushi

Preparation: 10 minutes   **Cooking: 15 minutes**   **Servings: 2**

Ingredients:

- 3 cups of brown rice
- 2 tbsp. of rice wine vinegar
- 2 avocados, longitudinally cut
- 2 carrots, longitudinally sliced
- 1 cucumber, longitudinally sliced
- 6 tbsp of cabbage
- Ponzu sauce, to taste

Directions:

1. Cook brown rice, as indicated in instructions. Fold rice to vinegar rice wine. Let the cooked rice cool down.
2. When cool, spread rice uniformly with a wooden spoon on a bamboo sushi mat, or dip your hands in a cold bowl of water and spread the rice with your fingertips, on top layer avocado, cabbage, and slices of cucumber.
3. Using the mat to roll it into a packed roll of rice and vegetable, slide the mat out and repeat.
4. Slice into circles of 1/2 inch. Serve.

Nutrition: Calories: 135 Fat: 3g Carbohydrates: 22g; Protein: 3g Sodium: 116mg

76. Fascinating Spinach and Beef Meatballs

Preparation: 10 minutes   **Cooking: 20 minutes**   **Servings: 4**

Ingredients:

- 1/2 cup onion
- 4 garlic cloves
- 1 whole egg
- 1/4 teaspoon oregano
- Pepper as needed
- 1-pound lean ground beef
- 10 ounces spinach

Directions:

1. Preheat your oven to 375 degrees F.
2. Take a bowl and mix in the rest of the ingredients, and using your hands, roll into meatballs.
3. Transfer to a sheet tray and bake for 20 minutes and serve.

Nutrition: Calorie: 200, Fat: 8g, Carbohydrates: 5g, Protein: 29g Sodium: 120mg.

77. Healthy Avocado Beef Patties

Preparation: 15 minutes   **Cooking: 10 minutes**   **Servings: 2**

Ingredients:

- 1 pound 85% lean ground beef
- 1 small avocado, pitted and peeled

- *Fresh ground black pepper as needed*

Directions:
1. Pre-heat and prepare your broiler to high.
2. Divide beef into two equal-sized patties.
3. Season the patties with pepper accordingly.
4. Broil the patties for 5 minutes per side.
5. Transfer the patties to a platter.
6. Slice avocado into strips and place them on top of the patties and serve!

Nutrition: Calories 468, Carbohydrates 9g, Protein 38g, Fat 43g, Sodium 120mg

78. Juicy and Peppery Tenderloin

Preparation: 10 minutes   **Cooking: 20 minutes**   **Servings: 2**

Ingredients:
- *2 teaspoons sage, chopped*
- *Sunflower seeds and pepper*
- *2 ½ pounds beef tenderloin*
- *2 teaspoons thyme, chopped*
- *2 garlic cloves, sliced*
- *2 teaspoons rosemary, chopped*
- *4 teaspoons olive oil*

Directions:
1. Preheat your oven to 425 º F.
2. Take a small knife and cut incisions in the tenderloin; insert one slice of garlic into the incision.
3. Rub meat with oil.
4. Take a bowl and add sunflower seeds, sage, thyme, rosemary, pepper and mix well.
5. Rub the spice mix over tenderloin.
6. Put rubbed tenderloin into the roasting pan and bake for 10 minutes.
7. Lower temperature to 350 degrees F and cook for 20 minutes more until an internal thermometer reads 145 degrees F.
8. Transfer tenderloin to a cutting board and let sit for 15 minutes; slice into 20 pieces and enjoy!

Nutrition: Calorie: 183 Fat: 9g Carbohydrates: 1g Protein: 24g Sodium: 130mg

79. Lovely Faux Mac and Cheese

Preparation: 15 minutes   **Cooking: 45 minutes**   **Servings: 2**

Ingredients:
- *5 cups cauliflower florets*
- *Sunflower seeds and pepper to taste*
- *1 cup coconut almond milk*
- *1/2 cup vegetable broth*
- *2 tablespoons coconut flour, sifted*
- *1 organic egg, beaten*
- *1 cup cashew cheese*

Directions:
1. Preheat your oven to 350 º F.
2. Season florets with sunflower seeds and steam until firm.
3. Place florets in a greased ovenproof dish.
4. Heat coconut almond milk over medium heat in a skillet; make sure to season the oil with sunflower seeds and pepper.
5. Stir in broth and add coconut flour to the mix, stir.
6. Cook until the sauce begins to bubble.
7. Remove heat and add beaten egg.
8. Pour the thick sauce over the cauliflower and mix in cheese.
9. Bake for 30-45 minutes and serve.

Nutrition: Calories: 229 Fat: 14g Carbohydrates: 9g Protein: 15g Sodium: 150mg

80. Almond Butternut Chicken

Preparation: 15 minutes   **Cooking: 30 minutes**   **Servings: 4**

Ingredients:

- *1/2-pound Nitrate-free bacon*
- *6 chicken thighs, boneless and skinless*
- *2-3 cups almond butternut squash, cubed*
- *Extra virgin olive oil*
- *Fresh chopped sage*
- *Sunflower seeds and pepper as needed*

Directions:

1. Prepare your oven by preheating it to 425°F.
2. Take a large skillet and place it over medium-high heat, add bacon and fry until crispy.
3. Take a slice of bacon and place it on the side, crumble the bacon.
4. Add cubed almond butternut squash in the bacon grease and sauté, season with sunflower seeds and pepper.
5. Once the squash is tender, remove the skillet and transfer it to a plate.
6. Add coconut oil to the skillet and add chicken thighs, cook for 10 minutes.
7. Season with sunflower seeds and pepper.
8. Remove skillet from the stove and transfer to oven.
9. Bake for 12-15 minutes, top with the crumbled bacon and sage.

Nutrition: Calories: 323; Fat: 19g; Carbohydrates: 8g; Protein: 12g Sodium: 96mg.

81. Zucchini Zoodles with Chicken

Preparation: 10 minutes   **Cooking: 10 minutes**   **Servings: 2**

Ingredients:

- *2 chicken fillets, cubed*
- *2 tablespoons ghee*
- *1-pound tomatoes, diced*
- *1/2 cup basil, chopped*
- *1/4 cup almond milk*
- *1 garlic clove, peeled, minced*
- *1 zucchini, shredded*

Directions:

1. Sauté cubed chicken in ghee until no longer pink.
2. Add tomatoes and season with sunflower seeds.
3. Simmer and reduce liquid.
4. Prepare your zucchini Zoodles by shredding zucchini in a food processor.
5. Add basil, garlic, coconut almond milk to the chicken and cook for a few minutes.
6. Add half of the zucchini Zoodles to a bowl and top with creamy tomato basil chicken and enjoy!

Nutrition: Calories: 540 Fat: 27g Carbohydrates: 13g Protein: 59g Sodium: 180mg

82. Crazy Japanese Potato and Beef Croquettes

Preparation: 10 minutes   **Cooking: 20 minutes**   **Servings: 2**

Ingredients:

- *3 medium russet potatoes, peeled and chopped*
- *1 tablespoon almond butter*
- *1 tablespoon vegetable oil*
- *3 onions, diced*
- *3/4-pound ground beef*
- *4 teaspoons light coconut aminos*
- *All-purpose flour for coating (1/2-1 cup)*
- *2 eggs, beaten*
- *Panko breadcrumbs for coating*
- *1/2 cup oil, frying*

Directions:

1. Take a saucepan and place it over medium-high heat; add potatoes and sunflower seeds water, boil for 16 minutes.
2. Remove water and put potatoes in another bowl, add almond butter and mash the potatoes.
3. Take a frying pan and place it over medium heat, add 1 tablespoon oil and let it heat up.
4. Add onions and stir fry until tender.
5. Add coconut aminos to beef to onions.

6. Keep frying until beef is browned.
7. Mix the beef with the potatoes evenly.
8. Take another frying pan and place it over medium heat; add half a cup of oil.
9. Form croquettes using the mashed potato mixture and coat them with flour, then eggs and finally breadcrumbs.
10. Fry patties until golden on all sides. Enjoy!

Nutrition: Calories: 239 Fat: 4g Carbohydrates: 20g Protein: 10g Sodium: 70mg

83. Spicy Chili Crackers

Preparation: 15 minutes   **Cooking: 60 minutes**   **Servings: 20**

Ingredients:

- *3/4 cup almond flour*
- *1/4 cup coconut flour*
- *1/2 teaspoon paprika*
- *1/2 teaspoon cumin*
- *1 1/2 teaspoons chili pepper spice*
- *1 teaspoon onion powder*
- *1/2 teaspoon sunflower seeds*
- *1 whole egg*
- *1/4 cup unsalted almond butter*

Directions:

1. Preheat your oven to 350 degrees F.
2. Line a baking sheet with parchment paper and keep it on the side.
3. Add ingredients to your food processor and pulse until you have a nice dough.
4. Divide dough into two equal parts.
5. Place one ball on a sheet of parchment paper and cover with another sheet; roll it out.
6. Cut into crackers and repeat with the other ball.
7. Transfer the prepped dough to a baking tray and bake for 8-10 minutes.
8. Remove from oven and serve.

Nutrition: Calories 225, Carbohydrates 3g, Protein 2g, Fat 4g, Sodium 70mg

84. Golden Eggplant Fries

Preparation: 10 minutes   **Cooking: 15 minutes**   **Servings: 2**

Ingredients:

- *2 eggs*
- *2 cups almond flour*
- *2 tablespoons coconut oil*
- *2 eggplants, peeled and cut thinly*
- *Sunflower seeds and pepper*

Directions:

1. Preheat your oven to 400 º F.
2. Take a bowl and mix with sunflower seeds and black pepper.
3. Take another bowl and beat eggs until frothy.
4. Dip the eggplant pieces into the eggs.
5. Then coat them with the flour mixture.
6. Add another layer of flour and egg.
7. Then, take a baking sheet and grease with coconut oil on top.
8. Bake for about 15 minutes and serve!

Nutrition: Calories 211, Carbohydrates 12g, Protein 9g, Fat 16g, Sodium 120mg

85. Traditional Black Bean Chili

Preparation: 10 minutes   **Cooking: 4 hours**   **Servings: 2**

Ingredients:

- *1 ½ cups red bell pepper, chopped*
- *1 cup yellow onion, chopped*
- *1 ½ cups mushrooms, sliced*
- *1 tablespoon olive oil*
- *1 tablespoon chili powder*
- *2 garlic cloves, minced*
- *1 teaspoon chipotle chili pepper, chopped*
- *1/2 teaspoon cumin, ground*

- 16 ounces canned black beans, drained and rinsed
- 2 tablespoons cilantro, chopped
- 1 cup tomatoes, chopped

Directions:
1. Add red bell peppers, onion, dill, mushrooms, chili powder, garlic, chili pepper, cumin, black beans, and tomatoes to your Slow Cooker.
2. Stir well.
3. Place lid and cook on HIGH for 4 hours.
4. Sprinkle cilantro on top and serve!

Nutrition: Calories: 211 Fat: 3g Carbohydrates: 22g Protein: 5g Sodium: 40mg

86. Pasta With Spinach, Garbanzos, And Raisins

Preparation: 10 minutes   **Cooking: 15 minutes**   **Servings: 2**

Ingredients:
- 8 ounces farfalle (bowtie) pasta
- 2 tablespoons olive oil
- 4 garlic cloves, crushed
- 1/2 can (19 ounces) garbanzos, rinsed and drained
- 1/2 cup unsalted chicken broth
- 1/2 cup golden raisins
- 4 cups fresh spinach, chopped
- 2 tablespoons Parmesan cheese
- Cracked black peppercorns to taste

Directions:
1. Fill about 75% of a large pot with water and bring to a boil.
2. Put in the pasta and cook until tender 10 to 12 minutes, or according to the package directions. Drain the pasta completely.
3. Warm olive oil and garlic on a skillet with medium heat.
4. Put in the garbanzos and chicken broth. Stir until warmed through.
5. Put raisins and spinach. Cook spinach for about 3 minutes. Do not overcook.
6. Divide the pasta among plates. Put 1/6 of the sauce, 1 teaspoon Parmesan cheese, and peppercorns on top of each serving to taste. Serve instantly.

Nutrition: Calories 283, Carbohydrates 21g, Protein 11g, Fat 7g, Sodium 106mg

87. Mango Salsa Pizza

Preparation: 10 minutes   **Cooking: 15 minutes**   **Servings: 2**

Ingredients:
- 12-inch prepared whole-grain pizza crust, purchased or made from a mix
- 1/2 cup onion
- 1/2 cup mango
- 1 cup red or green bell peppers
- 1/2 cup pineapple (tidbits)
- 1 tbsp. lime juice
- 1/2 cup fresh cilantro

Directions:
1. Prepare the oven to 425 F. Slightly covers a 12-inch round baking pan with cooking spray.
2. Chopped onion, bell peppers, and cilantro.
3. Prepare the mango, chopped, seeded, and peeled.
4. Put peppers, onions, mango, pineapple, lime juice, and cilantro in a small bowl. Set aside.
5. Get and roll out dough. Press into the baking pan. Keep in the oven and cook for about 15 minutes.
6. Get the pizza crust out of the oven and cover it with mango salsa. Put it back into the oven. Bake for 5 minutes or more until the toppings are hot and the crust is browned.
7. Slice the pizza into 8 even slices and serve instantly.

Nutrition: Calories 249, Carbohydrates 49g, Protein 8g, Fat 5g, Sodium 120mg

88. Stuffed Eggplant

Preparation: 15 minutes   **Cooking: 30 minutes**   **Servings: 2**

Ingredients:

- *1 medium eggplant*
- *1 cup of water*
- *1 tbsp. olive oil*
- *6 ounces boneless, skinless chicken breast*
- *1/4 cup onion, chopped*
- *1/4 cup red, green, or yellow bell peppers chopped*
- *1/4 cup celery chopped*
- *1/2 cup sliced fresh mushrooms*
- *1 cup whole-wheat breadcrumbs*
- *Freshly ground black pepper to taste*
- *1 cup unsalted tomatoes (canned), drained except for 1/4 cup liquid*

Directions:

1. Preheat the oven to 350 F. Slightly covers a baking dish with cooking spray.
2. Cut chicken breast into strips 1/2-inch-wide and 2 inches long.
3. Trim the ends off the eggplant and chop in half lengthwise. Using a spoon, remove the pulp, leaving a thick shell.
4. Prepare the baking dish and lay out the shells and then pour water into the bottom of the dish. Cut the eggplant pulp into cubes. Set aside.
5. Put oil in a large non-stick frying pan, heat over medium-high.
6. Put in the chicken strips and sauté until the chicken is slightly browned and no longer pink, about 5 minutes.
7. Put diced eggplant, onion, peppers, tomatoes, and reserved tomato juice, celery, and mushrooms to the chicken.
8. Let it simmer with lower heat until the vegetables are tender about 10 minutes.
9. Put black pepper and breadcrumbs. Add half mixture into each eggplant shell.
10. Enfold with aluminum foil. Bake for 15 minutes or more until the eggplant softened and stuffing is cooked through.
11. Move eggplant to individual plates and serve instantly.

Nutrition: Calories 310, Carbohydrates 33g, Protein 27g, Fat 9g, Sodium 116mg

89. Broiled White Sea Bass

Preparation: 5 minutes   **Cooking: 10 minutes**   **Servings: 2**

Ingredients:

- *2 white sea bass fillets (4 ounces)*
- *1 tablespoon lemon juice*
- *1 teaspoon garlic, minced*
- *1/4 teaspoon salt-free herbed seasoning blend*
- *Ground black pepper to taste*

Directions:

1. Preheat the broiler or grill.
2. Slightly coat a baking pan with cooking spray. Lay the fillets in the pan.
3. Drizzle the lemon juice, garlic, herbed seasoning, and pepper over the fillets.
4. Broil (grill) until the fish is opaque all over when tested with a tip of a knife, about 8 to 10 minutes.
5. Serve instantly.

Nutrition: Calories 114, Carbohydrates 2g, Protein 21g, Fat 2g, Sodium 96mg

90. Chicken Alfredo with Whole-Wheat Bowtie Pasta

Preparation: 10 minutes   **Cooking: 30 minutes**   **Servings: 2**

Ingredients:

- *12 ounces whole-wheat bowtie pasta*
- *2 tablespoons olive oil*
- *3 chicken breasts, boneless and skinless*
- *2 cloves garlic*
- *3/4 low-sodium chicken broth*
- *1/2 cup half-and-half*
- *3/4 cups grated Parmesan cheese*
- *2 tablespoons fresh parsley, minced*

- *Freshly ground black pepper to taste*

Directions:
1. Cook pasta per the package instructions. Set aside.
2. Put 2 tablespoons of olive oil on a skillet with medium-high heat.
3. Put in chicken breasts and cook until golden brown and done in the middle, about 5-6 minutes per side. Take out of the pan, chop into bite-size pieces, set aside.
4. Pour in the remaining 2 tablespoons of olive oil into the pan. Put garlic and sauté for a minute.
5. Add broth and let it boil for about 2 minutes. Put in half-and-half and whisk together. Carry on cooking, stirring regularly, for several minutes until liquid begins to become thick.
6. Turn off the heat and put in Parmesan cheese, chicken, and pasta. Sprinkle with black pepper.
7. Toss all ingredients together until well mixed.
8. Serve with parsley and additional parmesan cheese on top, if desired.

Nutrition: Calories 295, Carbohydrates 33g, Protein 17g, Fat 10g, Sodium 126mg

91.   Broccoli, Garlic, and Rigatoni

Preparation: 10 minutes   **Cooking: 25 minutes**   **Servings: 2**

Ingredients:
- *1/3-pound rigatoni noodles*
- *2 cups broccoli florets (tops)*
- *2 tablespoons Parmesan cheese*
- *2 teaspoons olive oil*
- *2 teaspoons minced garlic*
- *Freshly ground black pepper to taste*

Directions:
1. Fill about 75% of a large pot with water and bring to a boil. Put in the pasta and cook until tender, 10 to 12 minutes, or according to the package directions. Drain the pasta completely.
2. As the pasta cooks, in a pot fitted with a steamer basket, bring 1 inch of water to a boil. Put in the broccoli, cover, and steam until tender, about 10 minutes.
3. Get a large bowl, then mix the cooked pasta and broccoli. Toss with Parmesan cheese, olive oil, and garlic.
4. Sprinkle with pepper to taste. Serve instantly.

Nutrition: Calories 340, Carbohydrates 50g, Protein 16g, Fat 8g, Sodium 122mg

92.   Spinach Mushroom Frittata

Preparation: 10 minutes   **Cooking: 15 minutes**   **Servings: 4**

Ingredients:
- *3 cloves of garlic, minced*
- *1 cup chopped onion*
- *1 teaspoon olive oil*
- *1/2-pound fresh mushrooms, sliced*
- *1/2 teaspoon dried thyme*
- *10-ounce-bag fresh spinach*
- *1 tbsp. water*
- *1 tsp. dried dill or 1 tbsp. fresh dill*
- *Egg substitute equivalent to 10 eggs*
- *1/4 teaspoon black pepper*
- *1/4 cup feta cheese*

Directions:
1. Prepare oven to 350 degrees F.
2. In a 10- or 12-inch non-stick, ovenproof skillet, sauté garlic and onion in olive oil for around 5 minutes.
3. Put in mushrooms and thyme. Cook for 5 minutes more. Take the skillet off the stove.
4. Put spinach in a separate saucepan. Pour in 1 tablespoon of water. Cover and cook until just wilted. Drain spinach and let cool in a strainer. Squeeze out any liquid. Slice leaves.
5. In a large bowl, beat together egg substitute, dill, and pepper. Mix in the spinach, mushroom mixture, and feta cheese.
6. Clean non-stick skillet. Coat well with cooking spray. Put the skillet back on the stove over medium heat. When the skillet is hot, add egg mixture.
7. Place in the oven, uncovered. Check frittata in 10 minutes. Do not overcook.

8. When done, place a large serving platter over the skillet. Flip skillet over so that frittata falls onto the plate. Chop into six pieces and serve.

Nutrition: Calories 123, Carbohydrates 4g, Protein 15g, Fat 4g, Sodium 124mg

93. Creamy Chicken Breast

Preparation: 10 minutes   **Cooking: 20 minutes**   **Servings: 4**

Ingredients:

- *1 tablespoon olive oil*
- *A pinch of black pepper*
- *pounds chicken breasts, skinless, boneless, and cubed*
- *4 garlic cloves, minced*
- *2 and 1/2 cups low-sodium chicken stock*
- *2 cups coconut cream*
- *1/2 cup low-fat parmesan, grated 1 tablespoon basil, chopped*

Directions:

1. Heat-up a pan with the oil over medium-high heat, add chicken cubes, and brown them for 3 minutes on each side.
2. Add garlic, black pepper, stock, and cream, toss, cover the pan and cook everything for 10 minutes more.
3. Add cheese and basil, toss, divide between plates and serve for lunch. Enjoy!

Nutrition: Calories 221, Carbohydrates 14g, Protein 7g, Fat 6g, Sodium 197mg

94. Indian Chicken Stew

Preparation: 1 hour   **Cooking: 20 minutes**   **Servings: 4**

Ingredients:

- *1-pound chicken breasts, skinless, boneless, and cubed*
- *1 tablespoon garam masala*
- *1 cup fat-free yogurt*
- *1 tablespoon lemon juice*
- *A pinch of black pepper*
- *1/4 teaspoon ginger, ground*
- *15 ounces tomato sauce, no-salt-added*
- *5 garlic cloves, minced*
- *1/2 teaspoon sweet paprika*

Directions:

1. In a bowl, mix the chicken with garam masala, yogurt, lemon juice, black pepper, ginger, and fridge for 1 hour. Heat-up a pan over medium heat, add chicken mix, toss and cook for 5-6 minutes.
2. Add tomato sauce, garlic and paprika, toss, cook for 15 minutes, divide between plates and serve for lunch. Enjoy!

Nutrition: Calories 221, Carbohydrates 14g, Protein 16g, Fat 6g, Sodium 104mg

95. Sweet Potatoes and Zucchini Soup

Preparation: 10 minutes   **Cooking: 20 minutes**   **Servings: 8**

Ingredients:

- *4 cups veggie stock*
- *2 tablespoons olive oil*
- *2 sweet potatoes, peeled and cubed*
- *8 zucchinis, chopped*
- *2 yellow onions, chopped*
- *1 cup of coconut milk*
- *A pinch of black pepper*
- *1 tablespoon coconut aminos*
- *4 tablespoons dill, chopped*
- *1/2 teaspoon basil, chopped*

Directions:

1. Heat-up a pot with the oil over medium heat, add onion, stir and cook
2. for 5 minutes. Add zucchinis, stock, basil, potato, and pepper, stir and cook for 15 minutes more. Add milk, aminos, and dill, pulse using an immersion blender, ladle into bowls and serve for lunch.

Nutrition: Calories: 270 Carbohydrates: 50g Fat: 4g Protein: 11g Sodium 216 mg

96. Lemongrass and Chicken Soup

Preparation: 10 minutes   **Cooking: 25 minutes**   **Servings: 4**

Ingredients:

- 4 lime leaves, torn
- 4 cups veggie stock, low sodium
- 1 lemongrass stalk, chopped
- 1 tablespoon ginger, grated
- 1-pound chicken breast, skinless, boneless, and cubed
- 8 ounces mushrooms, chopped
- 4 Thai chilies, chopped
- 13 ounces of coconut milk
- 1/4 cup lime juice
- 1/4 cup cilantro, chopped A pinch of black pepper

Directions:

1. Put the stock into a pot, bring to a simmer over medium heat, add lemongrass, ginger, and lime leaves, stir, cook for 10 minutes, strain into another pot, and heat up over medium heat again.
2. Add chicken, mushrooms, milk, cilantro, black pepper, chilies, and lime juice, stir, simmer for 15 minutes, ladle into bowls and serve.

Nutrition: Calories: 105 Carbohydrates: 1g Fat: 2g Protein: 15g Sodium 200 mg

97. Chicken, Bamboo, and Chestnuts Mix

Preparation: 10 minutes   **Cooking: 20 minutes**   **Servings: 4**

Ingredients:

- 1-pound chicken thighs, boneless, skinless, and cut into medium chunks
- cup low-sodium chicken stock
- 1 tablespoon olive oil
- tablespoons coconut aminos
- 1-inch ginger, grated
- carrot, sliced
- garlic cloves, minced
- 8 ounces canned bamboo shoots, no-salt-added and drained 8 ounces water chestnuts

Directions:

1. Heat-up a pan with the oil over medium-high heat, add chicken, stir, and brown for 4 minutes on each side. Add the stock, aminos, ginger, carrot, garlic, bamboo, and chestnuts, toss, cover the pan, and cook everything over medium heat for 12 minutes.
2. Divide everything between plates and serve. Enjoy!

Nutrition: Calories 281, Carbohydrates 14g, Protein 14g, Fat 7g, Sodium 125mg

98. Salsa Chicken

Preparation: 10 minutes   **Cooking: 25 minutes**   **Servings: 4**

Ingredients:

- 1 cup mild salsa, no-salt-added
- 1/2 teaspoon cumin, ground Black pepper to the taste
- tablespoon chipotle paste
- 1-pound chicken thighs, skinless and boneless
- 2 cups corn
- Juice of 1 lime
- tablespoon olive oil
- tablespoons cilantro, chopped 1 cup cherry tomatoes, halved
- 1 small avocado, pitted, peeled, and cubed

Directions:

1. In a pot, combine the salsa with the cumin, black pepper, chipotle paste, chicken thighs, and corn, toss, bring to a simmer and cook over medium heat for 25 minutes. Add lime juice, oil, cherry tomatoes, and avocado, toss, divide into bowls and serve for lunch. Enjoy!

Nutrition: Calories 269, Carbohydrates 18g, Protein 7g, Fat 6g, Sodium 500mg

99. Rice with Chicken

Preparation: 10 minutes   **Cooking: 30 minutes**   **Servings: 4**

Ingredients:

- 1/2 cup coconut aminos
- 1/3 cup rice wine vinegar
- 2 tablespoons olive oil
- 2 chicken breast, skinless, boneless, and cubed
- 1/2 cup red bell pepper, chopped A pinch of black pepper
- 6 garlic cloves, minced
- 1/2 teaspoon ginger, grated
- 1/2 cup carrots, grated 1 cup white rice
- 2 cups of water

Directions:

1. Heat-up a pan with the oil over medium-high heat, add the chicken, stir and brown for 4 minutes on each side. Add aminos, vinegar, bell pepper, black pepper, garlic, ginger, carrots, rice and stock, stock, cover the pan and cook over medium heat for 20 minutes.
2. Divide everything into bowls and serve for lunch. Enjoy!

Nutrition: Calories: 70 Carbohydrates: 13g Fat: 2g Protein: 2g Sodium 105 mg

100. Tomato Soup

Preparation: 10 minutes   **Cooking: 20 minutes**   **Servings: 4**

Ingredients:

- 6 garlic cloves, minced
- 1 yellow onion, chopped
- 3 carrots, chopped
- 15 ounces tomato sauce, no-salt-added
- 1 tablespoon olive oil
- 15 ounces roasted tomatoes, no-salt-added
- 1 cup low-sodium veggie stock
- 1 tablespoon tomato paste, no-salt-added
- 1 tablespoon basil, dried
- 1/4 teaspoon oregano, dried
- 3 ounces coconut cream
- A pinch of black pepper

Directions:

1. Heat-up a pot with the oil over medium heat, add garlic and onion, stir and cook for 5 minutes. Add carrots, tomato sauce, tomatoes, stock, tomato paste, basil, oregano, and black pepper, stir, bring to a simmer, cook for 15 minutes, add cream, blend the soup using an immersion blender, divide into bowls and serve for lunch. Enjoy!

Nutrition: Calories: 90 Carbohydrates: 20g Fat: 0g Protein: 2g Sodium 480 mg

101. Cod Soup

Preparation: 10 minutes   **Cooking: 25 minutes**   **Servings: 4**

Ingredients:

- 1 yellow onion, chopped
- 12 cups low-sodium fish stock
- 1-pound carrots, sliced
- 1 Tablespoon olive oil Black pepper to the taste
- 1 tablespoons ginger, minced
- 1 cup of water
- 1-pound cod, skinless, boneless, and cut into medium chunks

Directions:

1. Heat-up a pot with the oil over medium-high heat, add onion, stir and cook for 4 minutes. Add water, stock, ginger, and carrots, stir and cook for 10 minutes more.
2. Blend soup using an immersion blender, add the fish and pepper, stir, cook for 10 minutes more, ladle into bowls and serve. Enjoy!

Nutrition: Calories: 344 Carbohydrates: 35g Fat: 4g Protein: 46g Sodium 334 mg

102. Sweet Potato Soup

Preparation: 10 minutes   **Cooking: 1 hour and 40 minutes**   **Servings: 6**

Ingredients:
- *4 big, sweet potatoes 28 ounces veggie stock*
- *A pinch of black pepper*
- *1/4 teaspoon nutmeg, ground*
- *1/3 cup low-sodium heavy cream*

Directions:
1. Put the sweet potatoes on a lined baking sheet, bake them at 350 degrees F for 1 hour and 30 minutes, cool them down, peel, roughly chop them, and put them in a pot.
2. Add stock, nutmeg, cream, and pepper pulse well using an immersion blender, heat the soup over medium heat, cook for 10 minutes, ladle into bowls and serve. Enjoy!

Nutrition: Calories: 110 Carbohydrates: 23g Fat: 1g Protein: 2g Sodium 140 mg

103. Light Balsamic Salad

Preparation: 10 minutes   **Servings: 3**

Ingredients:
- *1 orange, cut into segments*
- *2 green onions, chopped*
- *1 romaine lettuce head, torn*
- *1 avocado, pitted, peeled, and cubed*
- *1/4 cup almonds, sliced*

For the salad dressing:
- *teaspoon mustard*
- *1/4 cup olive oil*
- *Tbsp balsamic vinegar Juice of 1/2 orange*
- *Salt and black pepper*

Directions:
1. In a salad bowl, mix oranges with avocado, lettuce, almonds, and green onions. In another bowl, mix olive oil with vinegar, mustard, orange juice, salt, and pepper, whisk well, add this to your salad, toss and serve.

Nutrition: Calories: 35 Carbohydrates: 5g Fat: 2g Protein: 1g Sodium 400 mg

104. Purple Potato Soup

Preparation: 10 minutes   **Cooking: 1 hour and 15 minutes**   **Servings: 6**

Ingredients:
- *6 purple potatoes, chopped*
- *1 cauliflower head, florets separated Black pepper to the taste*
- *4 garlic cloves, minced 1 yellow onion, chopped 3 tablespoons olive oil*
- *tablespoon thyme, chopped 1 leek, chopped*
- *shallots, chopped*
- *4 cups chicken stock, low sodium*

Directions:
1. In a baking dish, mix potatoes with onion, cauliflower, garlic, pepper,
2. thyme, and half of the oil, toss to coat, introduce in the oven and bake for 45 minutes at 400 degrees F.
3. Heat a pot with the rest of the oil over medium-high heat, add leeks and shallots, stir and cook for 10 minutes.
4. Add roasted veggies and stock, stir, bring to a boil, cook for 20 minutes, transfer soup to your food processor, blend well, divide into bowls, and serve.

Nutrition: Calories: 70 Carbohydrates: 15g Fat: 0g Protein: 2g Sodium 106 mg

105. Leeks Soup

Preparation: 10 minutes **Cooking: 1 hour and 15 minutes** **Servings: 6**

Ingredients:

- 2 gold potatoes, chopped
- 1 cup cauliflower florets Black pepper to the taste
- 5 leeks, chopped
- garlic cloves, minced
- 1 yellow onion, chopped
- 3 tablespoons olive oil
- Handful parsley, chopped
- 4 cups low-sodium chicken stock

Directions:

1. Heat-up a pot with the oil over medium-high heat, add onion and garlic, stir and cook for 5 minutes.
2. Add potatoes, cauliflower, black pepper, leeks, and stock, stir, bring to a simmer, cook over medium heat for 30 minutes, blend using an immersion blender, add parsley, stir, ladle into bowls and serve.

Nutrition: Calories: 125 Carbohydrates: 29g Fat: 1g Protein: 4g Sodium 152 mg

106. Cauliflower Lunch Salad

Preparation: 2 hours **Cooking: 10 minutes** **Servings: 4**

Ingredients:

- 1/3 cup low-sodium veggie stock 2 tablespoons olive oil
- 6 cups cauliflower florets, grated
- Black pepper to the taste
- 1/4 cup red onion, chopped 1 red bell pepper, chopped Juice of 1/2 lemon
- cup kalamata olives halved 1 teaspoon mint, chopped
- tablespoon cilantro, chopped

Directions:

1. Heat-up a pan with the oil over medium-high heat, add cauliflower, pepper and stock, stir, cook within 10 minutes, transfer to a bowl, and keep in the fridge for 2 hours. Mix cauliflower with olives, onion, bell pepper, black pepper, mint, cilantro, and lemon juice, toss to coat, and serve.

Nutrition: Calories: 102 Carbohydrates: 3g Fat: 10g Protein: 1g Sodium 97 mg

107. Fish Stew

Preparation: 10 minutes **Cooking: 30 minutes** **Servings: 4**

Ingredients:

- 1 red onion, sliced
- 1 tablespoons olive oil
- 1-pound white fish fillets, boneless, skinless, and cubed 1 avocado, pitted and chopped
- tablespoon oregano, chopped
- 1 cup chicken stock
- 1 tomato, cubed
- 1 teaspoon sweet paprika
- A pinch of salt and black pepper 1 tablespoon parsley, chopped
- Juice of 1 lime

Directions:

1. Warm-up oil in a pot over medium heat, add the onion, and sauté within 5 minutes. Add the fish, the avocado, and the other ingredients, toss, cook over medium heat for 25 minutes more, divide into bowls and serve for lunch.

Nutrition: Calories: 78 Carbohydrates: 8g Fat: 1g Protein: 11g Sodium: 151 mg

108. Shrimp and Broccoli Soup

Preparation: 5 minutes **Cooking: 25 minutes** **Servings: 4**

Ingredients:

- 1 tablespoons olive oil
- 1 yellow onion, chopped
- 4 cups chicken stock
- Juice of 1 lime
- 1-pound shrimp, peeled and deveined
- 1/2 cup coconut cream

- *1/2-pound broccoli florets*
- *1 tablespoon parsley, chopped*

Directions:
1. Heat a pot with the oil over medium heat, add the onion and sauté for 5 minutes. Add the shrimp and the other ingredients, simmer over medium heat for 20 minutes more. Ladle the soup into bowls and serve.

Nutrition: Calories: 220 Carbohydrates: 12g Fat: 7g Protein: 26g Sodium: 577 mg

109. Coconut Turkey Mix

Preparation: 10 minutes   **Cooking: 30 minutes**   **Servings: 4**

Ingredients:
- *1 yellow onion, chopped*
- *1-pound turkey breast, skinless, boneless, and cubed*
- *2 tablespoons olive oil*
- *5 garlic cloves, minced*
- *1 zucchini, sliced*
- *1 cup coconut cream*
- *A pinch of sea salt black pepper*

Directions:
1. Bring the pan to medium heat, add the onion and the garlic and sauté for 5 minutes. Put the meat and brown within 5 minutes more. Add the rest of the ingredients, toss, bring to a simmer and cook over medium heat for 20 minutes more. Serve for lunch.

Nutrition: Calories 200 Fat 4g Carbohydrates 14g Protein 7g Sodium 111mg

110. Salmon and Cabbage Mix

Preparation: 5 minutes   **Cooking: 25 minutes**   **Servings: 4**

Ingredients:
- *4 salmon fillets, boneless*
- *1 yellow onion, chopped*
- *2 tablespoons olive oil*
- *1 cup red cabbage, shredded*
- *1 red bell pepper, chopped*
- *1 tablespoon rosemary, chopped*
- *1 tablespoon coriander, ground*
- *1 cup tomato sauce*
- *A pinch of sea salt*
- *Pinch of black pepper*

Directions:
1. Bring the pan to medium heat, add the onion and sauté for 5 minutes.
2. Put the fish and sear it within 2 minutes on each side. Add the cabbage and the remaining ingredients, toss, cook over medium heat for 20 minutes more, divide between plates and serve.

Nutrition: Calories: 130 Carbohydrates: 8g Fat: 6g Protein: 12g Sodium: 345 mg

111. Shrimp and Onion Ginger Dressing

Preparation:10 minutes   **Cooking: 5 minutes**   **Servings: 2**

Ingredients:
- *8 medium shrimp, peeled and deveined*
- *12 ounces package mixed salad leaves*
- *10 cherry tomatoes, halved*
- *2 green onions, sliced*
- *2 medium mushrooms, sliced*
- *1/3 cup rice vinegar*
- *1/4 cup sesame seeds, toasted*
- *tablespoon low-sodium soy sauce*
- *2 teaspoons ginger, grated*
- *teaspoons garlic, minced*
- *2/3 cup canola oil*
- *1/3 cup sesame oil*

Directions:
1. In a bowl, mix rice vinegar with sesame seeds, soy sauce, garlic, ginger, and stir well. Pour this into your kitchen blender, add canola oil and sesame oil, pulse very well, and leave aside. Brush shrimp with 3 tablespoons of the ginger dressing you've prepared.
2. Heat your kitchen grill over high heat, add shrimp and cook for 3 minutes, flipping once. In a salad bowl, mix salad leaves with grilled shrimp, mushrooms, green onions, and tomatoes. Drizzle ginger dressing on top and serve right away!

Nutrition: Calories: 360 Carbohydrates: 14g Fat 11g Protein: 49g Sodium: 469 mg

112. Lime Shrimp and Kale

Preparation: 10 minutes   **Cooking: 20 minutes**   **Servings: 4**

Ingredients:

- *1-pound shrimp, peeled and deveined 4 scallions, chopped*
- *1 teaspoon sweet paprika*
- *1 tablespoon olive oil Juice of 1 lime*
- *Zest of 1 lime, grated*
- *A pinch of salt and black pepper 2 tablespoons parsley, chopped*

Directions:

1. Bring the pan to medium heat, add the scallions and sauté for 5 minutes. Add the shrimp and the other ingredients, toss, cook over medium heat for 15 minutes more, divide into bowls and serve.

Nutrition: Calories: 149 Carbohydrates: 12g Fat: 4g Protein: 21g Sodium: 250 mg

113. Parsley Cod Mix

Preparation: 10 minutes   **Cooking: 20 minutes**   **Servings: 4**

Ingredients:

- *1 tablespoon olive oil 2 shallots, chopped*
- *4 cod fillets, boneless and skinless*
- *2 garlic cloves, minced*
- *2 tablespoons lemon juice 1 cup chicken stock*
- *A pinch of salt and black pepper*

Directions:

1. Bring the pan to medium heat -high heat, add the shallots and the garlic and sauté for 5 minutes. Add the cod and the other ingredients, cook everything for 15 minutes more, divide between plates and serve for lunch.

Nutrition: Calories: 216 Carbohydrates: 7g Fat: 5g Protein: 34g Sodium: 380 mg

SALADS

114. Apple Lettuce Salad

Preparation: 20 minutes   **Servings: 4**

Ingredients

- 1/4 cup unsweetened apple juice
- 2 tbsp. lemon juice
- 1 tbsp. canola oil
- 2 ½ tsp. brown sugar
- 1/2 tsp. Dijon mustard
- 1/4 tsp. apple pie spice
- 1 medium red apple, chopped
- 8 cups mixed salad greens

Directions

1. Combine apple juice, lemon juice, oil, brown sugar, mustard, and apple pie spice in a large bowl.
2. Add the apple and toss to coat.
3. Add the green salad and toss just before serving.

Nutrition: Calories 124, Protein 2 g, Carbohydrates 20 g, Fat 4 g Sodium 145 mg

115. Apple Salad with Figs

Preparation: 15 minutes   **Servings: 6**

Ingredients

- 6 dried figs, chopped
- 2 large red apples, cored and diced
- 2 carrots, peeled and grated
- 1/2 cup fat-free lemon yogurt
- 2 ribs of celery, diced
- 2 tbsp. slivered almonds

Directions

1. In a portable bowl, combine the apples, figs, carrots, and celery.
2. Add the yogurt and mix well.
3. Top it with the slivered almonds and serve.

Nutrition: Calories 93, Protein 2 g, Carbohydrates 19 g, Fat 1 g, Sodium 133 mg

116. Apple-Fennel Slaw

Preparation: 15 minutes   **Cooking: 10 minutes**   **Servings: 4**

Ingredients

- 1 medium-sized fennel bulb, thinly sliced
- 1 large Granny Smith apple, cored and thinly sliced
- 2 carrots, grated
- 2 tbsp. raisins
- 1 tbsp. olive oil
- 1 tsp. sugar
- 1/2 cup apple juice
- 2 tbsp. apple cider vinegar
- 4 lettuce leaves

Directions

1. In an enormous bowl, combine the fennel, apple, carrots, and raisins to make the slaw.
2. Drizzle with olive oil, cover, and refrigerate while you prepare the rest of the ingredients.
3. In a saucepan, combine the sugar and apple juice. Put on medium heat and cook until reduced to about 1/4 cup, about 10 minutes. Remove from heat and let cool.
4. Include the apple cider vinegar. Pour the apple juice mixture over the slaw and mix well.
5. Let cool completely. Serve on lettuce leaves.

Nutrition: Calories 124, Protein 2 g, Carbohydrates 22 g, Fat 1 g, Sodium 61 mg

117. Arugula Peach Almond Salad

Preparation: 5 minutes   **Servings: 4**

Ingredients

- 1 tbsp. balsamic vinegar
- 1 tbsp. olive oil, preferably extra-virgin
- 1 tbsp. water
- 1/8 tsp. of kosher salt

- *6 cups baby arugula, well washed and dried*
- *3 ripe peaches, pitted and sliced*
- *1/2 cup sliced natural almonds, toasted*
- *Freshly ground black pepper*

Directions

1. In an enormous bowl, combine the vinegar, oil, water, and salt.
2. Add the arugula, peaches, and almonds and mix.
3. Season with pepper and serve immediately

Nutrition: Calories 152, Protein 4 g, Carbohydrates 15 g, Fat 10 g, Sodium 73 mg

118. Asian Vegetable Salad

Preparation: 25 minutes   **Servings: 4**

Ingredients

- *1 ½ cup julienned carrot*
- *1/2 cup julienned red bell pepper*
- *1 ½ cup julienned bok choy*
- *1/2 cup julienned yellow onion*
- *1 cup thinly sliced red cabbage*
- *1 ½ cup thinly sliced spinach*
- *1 tbsp. thinly sliced cilantro*
- *1 tbsp. minced garlic*
- *1 ½ tbsp. chopped cashews*
- *1 ½ cups snow peas*
- *2 tsp. toasted sesame oil*
- *2 tsp. low-sodium soy sauce*

Directions

1. Rinse all the vegetables under cold running water. Leave to drain.
2. Julienne (cut into very thin strips like matches) carrot, pepper, bok choy, and onion.
3. Chiffonade (cut along the grain into very thin strips) the cabbage, spinach, and cilantro.
4. In a large bowl, combine the chopped vegetables, garlic, cashews, and peas. Dress the salad with sesame oil and soy sauce.
5. Toss again to combine and serve.

Nutrition: Calories 113, Protein 3 g, Carbohydrates 14 g, Fat 4 g, Sodium 168 mg

119. Baby Beet and Orange Salad

Preparation: 30 minutes   **Cooking: 50 minutes**   **Servings: 4**

Ingredient

- *2 bunches baby beets with greens*
- *2 ribs celery, chopped (1/2 cup)*
- *1/4 head Napa cabbage, chopped*
- *1 chopped small yellow onion, chopped (1/2 cup)*
- *1 orange, peeled, and cut into segments*
- *Juice and zest of 1 orange*
- *1/2 tbsp. olive oil*
- *Pinch of black pepper to taste*

Directions

1. Warm the oven to 400°F. Cut the greens from the beets. Rinse the greens under cold water, drain well, and set aside. Wash the beets.
2. Pour a drizzle of olive oil on your hands and rub the beets to coat them lightly.
3. Wrap beets in foil and cook for about 45 minutes or until tender. Allow it to cool until you can be able to handle it, then peel off the outer skin. Cut and reserve.
4. Cut the beets into strips and put them in the bowl.
5. Chop the celery, cabbage, and onion and add them to the bowl. Zest and juice one orange in the bowl.
6. Cut the already peeled orange into quarters. Add to bowl. Pour half tbsp. of olive oil over the salad.
7. Top with black pepper and toss to combine.
8. Place the salad on cold plates and garnish with sliced beets. Serve immediately.

Nutrition: Calories 118, Protein 3 g, Carbohydrates 22 g, Fat 2 g Sodium 135 mg

120. Bean Salad with Vinaigrette

Preparation: 25 minutes   **Servings: 6**
Ingredients
For the vinaigrette:
- *1/3 cup of fresh parsley, chopped*
- *Ground black pepper, to taste*
- *2 tbsp. balsamic vinegar*

- *4 garlic cloves, finely chopped*
- *1/4 cup of extra-virgin olive oil*

For the salad:
- *1 can (15 oz.) of low-sodium garbanzo beans, rinsed and drained*
- *1 can (15 oz.) of black beans (low sodium), rinsed and drained*

- *6 lettuce leaves*
- *1 medium red onion, diced*
- *1/2 cup celery, finely chopped*

Directions
1. To make the dressing, in a portable bowl, combine the parsley, garlic, balsamic vinegar, and pepper. While whisking, add the olive oil slowly. Set aside.
2. Combine the beans and onion in an enormous bowl. Pour the dressing over the mixture and toss gently to combine well and evenly coat.
3. Cover and refrigerate until serving.
4. To serve, place 1 lettuce leaf on each plate.
5. Divide the salad between individual plates and garnish with chopped celery and serve.

Nutrition: Calories 206, Protein 7 g, Carbohydrates 22 g, Fat 10 g Sodium 174 mg

121. Beet Walnut Salad

Preparation Time: 1h 20 minutes   **Servings: 8**
Ingredients
- *1 small bunch of beets, or enough canned beets (no salt added) to make 3 cups, drained*
- *1/4cup red wine vinegar*
- *3 tbsp. balsamic vinegar*
- *1 tbsp. olive oil*
- *tbsp. water*

- *8 cups fresh salad greens*
- *1/4 cup chopped apple*
- *1/4 cup chopped celery*
- *Freshly ground pepper*
- *3 tbsp. chopped walnuts*
- *1/4 cup gorgonzola cheese, crumbled*

Directions
1. Steam the raw beets in water in a saucepan until tender. Remove the skins. Rinse to cool.
2. Cut into 1/2-inch slices. In a medium bowl, season with red wine vinegar.
3. In an enormous bowl, combine the balsamic vinegar, olive oil, and water. Add the salad greens and mix.
4. Arrange the salad greens on individual salad plates.
5. Garnish with sliced beets and chopped apples and celery.
6. Sprinkle with pepper, nuts, and cheese. Serve immediately.

Nutrition: Calories 105, Protein 3 g, Carbohydrates 12 g, Fat 5 g, Sodium 131 mg

122. Blue Cheese Spinach Salad

Preparation: 20 minutes   **Servings: 12**
Ingredients
Dressing:
- *4 tsp. olive oil*
- *2 tbsp. balsamic vinegar*
- *1 tbsp. maple syrup*

- *1/4 tsp. nutmeg*
- *1 tbsp. plain low-fat yogurt*

Salad:

- *2 pounds spinach, roughly chopped (or 3 10 oz. packages)*
- *1/2 cup sliced red onion*
- *1 ½ cups sliced cucumbers*
- *1 ½ cups grape tomatoes*
- *1/4 cup chopped walnuts*
- *1/4 cup blue cheese crumbles*

Directions
1. Combine all the ingredients together for the seasoning in a blender or food processor.
2. Toss spinach with seasoning and whisk 2 generous cups on cold plates.
3. Place the grated vegetables, nuts, and blue cheese on the spinach and serve.

Nutrition: Calories 70, Protein 4 g, Carbohydrates 27 g, Fat 4 g Sodium 95 mg

123. Braised Celery Root

Preparation: 25 minutes　　**Cooking: 1 hour**　　　　**Servings: 6**

Ingredients

- *1 cup vegetable stock or broth*
- *1 celery root (celeriac), peeled and diced (about 3 cups)*
- *1/4 cup sour cream*
- *1 tsp. Dijon mustard*
- *1/4 tsp. salt*
- *1/4 tsp. freshly ground black pepper*
- *2 tsp. fresh thyme leaves*

Directions
1. In an enormous saucepan, bring the stock to a boil over high heat. Add the celeriac.
2. When the stock comes back to a boil, reduce the heat to low. Cover and cook over low heat, occasionally stirring, until the celery root is tender, 10 to 12 minutes.
3. With a slotted spoon, transfer the celeriac to a bowl, cover, and keep warm. Increase the heat to high heat and bring the cooking liquid to a boil. Cook, uncovered until reduced to 1 tbsp., about 5 minutes.
4. Remove from heat and add sour cream, mustard, salt, and pepper. Add the celeriac and thyme to the sauce and stir over medium heat until heated through.
5. Move to a warm plate and serve right away.

Nutrition: Calories 54, Protein 2 g, Carbohydrates 7 g, Fat 2 g Sodium 206 mg

124. Butternut Squash Apple Salad

Preparation: 5 minutes　　**Cooking: 20 minutes**　　　　**Servings: 6**

Ingredients

- *2 tsp. of olive oil*
- *A butternut squash, seeded and peeled, cut into 1/2-inch pieces*
- *2 big apples, cored and cut 1/2-inch pieces*

Dressing:

- *1/2 cup low-fat plain yogurt*
- *2 tsp. balsamic vinegar*
- *2 cups chopped carrots*
- *1 ½ cups chopped celery*
- *6 cups spinach, chopped*
- *6 cups arugula, chopped*
- *1 1/2 tsp. honey*

Directions
1. Heat oven to 400°F. Stirs squash in olive oil, roast in the oven for 20-30 minutes until golden and tender. Let it cool completely.
2. Mix all the vegetables in a large bowl.
3. Prepare the vinaigrette by mixing yogurt, vinegar, and honey. Beat until smooth.
4. Pour the vinaigrette over the salad.
5. Toss and serve immediately.

Nutrition: Calories: 215, Protein 5 g, Carbohydrates 42 g, Fat 3 g Sodium 97 mg

125. Chicken Salad with Pineapple

Preparation: 15 minutes   **Cooking: 15 minutes**   **Servings: 8**

Ingredients

- *4 boneless, skinless chicken breasts, each about 5 oz.*
- *1 tbsp. olive oil*
- *1 can (8 oz.) unsweetened pineapple chunks, drained except for 2 tbsp. juice*

- *2 cups broccoli florets*
- *4 cups fresh baby spinach leaves*
- *1/2 cup thinly sliced red onions*

For the vinaigrette:

- *1/4 cup olive oil*
- *2 tbsp. balsamic vinegar*

- *2 tsp. sugar*
- *1/4 tsp. ground cinnamon*

Directions

1. Cut each chicken breast into cubes. In an enormous nonstick skillet, heat olive oil over medium heat.
2. Add the chicken and cook until golden brown, about 10 minutes.
3. In a large bowl, combine the cooked chicken, pineapple chunks, broccoli, spinach, and onion.
4. To prepare the vinaigrette, combine the olive oil, vinegar, reserved pineapple juice, sugar, and cinnamon in a small bowl. Pour over the salad.
5. Stir gently to coat evenly. Serve immediately.

Nutrition: Calories 186, Protein 17 g, Carbohydrates 7g, Fat 10 g, Sodium 250 mg

126. Chopped Greek Salad

Preparation: 35 minutes   **Servings: 4**

Ingredients

- *1 small red onion, cut into very thin half-moons*
- *1 tbsp. red wine vinegar*
- *1 tbsp. water*
- *1 tsp. dried oregano*
- *1 clove garlic, minced*
- *1/8 tsp. freshly ground black pepper*
- *1 tbsp. extra-virgin olive oil*

- *1-pint grape tomatoes, cut in halves*
- *1 medium cucumber, peeled, halved lengthwise, seeded, and cut into thin half-moons*
- *1/2 cup diced (1/2-inch) green bell pepper*
- *2 oz. (1/2 cup) crumbled regular rindless goat cheese*

Directions

1. Soak the red onion in a portable bowl of cold water for 30 minutes; drain and dry. (This step is optional, but it helps soften the strong onion flavor.)
2. In a large bowl, combine the vinegar, water, oregano, garlic, and pepper. Gradually add the oil.
3. Add the drained onion, tomatoes, cucumber, and bell pepper and mix well.
4. Sprinkle with goat cheese and serve immediately.

Nutrition: Calories 95, Protein 5 g, Carbohydrates 10 g, Fat 5 g, Sodium 81 mg

127. Classic Chicken Salad

Preparation: 30 minutes   **Servings: 2**

Ingredients

- *2 tbsp. light mayonnaise*
- *2 tbsp. plain low-fat yogurt*
- *1/4 tsp. kosher salt (optional)*
- *1/8 tsp. freshly ground black pepper*
- *8 oz. Basic Roast Chicken Breast*

- *2 small celery ribs, finely diced*
- *1 finely chopped scallion, white and green parts*
- *4 romaine lettuce leaves, for serving*

Directions

1. In a medium-sized bowl, combine mayonnaise, yogurt, and pepper.
2. Add the chicken, celery, and scallion and mix well.

3. Divide equal portions of the chicken salad between two plates, add the lettuce, and serve.
Nutrition: Calories 197, Protein 25 g, Carbohydrates 4 g, Fat 8 g, Sodium 276 mg

128. Corn Salad

Preparation: 20 minutes   **Cooking: 10 minutes**   **Servings: 4**
Ingredients

- 1/4 cup coarsely chopped cilantro
- 6 ears corn, shucked
- 1/4 cup nicely chopped red onion
- 2 roasted red bell peppers, diced (about 1 cup)
- 1-pint grape tomatoes, cut in half
- 1/4 tsp. kosher salt
- Juice of 1 lime
- 1/4 tsp. freshly ground black pepper
- 1 ½ tbsp. extra-virgin olive oil

Directions
1. In an enormous pot of boiling water, cook the ears of corn until the kernels have turned bright yellow, 3 to 4 minutes. Drain and let cool.
2. When cool enough to handle, remove the corn kernels from the cob using a knife. Put the corn in a large bowl, and add the cilantro, red onion, tomatoes, bell peppers, salt, black pepper, lime juice, and olive oil.
3. Mix the salad, taste, and adjust the seasonings as needed. Serve.

Nutrition: Calories 243, Protein 6 g, Carbohydrates 43 g, Fat 7 g, Sodium 153 mg

129. Spring Greens Salad

Preparation: 5 minutes   **Servings: 2**
Ingredients:

- 1/2 cup radish, sliced
- 1 cup fresh spinach, chopped
- 1/2 cup green peas, cooked
- 1/2 lemon
- 1 cup arugula, chopped
- 1 tablespoon avocado oil
- 1/2 teaspoon dried sage

Directions:
1. In the salad bowl, mix up radish, spinach, green peas, arugula, and dried sage.
2. Then squeeze the lemon over the salad.
3. Add avocado oil and shake the salad.

Nutrition: 54 calories, 3.1g protein 9g carbohydrates 3g fat Sodium: 122mg

130. Tuna Salad

Preparation: 7 minutes   **Servings: 2**
Ingredients:

- 1/2 cup low-fat Greek yogurt
- 8 oz tuna, canned
- 1/2 cup fresh parsley, chopped
- 1 cup corn kernels, cooked
- 1/2 teaspoon ground black pepper

Directions:
1. Mix up tuna, parsley, kernels, and ground black pepper.
2. Then add yogurt and stir the salad until it is homogenous.

Nutrition: Calories: 172 Fat: 10g Carbohydrates: 5g Protein: 14g Sodium: 155mg

131. Fish Salad

Preparation: 5 minutes   **Servings: 2**
Ingredients:

- 7 oz canned salmon, shredded
- 1 tablespoon lime juice
- 1 tablespoon low-fat yogurt
- 1 cup baby spinach, chopped
- 1 teaspoon capers, drained and chopped

Directions:
1. Mix up all ingredients together and transfer them into the salad bowl.

Nutrition: Calories 71, Carbohydrates 3g, Protein 1g, Fat 3g, Sodium 52mg

132. Salmon Salad

Preparation: 10 minutes   **Servings: 2**

Ingredients:
- *4 oz canned salmon, flaked*
- *1 tablespoon lemon juice*
- *2 tablespoons red bell pepper, chopped*
- *1 tablespoon red onion, chopped*
- *1 teaspoon dill, chopped*
- *1 tablespoon olive oil*

Directions:
1. Mix up all ingredients in the salad bowl.

Nutrition: Calories 119, Carbohydrates 7g, Protein 8g, Fat 7g, Sodium 121mg

133. Arugula Salad with Shallot

Preparation: 10 minutes   **Servings: 2**

Ingredients:
- *1 cup cucumber, chopped*
- *1 tablespoon lemon juice*
- *1 tablespoon avocado oil*
- *2 shallots, chopped*
- *1/2 cup black olives, sliced*
- *3 cups arugula, chopped*

Directions:
1. Mix up all ingredients from the list above in the salad bowl and refrigerate in the fridge for 5 minutes.

Nutrition: Calories 133, Carbohydrates 3g, Protein 12g, Fat 2g, Sodium 186mg

134. Watercress Salad

Preparation: 10 minutes   **Cooking: 4 minutes**   **Servings: 2**

Ingredients:
- *2 cups asparagus, chopped*
- *16 ounces shrimp, cooked*
- *4 cups watercress, torn*
- *1 tablespoon apple cider vinegar*
- *1/4 cup olive oil*

Directions:
1. In the mixing bowl mix up asparagus, shrimps, watercress, and olive oil.

Nutrition: Calories 264, Carbohydrates 25g, Protein 5g, Fat 15g, Sodium 300mg

135. Seafood Arugula Salad

Preparation: 5 minutes   **Cooking: 10 minutes**   **Servings: 2**

Ingredients:
- *1 tablespoon olive oil*
- *2 cups shrimps, cooked*
- *1 cup arugula*
- *1 tablespoon cilantro, chopped*

Directions:
1. Put all ingredients in the salad bowl and shake well.

Nutrition: Calories 161, Carbohydrates 4g, Protein 1g, Fat 3g, Sodium 216mg

136. Smoked Salad

Preparation: 10 minutes   **Servings: 2**

Ingredients:
- *1 mango, chopped*
- *4 cups lettuce, chopped*
- *8 oz smoked turkey, chopped*
- *2 tablespoons low-fat yogurt*
- *1 teaspoon smoked paprika*

Directions:
1. Mix up all ingredients in the bowls and transfer them to the serving plates.

Nutrition: Calories 88, Carbohydrates 2g, Protein 12g, Fat 2g, Sodium 350mg

137. Avocado Salad

Preparation: 5 minutes   **Servings: 2**

Ingredients:
- 1/2 teaspoon ground black pepper
- 1 avocado, peeled, pitted and sliced
- 4 cups lettuce, chopped
- 1 cup black olives, pitted and halved
- 1 cup tomatoes, chopped
- 1 tablespoon olive oil

Directions:
1. Put all ingredients in the salad bowl and mix up well.

Nutrition: Calories 197, Carbohydrates 10g, Protein 1g, Fat 17g, Sodium 301mg

138. Berry Salad with Shrimps

Preparation : 7 minutes   **Servings: 2**

Ingredients:
- 1 cup corn kernels, cooked
- 1 endive, shredded
- 1 pound shrimp, cooked
- 1 tablespoon lime juice
- 2 cups raspberries, halved
- 2 tablespoons olive oil
- 1 tablespoon parsley, chopped

Directions:
1. Put all ingredients from the list above in the salad bowl and shake well.

Nutrition: Calories 283, Carbohydrates 21g, Protein 20g, Fat 4g, Sodium 313mg

139. Sliced Mushrooms Salad

Preparation: 10 minutes   **Cooking: 20 minutes**   **Servings: 2**

Ingredients:
- 1 cup mushrooms, sliced
- 1 tablespoon margarine
- 1 cup lettuce, chopped
- 1 teaspoon lemon juice
- 1 tablespoon fresh dill, chopped
- 1 teaspoon cumin seeds

Directions:
1. Melt the margarine in the skillet.
2. Add mushrooms and lemon juice. Sauté the vegetables for 20 minutes over medium heat.
3. Then transfer the cooked mushrooms to the salad bowl, add lettuce, dill, and cumin seeds.
4. Stir the salad well.

Nutrition: Calories 135, Carbohydrates 13g, Protein 2g, Fat 5g, Sodium 138mg

140. Tender Green Beans Salad

Preparation: 5 minutes   **Servings: 2**

Ingredients:
- 2 cups green beans, trimmed, chopped, cooked
- 2 tablespoons olive oil
- 2 pounds shrimp, cooked, peeled
- 1 cup tomato, chopped
- 1/4 cup apple cider vinegar

Directions:
1. Mix up all ingredients together.
2. Then transfer the salad to the salad bowl.

Nutrition: Calories 179, Carbohydrates 6g, Protein 26g, Fat 5g, Sodium 280mg

141. Spinach and Chicken Salad

Preparation: 7 minutes   **Servings: 2**
Ingredients:
- 1 tablespoon olive oil
- A pinch of black pepper
- 1-pound chicken breast, cooked, skinless, boneless, shredded
- 1 pound cherry tomatoes, halved
- 1 red onion, sliced
- 3 cups spinach, chopped
- 1 tablespoon lemon juice
- 1 tablespoon nuts, chopped

Directions:
1. Put all ingredients in the salad bowl and gently stir with the help of a spatula.

Nutrition: Calories 209, Carbohydrates 8g, Protein 26g, Fat 8g, Sodium 162mg

142. Cilantro Salad

Preparation: 10 minutes   **Cooking: 8 minutes**   **Servings: 2**
Ingredients:
- 1 tablespoon avocado oil
- 1 pound shrimp, peeled and deveined
- 2 cups lettuce, chopped
- 1 tablespoon balsamic vinegar
- 1 tablespoon lemon juice
- 1 cup fresh cilantro, chopped

Directions:
1. Heat up a pan with the oil over medium heat, add the shrimps and cook them for 4 minutes per side or until they are light brown.
2. Transfer the shrimps to the salad bowl and add all remaining ingredients from the list above. Shake the salad.

Nutrition: Calories 146, Carbohydrates 3g, Protein 26.1g, Fat 3g, Sodium 281mg

143. Iceberg Salad

Preparation: 10 minutes   **Servings: 2**
Ingredients:
- 1 cup iceberg lettuce, chopped
- 2 oz scallions, chopped
- 1 cup carrot, shredded
- 1 cup radish, sliced
- 2 tablespoons red vinegar
- 1/4 cup olive oil

Directions:
1. Make the dressing: mix up olive oil and red vinegar.
2. Then mix up all remaining ingredients in the salad bowl.
3. Sprinkle the salad with dressing.

Nutrition: Calories 191, Carbohydrates 5g, Protein 1g, Fat 12g, Sodium 166mg

144. Seafood Salad with Grapes

Preparation: 5 minutes   **Servings: 2**
Ingredients:
- 2 tablespoons low-fat mayonnaise
- 2 teaspoons chili powder
- 1-pound shrimp, cooked, peeled
- 1 cup green grapes, halved
- 1 oz nuts, chopped

Directions:
1. Mix up all ingredients in the mixing bowl and transfer the salad to the serving plates.

Nutrition: Calories 225, Carbohydrates 8g, Protein 9g, Fat 4g, Sodium 390mg

145. Toasted Almond Ambrosia

Preparation: 10 Minutes   **Cooking: 20 minutes**   **Servings: 2**

Ingredients:

- *1/2 Cup Almonds, Slivered*
- *1/2 Cup Coconut, Shredded & Unsweetened*
- *3 Cups Pineapple, Cubed*
- *5 Oranges, Segment*
- *1 Banana, Halved Lengthwise, Peeled & Sliced*
- *2 Red Apples, Cored & Diced*
- *2 Tablespoons Cream Sherry*
- *Mint Leaves, Fresh to Garnish*

Directions:

1. Start by heating your oven to 325, and then get out a baking sheet. Roast your almonds for ten minutes, making sure they're spread out evenly.
2. Transfer them to a plate and then toast your coconut on the same baking sheet. Toast for ten minutes.
3. Mix your banana, sherry, oranges, apples and pineapple in a bowl.
4. Divide the mixture not serving bowls and top with coconut and almonds.
5. Garnish with mint before serving.

Nutrition: Calories 177, Carbohydrates 36g, Protein 4g, Fat 5g, Sodium 123mg

146. Healthy Cauliflower Salad

Preparation: 10 minutes   **Serving: 4**

Ingredients:

- *1 head cauliflower, broken into florets*
- *1 small onion, chopped*
- *1/8 cup extra virgin olive oil*
- *1/4 cup apple cider vinegar*
- *1/2 teaspoon sea salt*
- *1/2 teaspoon black pepper*
- *1/4 cup dried cranberries*
- *1/4 cup pumpkin seeds*

Directions:

1. Wash the cauliflower thoroughly and break down into florets.
2. Transfer the florets to a bowl.
3. Take another bowl and whisk in oil, salt, pepper and vinegar.
4. Add pumpkin seeds, cranberries to the bowl with dressing.
5. Mix well and pour dressing over cauliflower florets.
6. Toss well.
7. Add onions and toss.
8. Chill and serve.

Nutrition: Calories: 163 Fat: 11g Carbohydrates: 16g Protein: 3g Sodium: 112mg

147. Chickpea Salad

Preparation: 6 minutes   **Serving: 4**

Ingredients:

- *1 cup canned chickpeas drained and rinsed.*
- *2 spring onions thinly sliced.*
- *1 small cucumber, diced.*
- *2 green bell peppers, chopped.*
- *2 tomatoes, diced.*
- *2 tablespoons fresh parsley, chopped.*
- *1 teaspoon capers drained and rinsed.*
- *Half a lemon, juiced.*
- *2 tablespoons sunflower oil.*
- *1 tablespoon red wine vinegar.*
- *Pinch of dried oregano.*
- *Sunflower seeds and pepper to taste*

Directions:

1. Take a medium sized bowl and add chickpeas, spring onions, cucumber, bell pepper, tomato, parsley and capers.
2. Take another bowl and mix in the rest of the ingredients, pour mixture over chickpea salad and toss well.

3. Coat and serve, enjoy!

Nutrition: Calories: 174 Fat: 1g Carbohydrates: 16g Protein: 12g Sodium: 112mg

148. Tart Apple Salad with Fennel and Honey Yogurt Dressing

Preparation: 15 minutes   **Servings: 6**

Ingredients:

- 2 tart green apples, diced
- 1 small bulb fennel, chopped
- 1 ½ cups seedless red grapes, halved
- 2 tablespoons freshly squeezed lemon juice
- 1/4 cup low-fat vanilla yogurt
- 1 teaspoon honey

Directions:

1. Mix all the fixing into a mixing bowl, then serve immediately.

Nutrition: Calories: 70 Fat: 1g Protein: 2 g Carbohydrates: 16 g Sodium: 116 mg

149. Orchid Salad

Preparation: 15 minutes   **Servings: 4**

Ingredients:

- 2 cups shredded red cabbage
- 3 tablespoons freshly squeezed orange juice
- 1 teaspoon balsamic vinegar
- 1/8 teaspoon freshly ground black pepper
- 2 tart green apples, sliced thinly
- 1/2 teaspoon freshly squeezed lemon juice
- 1 medium ripe cantaloupe
- 1/4 cup chopped walnuts

Directions:

1. Place the cabbage into a mixing bowl. Add the orange juice, vinegar, and pepper and toss well to coat. Set aside. Place the apple slices in another bowl, add the lemon juice, and toss gently to coat. Set aside.
2. Slice the cantaloupe in half and discard the seeds. Slice each half into 8 wedges and remove the rind. Slice each wedge in half across the middle, so you're left with 16 triangular parts.
3. Place 2 cantaloupe parts in the middle of a plate, cut sides, so they look rejoined. Pull them slightly apart and then do the same with another two parts so that you have a sort of X with a space in the middle.
4. Arrange a trio of fanned apple slices in each of the 4 empty spots between the cantaloupe points. Then place 1/4 of the cabbage mixture in the space in the middle of the X. Top with 1/4 of the chopped walnuts. Serve immediately.

Nutrition: Calories: 166 Fat: 5g Protein: 3g Carbohydrates: 30g Sodium: 106 mg

150. Delicious Blueberry Breakfast Salad

Preparation: 10 minutes   **Servings: 4**

Ingredients:

- 2 pounds salad greens, torn
- 4 cups blueberries
- 3 cups orange, peeled and cut into segments
- 2 tablespoons coconut sugar
- 2 teaspoons shallot, minced
- A pinch of black pepper
- 2 cups granola
- For the vinaigrette:
- 1 cup blueberries
- 1 cup olive oil
- 1/2 teaspoon sweet paprika

Directions:

1. In your food processor, combine 1 cup blueberries with the oil, sugar, shallot, paprika and black pepper and pulse well.
2. In a salad, bowl, combine 4 cups blueberries with salad greens, granola and oranges and toss.
3. Add the blueberry vinaigrette, toss and serve for breakfast.

Nutrition: Calories 171, Fat 2g, Carbohydrates 8g, Protein 8g, Sodium: 122mg.

151. Kale Salad with Quinoa

Preparation: 10 minutes   **Servings: 4**

Ingredients:

- *6 cups kale, chopped*
- *1/4 cup lemon juice*
- *1/2 cup olive oil*
- *1 teaspoon mustard*
- *1 ½ cups quinoa, cooked*
- *1 ½ cups cherry tomatoes, halved*
- *A pinch of black pepper*
- *3 tablespoons pine nuts, toasted*

Directions:

1. In a large salad bowl, combine the kale with quinoa and cherry tomatoes.
2. Add lemon juice, oil, mustard, black pepper and pine nuts, toss well, divide between plates and serve for breakfast.

Nutrition: Calories 165, fat 5g, Carbohydrates 14g, Protein 6g Sodium: 112mg

152. Salmon Breakfast Salad

Preparation: 10 minutes   **Servings: 2**

Ingredients:

- *3 tablespoons nonfat yogurt*
- *1 teaspoon horseradish sauce*
- *1 tablespoon dill, chopped*
- *1 teaspoon lemon juice*
- *4 ounces smoked salmon, boneless, skinless and torn*
- *3 ounces salad greens*
- *2 ounces cherry tomatoes, halved*
- *2 ounces black olives, pitted and sliced*

Directions:

1. In a salad bowl, combine the salmon with salad greens, tomatoes and black olives.
2. In another bowl, combine the yogurt with horseradish, dill and lemon juice, whisk well, pour over the salad, toss well and serve for breakfast and serve.

Nutrition: Calories 177, Fat 4g, Carbohydrates 14g, Protein 8g Sodium: 112mg

153. Pear and Banana Salad

Preparation: 10 minutes   **Servings: 2**

Ingredients:

- *1 banana, peeled and sliced*
- *1 Asian pear, cored and cubed*
- *Juice of 1/2 lime*
- *1/2 teaspoon cinnamon powder*
- *2 ounces pepitas, toasted*

Directions:

1. In a bowl, combine the banana with the pear, lime juice, cinnamon and pepitas, toss, divide between small plates and serve for breakfast.

Nutrition: Calories 188, Carbohydrates 5g, Protein 7g, Fat 3g, Sodium 120mg

154. Easy Plum and Avocado Salad

Preparation: 10 minutes   **Servings: 3**

Ingredients:

- *2 avocados, peeled, pitted and cubed*
- *4 plums, stones removed and cubed*
- *1 cup cilantro, chopped*
- *1 garlic clove, minced*
- *Juice of 1 lemon*
- *A drizzle of olive oil*
- *1 red chili pepper, minced*

Directions:

1. In a salad bowl, combine the avocados with plums, cilantro, garlic, lemon juice, oil and chili pepper, toss well, divide between plates and serve for breakfast.

Nutrition: Calories 212, Carbohydrates 14g, Protein 11g, Fat 2g, Sodium 112mg

155. Pork, Water Chestnuts and Cabbage Salad

Preparation: 10 minutes   **Servings: 10**
Ingredients:

- 1 green cabbage head, shredded
- 1 and 1/2 cups brown rice, already cooked
- 2 cups pork roast, already cooked and shredded
- 10 ounces peas
- 8 ounces water chestnuts, drained and sliced
- 1/2 cup low-fat sour cream
- 1/2 cup avocado mayonnaise
- A pinch of black pepper

Directions:

1. In a bowl, combine the cabbage with the rice, shredded meat, peas, chestnuts, sour cream, mayo and black pepper, toss and serve cold.

Nutrition: Calories 310, Carbohydrates 11g, Protein 17g, Fat 5g, Sodium 100mg

156. Garlic Meatballs Salad

Preparation: 10 minutes   **Cooking: 15 minutes**   **Servings: 6**
Ingredients:

- 17 ounces pork ground
- 1 yellow onion, grated
- 1 egg, whisked
- 1/4 cup parsley, chopped
- Black pepper to the taste
- 2 garlic cloves, minced
- 1/4 cup mint, chopped
- 2 and 1/2 teaspoons oregano, dried
- 1/4 cup olive oil
- 7 ounces cherry tomatoes, halved
- 1 cucumber, thinly sliced
- 1 cup baby spinach
- 1 and 1/2 tablespoons lemon juice
- A drizzle of avocado oil

Directions:

1. In a bowl, combine the pork with the onion, egg, parsley, black pepper, mint, garlic and oregano, stir well and shape medium meatballs out of this mix.
2. Heat up a pan with the olive oil over medium-high heat, add the meatballs and cook them for 5 minutes on each side.
3. In a salad bowl, combine the meatballs with the tomatoes, cucumber, spinach, lemon juice and avocado oil, toss and serve.

Nutrition: Calories 220, Carbohydrates 8g, Protein 12g, Fat 4g, Sodium 112mg

157. Delicious Lemon Chicken Salad

Preparation: 15 minutes   **Cooking: 5 minutes**   **Servings: 4**
Ingredients:

- 1 lb. chicken breast, cooked and diced
- 1 tbsp fresh dill, chopped
- 2 tsp olive oil
- 1/4 cup low-fat yogurt
- 1 tsp lemon zest, grated
- 2 tbsp onion, minced
- 1/4 tsp pepper
- 1/4 tsp salt

Directions:

1. Put all your fixing into the large mixing bowl and toss well. Season with pepper and salt. Cover and place in the refrigerator. Serve chilled and enjoy.

Nutrition: Calories 165, Carbohydrates 2g, Protein 25g, Fat 6g, Sodium 153mg

158. Fruity Chicken Salad

Preparation: 10 minutes   **Cooking: 30 minutes**   **Servings: 4**
Ingredients:

- 1 whole chicken, chopped
- 8 black tea bags
- 4 scallions, chopped
- 2 celery ribs, chopped
- 1 cup mandarin orange, chopped
- 1/2 cup fat free yogurt

- *1 cup cashews, toasted and chopped*
- *Black pepper to the taste*

Directions:
2. Put chicken pieces in a pot, add water to cover, also add tea bags, bring to a boil over medium heat and cook for 25 minutes until chicken is tender.
3. Discard liquid and tea bags but reserve about 4 ounces.
4. Transfer chicken to a cutting board, leave aside to cool down, discard bones, shred meat and put it in a bowl.
5. Add celery, orange pieces, cashews, scallion and reserved liquid and toss everything.
6. Add salt, pepper, mayo and yogurt, toss to coat well and keep in the fridge until you serve it.

Nutrition: Calories 150, Carbohydrates 7g, Protein 6g, Fat 3g, Sodium 144mg

159. Cod Salad with Mustard

Preparation: 12 minutes   **Cooking: 12 minutes**   **Servings: 4**
Ingredients:
- *4 medium cod fillets, skinless and boneless*
- *2 tablespoons mustard*
- *1 tablespoon tarragon, chopped*
- *1 tablespoon capers, drained*
- *4 tablespoons olive oil+ 1 teaspoon*
- *Black pepper to the taste*
- *2 cups baby arugula*
- *1 small red onion, sliced*
- *1 small cucumber, sliced*
- *2 tablespoons lemon juice*

Directions:
1. In a bowl, mix mustard with 2 tablespoons olive oil, tarragon and capers and whisk.
2. Heat up a pan with 1 teaspoon oil over medium-high heat, add fish, season with black pepper to the taste, cook for 6 minutes on each side and cut into medium cubes.
3. In a salad bowl, combine the arugula with onion, cucumber, lemon juice, cod and mustard mix, toss and serve.

Nutrition: Calories 258, Carbohydrates 12g, Protein 18g, Fat 12g, Sodium 116mg

160. Salmon And Easy Cucumber Salad

Preparation: 10 minutes   **Servings: 4**
Ingredients:
- *2 cucumbers, cubed*
- *2 teaspoons lemon juice*
- *4 ounces non-fat yogurt*
- *1 teaspoon lemon zest, grated*
-
- *Black pepper to the taste*
- *2 teaspoons dill, chopped*
- *8 ounces smoked salmon, flaked*

Directions:
1. In a bowl, the cucumbers with the lemon juice, lemon zest, black pepper, dill, salmon and yogurt, toss and serve cold.

Nutrition: Calories 242, Carbohydrates 8g, Protein 3g, Fat 3g, Sodium 126mg

161. Salmon and Tomatoes Salad

Preparation: 10 minutes   **Servings: 2**
Ingredients:
- *4 cups cherry tomatoes, halved*
- *1 red onion, sliced*
- *8 ounces smoked salmon, thinly sliced*
- *4 tablespoons olive oil*
- *1/2 teaspoon garlic, minced*
- *2 tablespoons lemon juice*
- *1 tablespoon oregano, chopped*
- *Black pepper to the taste*
- *1 teaspoon balsamic vinegar*

Directions:
1. In a salad bowl, combine the tomatoes with the onion, salmon, oil, garlic, lemon juice, oregano, black pepper, and vinegar, toss and serve cold.

Nutrition: Calories 159, Carbohydrates 7g, Protein 7g, Fat 8g, Sodium 100mg

162. Southwestern Bean-And-Pepper Salad

Preparation: 6 minutes   **Servings: 4**

Ingredients:
- *1 can pinto beans, drained*
- *2 bell peppers, cored and chopped*
- *1 cup corn kernels*
- *Salt*
- *Freshly ground black pepper*
- *Juice of 2 limes*
- *1 tablespoon olive oil*
- *1 avocado, chopped*

Directions:
1. Mix beans, peppers, corn, salt, plus pepper in a large bowl. Press fresh lime juice, then mix in olive oil. Let the salad stand in the fridge within 30 minutes. Add avocado just before serving.

Nutrition: Calories: 245 Fat: 11g Carbohydrate: 32g Protein: 8g Sodium: 97mg

163. Pan-Fried Salmon with Salad

Preparation: 15 minutes   **Cooking: 20 minutes**   **Servings: 4**

Ingredients:
- *Pinch of salt and pepper*
- *1 tablespoon extra-virgin olive oil*
- *2 tablespoon unsalted butter*

Salad Dressing:
- *3 tablespoons olive oil*
- *2 tablespoons balsamic vinaigrette*
- *1/2 teaspoon fresh dill*
- *1 tablespoon fresh lemon juice*
- *100g salad leaves, or bag of mixed leaves*
- *1/2 teaspoon maple syrup (honey)*

Directions:
1. Pat-dry the salmon fillets with a paper towel and season with a pinch of salt and pepper. In a skillet, warm-up oil over medium-high heat and add fillets. Cook each side within 5 to 7 minutes until golden brown.
2. Dissolve butter, dill, and lemon juice in a small saucepan. Put the butter mixture onto the cooked salmon. Lastly, combine all the salad dressing ingredients and drizzle to mixed salad leaves in a large bowl. Toss to coat. Serve with fresh salads on the side. Enjoy!

Nutrition: Calories 307 Fat 22g Protein 34g Carbohydrate 2g Sodium 80mg

SOUP

164. Chicken Squash Soup

Preparation: 15 minutes   **Cooking: 5 hours & 30 minutes**   **Servings: 3**

Ingredients:

- 1/2 Butternut Squash (large)
- 1 clove Garlic
- 1 1/4 quarts broth (vegetable or chicken)
- 1/8 tsp. Pepper (white)
- 1/2 tbsp. chopped Parsley
- 2 minced Sage leaves
- 1 tbsp. Olive Oil
- 1/4 chopped onion (white)
- A pinch of Black Pepper (cracked)
- 1/2 tbsp. of Pepper Flakes (chili)
- 1/2 tsp. chopped rosemary

Directions:

1. Preheat oven to 400 degrees. Grease a baking sheet. Roast the squash in a preheated oven for 30 mins. Transfer it to a plate and let it cool. Sauté onion and garlic in the oil.
2. Now, scoop out the flesh from the roasted squash and add to the sautéed onion & garlic. Mash all of it well. Pour 1/2 quart of the broth into the slow cooker. Add the squash mixture. Cook on "low" for 4 hrs. Using a blender, make a smooth puree.
3. Transfer the puree to the slow cooker. Add in the rest of the broth and other ingredients. Cook again for 1 hr. on "high". Serve in heated soup bowls.

Nutrition: Calorie 158, Carbohydrate 25g, Protein 3g, Fat 6g, Sodium 188mg

165. Veggie and Beef Soup

Preparation: 15 minutes   **Cooking: 4 hours**   **Servings: 4**

Ingredients:

- 1 chopped Carrot
- 1 chopped Celery Rib
- 3/4 l. Sirloin (ground)
- 1 cup Water
- 1/2 Butternut Squash (large)
- 1 clove Garlic
- 1/2-quart Beef broth
- 7 ounces diced Tomatoes (unsalted)
- 1/2 tsp. Kosher Salt
- 1 tbsp. chopped parsley
- 1/4 tsp. Thyme (dried)
- 1/4 tsp. Black Pepper (ground)
- 1/2 Bay Leaf

Directions:

1. Sauté all the vegetables in oil. Put the vegetables to the side, then place sirloin in the center. Sauté, using a spoon to crumble the meat. When cooked, combine with the vegetables on the sides of the pan.
2. Now, pour the rest of the ingredients into the slow cooker. Add cooked meat and vegetables. Stir well. Cook on "low" for 3 hrs. Serve in soup bowls.

Nutrition: Calorie 217, Carbohydrate 17g, Protein 22g, Fat 7g, Sodium 88mg

166. Collard, Sweet Potato and Pea Soup

Preparation: 15 minutes   **Cooking: 4 hours**   **Servings: 4**

Ingredients:

- 3 ½ oz. Ham Steak, chopped
- 1/2 chopped Yellow Onion
- 1/2 lb. sliced Sweet Potatoes
- 1/4 tsp. Red Pepper (hot and crushed)
- 1/2 cup frozen Peas (black-eyed)
- 1/2 tbsp. Canola Oil
- 1 minced clove of Garlic
- 1 ½ cup Water
- 1/4 tsp. Salt
- 2 cups Collard Greens (julienned and without stems)

Directions:
1. Sauté ham with garlic and onion in oil. In a slow cooker, place other ingredients except for collard greens and peas.
2. Add in the ham mixture. Cook on "low" for 3 hrs. Now, add collard green and peas and cook again for an hour on "low." Serve in soup bowls.

Nutrition: Calorie 172, Carbohydrate 24g, Protein 11g, Fat 4g, Sodium 112mg

167. Bean Soup

Preparation: 15 minutes   **Cooking: 5 hours**   **Servings: 4**

Ingredients:
- 1/2 cup Pinto Beans (dried)
- 1/2 Bay Leaf
- 1 clove Garlic
- 1/2 onion (white)
- 2 cups Water
- 2 tbsp. Cilantro (chopped)
- 1 cubed Avocado
- 1/8 cup White Onion (chopped)
- 1/4 cup Roma Tomatoes (chopped)
- 2 tbsp. Pepper Sauce (chipotle)
- 1/4 tsp. Kosher Salt
- 2 tbsp. chopped Cilantro
- 2 tbsp. Low Fat Monterrey Jack Cheese, shredded

Directions:
1. Place water, salt, onion, pepper, garlic, bay leaf, and beans in the slow cooker.
2. Cook on high for 5-6 hours. Discard the Bay leaf.
3. Serve in heated bowls.

Nutrition: Calorie 258, Carbohydrate 25g, Protein 8g, Fat 19g, Sodium 122mg

168. Brown Rice and Chicken Soup

Preparation: 15 minutes   **Cooking: 4 hours**   **Servings: 4**

Ingredients:
- 1/3 cups Brown Rice
- 1 chopped Leek
- 1 sliced Celery Rib
- 1 1/2 cups water
- 1/2 tsp. Kosher Salt
- 1/2 Bay Leaf
- 1/8 tsp. Thyme (dried)
- 1/4 tsp. Black Pepper (ground)
- 1 tbsp. chopped parsley
- 1/2-quart Chicken Broth (low sodium)
- 1 sliced Carrot
- 3/4 lb. of Chicken Thighs (skin and boneless)

Directions:
1. Boil 1 cup of water with 1/2 tsp. of salt in a saucepan. Add the rice. Cook for 30 minutes on medium flame. Brown chicken pieces in the oil. Transfer the chicken to a plate when done.
2. In the same pan, sauté the vegetables for 3 mins. Now, place the chicken pieces in the slow cooker. Add water and broth. Cook on "low" for 3 hrs. Put the rest of the fixing, the rice last. Cook again for 10 minutes on "high." After discarding Bay leaf, serve in soup bowls

Nutrition: Calorie 208, Carbohydrate 18g, Protein 20g, Fat 6g, Sodium 167mg

169. Broccoli Soup

Preparation: 15 minutes   **Cooking: 3 hours**   **Servings: 2**

Ingredients:
- 4 cups chopped broccoli
- 1/2 cup chopped onion (white)
- 1 ½ cup Chicken Broth (low sodium)
- 1/8 tsp. Black Pepper (cracked)
- 1 tbsp. Olive Oil
- 1 Garlic Clove
- 1/16 tsp. Pepper Flakes (chili)
- 1/4 cup Milk (low fat)

Directions:

1. In the slow cooker, cover the broccoli with water and cook for an hour on "high." Set aside after draining. Sauté onion and garlic in oil and transfer them to slow cooker when done. Add the broth.
2. Cook on "low" for 2 hrs. Transfer the mixture to a blender and make a smooth puree. Add black pepper, milk, and pepper flakes to the puree. Boil briefly. Serve the soup in heated bowls.

Nutrition: Calories 291 Fat 14 g; Carbohydrate 28g Protein 17 g Sodium: 123mg

170. Hearty Ginger Soup

Preparation: 5 minutes   **Cooking: 5 minutes**   **Servings: 4**

Ingredients:

- 3 cups coconut almond milk
- 2 cups of water
- 1/2-pound boneless chicken breast halves, cut into chunks
- 3 tablespoons fresh ginger root, minced
- 2 tablespoons fish sauce
- 1/4 cup fresh lime juice
- 2 tablespoons green onions, sliced
- 1 tablespoon fresh cilantro, chopped

Directions:

1. Take a saucepan and add coconut almond milk and water. Bring the mixture to a boil and add the chicken strips. Adjust the heat to medium, then simmer for 3 minutes.
2. Stir in the ginger, lime juice, and fish sauce.
3. Sprinkle a few green onions and cilantro.

Nutrition: Calories: 415 Fat: 39g Carbohydrates: 8g Protein: 14g Sodium: 150 mg

171. Tasty Tofu and Mushroom Soup

Preparation: 15 minutes   **Cooking: 10 minutes**   **Servings: 8**

Ingredients:

- 3 cups prepared dashi stock
- 1/4 cup shiitake mushrooms, sliced
- 1 tablespoon miso paste
- 1 tablespoon coconut aminos
- 1/8 cup cubed soft tofu
- 1 green onion, diced

Directions:

1. Take a saucepan and add the stock; bring to a boil. Add mushrooms, cook for 4 minutes.
2. Take a bowl and add coconut aminos, miso pastes, and mix well. Pour the mixture into stock and let it cook for 6 minutes on simmer.
3. Add diced green onions and enjoy!

Nutrition: Calories: 100 Fat: 4g Carbohydrates: 5g Protein: 11 Sodium: 87 mg

172. Ingenious Eggplant Soup

Preparation: 15 minutes   **Cooking: 15 minutes**   **Servings: 8**

Ingredients:

- 1 large eggplant, washed and cubed
- 1 tomato, seeded and chopped
- 1 small onion, diced
- 2 tablespoons parsley, chopped
- 2 tablespoons extra virgin olive oil
- 2 tablespoons distilled white vinegar
- 1/2 cup parmesan cheese, crumbled
- Sunflower seeds as needed

Directions:

1. Preheat your outdoor grill to medium-high. Pierce the eggplant a few times using a knife/fork. Cook the eggplants on your grill for about 15 minutes until they are charred. Put aside and allow them to cool.
2. Remove the eggplant's skin and dice the pulp. Put it in a mixing bowl and add parsley, onion, tomato, olive oil, feta cheese, and vinegar. Mix well and chill for 1 hour. Season with sunflower seeds and enjoy!

Nutrition: Calories: 99 Fat: 7g Carbohydrates: 7g Protein:3.4g Sodium: 90 mg

173. Loving Cauliflower Soup

Preparation: 15 minutes   **Cooking: 10 minutes**   **Servings: 6**

Ingredients:

- 4 cups vegetable stock
- 1-pound cauliflower, trimmed and chopped
- 7 ounces Kite ricotta/cashew cheese
- 4 ounces almond butter
- Sunflower seeds and pepper to taste

Directions:

1. Put almond butter and melt in a skillet over medium heat. Add cauliflower and sauté for 2 minutes. Add stock and bring the mix to a boil.
2. Cook until cauliflower is al dente. Stir in cream cheese, sunflower seeds, and pepper. Puree the mix using an immersion blender. Serve and enjoy!

Nutrition: Calories: 143 Fat: 16g Carbohydrates: 6g Protein: 3.4g Sodium: 510 mg

174. Garlic and Lemon Soup

Preparation: 15 minutes   **Servings: 3**

Ingredients:

- 1 avocado, pitted and chopped
- 1 cucumber, chopped
- 2 bunches spinach
- 1 1/2 cups watermelon, chopped
- 1 bunch cilantro, roughly chopped
- Juice from 2 lemons
- 1/2 cup coconut aminos
- 1/2 cup lime juice

Directions:

1. Add cucumber, avocado to your blender, and pulse well. Add cilantro, spinach, and watermelon and blend. Add lemon, lime juice, and coconut amino.
2. Pulse a few more times. Transfer to a soup bowl and enjoy!

Nutrition: Calories: 100 Fat: 7g Carbohydrates: 6g Protein: 3g Sodium: 100 mg

175. Cucumber Soup

Preparation: 15 minutes   **Servings: 4**

Ingredients:

- 2 tablespoons garlic, minced
- 4 cups English cucumbers, peeled and diced
- 1/2 cup onions, diced
- 1 tablespoon lemon juice
- 1 ½ cups vegetable broth
- 1/2 teaspoon sunflower seeds
- 1/4 teaspoon red pepper flakes
- 1/4 cup parsley, diced
- 1/2 cup Greek yogurt, plain

Directions:

1. Put the listed fixing in a blender and blend to emulsify (keep aside 1/2 cup of chopped cucumbers). Blend until smooth.
2. Divide the soup amongst 4 servings and top with extra cucumbers. Enjoy chilled!

Nutrition: Calories: 371 Fat: 36g Carbohydrates: 8g Protein: 4g Sodium: 40 mg

176. Vegetable Pasta Soup

Preparation: 5 minutes   **Cooking: 10 minutes**   **Serve:4**

Ingredients

- (3/4-cup) appetizer
- 2 teaspoons olive oil
- 6 cloves garlic, minced
- 1 1/2 cups coarsely shredded carrot
- 1 cup chopped onion
- 1 cup thinly sliced celery
- 1 32-ounce box reduced-sodium chicken broth
- 4 cups water
- 1 1/2 cups dried ditalini pasta
- 1/4 cup shaved Parmesan cheese
- 2 tablespoons snipped fresh parsley

Directions:
1. Heat oil over medium heat in a 5- to 6-quart Dutch oven. Combine with garlic; simmer for 15 seconds. Connect the carrot, onion, and celery; roast, stirring regularly, for 5 to 7 minutes or until tender. Connect the water and chicken broth; bring to a boil. Stir in uncooked pasta; boil for 7 to 8 minutes or until tender.
2. Cover individual pieces of Parmesan cheese and parsley to eat. Allows 12 servings of (3/4-cup) appetizer.

Nutrition: Calories: 200, Fat: 5g, Carbohydrates: 10g, Protein: 6g. Sodium: 121mg.

177. Easy Black-Bean Soup

Preparation: 5-6minutes   **Cooking: 15 minutes**   **Serve:4**

Ingredients

- *2 teaspoons vegetable oil*
- *1 medium onion, chopped*
- *1 and ½ teaspoons cinnamon*
- *2 cans (19 ounces each) black beans, with liquid*
- *1 package (32 ounces) reduced-sodium chicken broth*
- *1 large sweet potato, diced*
- *Plain Greek-style yogurt, optional*

Directions:
1. In a saucepan, heat oil over medium heat. Add onion and cinnamon and cook for 6 minutes. Stir in beans, chicken broth, and sweet potato. Bring mixture to a boil; reduce heat and simmer 10 minutes.
2. Let soup cool 5-minutes, puree in a blender in two batches until smooth. Reheat on low until warm before serving. Top with yogurt, if desired.

Nutrition: Calories: 200, Fat: 5g, Carbohydrates: 10g, Protein: 6g. Sodium: 110mg

178. Curried Carrot Soup

Preparation: 5-6minutes   **Cooking: 20 minutes**   **Serve:6**

Ingredients

- *3 tablespoons canola oil*
- *2 teaspoons curry powder*
- *8 medium carrots, peeled and thinly sliced*
- *4 medium stalks celery, thinly sliced*
- *1 medium onion, coarsely chopped*
- *5 cups reduced-sodium chicken broth*
- *1 tablespoon lemon juice*
- *1/2 teaspoon salt*
- *Freshly ground pepper, to taste*

Directions:
1. In a large saucepan over medium heat, simmer the oil and curry powder, stirring, until fragrant, for 1 to 2 minutes. Stir in the carrots, onion, and celery; toss to cover with the oil. Cook for ten minutes, stirring constantly. Stir in the bouillon. Just get it to a boil. Reduce the heat and simmer for about 10 minutes, until the vegetables are very tender. Delete from the heat; quit to stand for ten minutes.
2. To blot away the oil that has risen to the tip, lay a paper towel over the surface of the broth. Discard the towel with paper.
3. Switch the soup to a blender and purée in increments of no more than 2 cups at a time (use caution when pureeing hot liquids). Return to the bowl, put the pureed soup over medium heat, and heat through. Using lemon juice, salt, and pepper to season.

Nutrition: Calories: 200, Fat: 5g, Carbohydrates: 10g, Protein: 6g. Sodium: 121mg

179. Chicken Noodle Soup

Preparation: 5-6minutes   **Cooking: 20 minutes**   **Servings: 4**

Ingredients

- *1 teaspoon olive oil*
- *1 cup chopped onion*
- *3 cloves garlic, minced*
- *1 cup chopped celery*
- *1 cup sliced, peeled carrots (2 medium)*
- *4 cups Maureen's Chicken Broth (separate recipe)*
- *4 ounces dried linguini, broken*

- *1 cup cooked non-brined chicken breast, cut into desired size (skin and bones removed)*
- *2 tablespoons snipped fresh parsley*

Directions:

1. In a large saucepan, heat olive oil over medium heat and sauté onion and garlic until translucent. Add celery and carrots and continue to sauté for another 3 minutes. Add Maureen's Chicken Broth. Bring to a boil; reduce heat and simmer, covered, 5 minutes. Stir in linguini; cook and stir until mixture returns to a boil. Reduce heat and simmer, covered, 10 minutes more or until pasta and vegetables are tender, stirring occasionally.
2. Add cooked chicken and fresh parsley. Heat through.

Nutrition: Calories: 199, Fat: 3g, Carbohydrates: 12g, Protein: 4g. Sodium: 109mg

180. Chicken and Veggie Soup

Preparation: 5-6minutes   **Cooking: 15 minutes**   **Servings: 4**

Ingredients

- *2 14-ounce cans reduced-sodium chicken broth*
- *2 cups water*
- *1/4 teaspoon black pepper*
- *1 cup dried whole wheat rotini or twisted spaghetti or broken fusilli*
- *3 cups vegetable pieces (such as thinly sliced carrots, small broccoli florets,*
- *chopped green or red sweet pepper, and/or fresh or frozen whole kernel corn)*
- *1 and 1/2 cups cubed cooked chicken (about 8 ounces)*
- *1 tablespoon snipped fresh basil*
- *1/4 cup finely shredded Parmesan cheese (1 ounce)*

Preparation:

1. In a Dutch oven, combine the broth, the water, and black pepper; bring to boiling. Stir in the pasta. Return to boiling; reduce heat. Simmer, covered, for 5 minutes. Stir in vegetables.
2. Return to boiling; reduce heat. Simmer, covered, for 5 to 8 minutes more or until vegetables and pasta are tender. Stir in chicken and basil, heat through.
3. To serve, top with Parmesan cheese.

Nutrition: Calories 200, Carbohydrates 10g, Protein 6g, Fat 5g, Sodium 102mg

181. Sweet Potato & Lentil Soup

Preparation :12minutes   **Cooking time: 25 minutes**   **Serve 6**

Ingredients

- *2 tsp medium curry powder*
- *3 tbsp olive oil*
- *2 onions, grated*
- *1 eating apple, peeled, cored and grated*
- *3 garlic cloves, crushed*
- *20g pack coriander, stalks chopped*
- *thumb-size piece fresh root ginger, grated*
- *800g sweet potatoes*
- *1.2l vegetable stock*
- *100g red lentils*
- *300ml milk*
- *juice 1 lime*

Directions:

1. Put the curry powder into a large saucepan, then toast over a medium heat for 2 mins. Add the olive oil, stirring as the spice sizzles in the pan. Tip in the onions, apple, garlic, coriander stalks and ginger, season, then gently cook for 5 mins, stirring every so often.
2. Meanwhile, peel, then grate the sweet potatoes. Tip into the pan with the stock, lentils, milk and seasoning, then simmer, covered, for 20 mins. Blend until smooth using a stick blender. Stir in the lime juice, check the seasoning and serve, topped with roughly chopped coriander leaves.

Nutrition: Calories: 200, Fat: 5g, Carbohydrates: 10g, Protein: 6g Sodium: 112mg.

182. Curried Squash, Lentil & Coconut Soup

Preparation:35 minutes   **Cooking time: 20 minutes**   **Serve:**4

Ingredients

- *1 tbsp olive oil*
- *1 butternut squash, peeled, deseeded and diced*
- *200g carrots, diced*
- *1 tbsp curry powder containing turmeric*
- *100g red lentils*
- *700ml vegetable stock*
- *1 can reduced-fat coconut milk*
- *coriander and naan bread, to serve*

Directions:

1. Heat the oil in a large saucepan, add the squash and carrots, sizzle for 1 min, then stir in the curry powder and cook for 1 minutes more. Tip in the lentils, the vegetable stock, and coconut milk and give everything a good stir. Bring to the boil, then turn the heat down and simmer for 15-18 minutes until everything is tender.
2. Using a hand blender or in a food processor, blitz until as smooth as you like. Season and serve scattered with roughly chopped coriander and some naan bread alongside.

Nutrition: Calories: 199, Fat: 3g, Carbohydrates: 12g, Protein: 4g. Sodium: 112mg

183. Courgette, Pea & Pesto Soup

Preparation: 5minutes   **Cooking: 10 minutes**   **Serve:**4

Ingredients

- *1 tbsp olive oil*
- *1 garlic clove, sliced*
- *500g courgettes, quartered lengthways and chopped*
- *200g frozen peas*
- *400g can cannellini beans, drained and rinsed*
- *1l hot vegetable stock*
- *2 tbsp basil pesto, or vegetarian alternative*

Directions:

1. Heat the oil in a large saucepan. Cook the garlic for a few seconds, then add the courgettes and cook for 3 minutes until they start to soften. Stir in the peas and cannellini beans, pour on the hot stock, and cook for a further 3 mins.
2. Stir the pesto through the soup with some seasoning, then ladle into bowls and serve with crusty brown bread, if you like. Or pop in a flask to take to work.

Nutrition: Calories: 200, Fat: 5g, Carbohydrates: 10g, Protein: 6g Sodium: 123mg.

184. Cauliflower Carrot Soup

Preparation:6-8minutes   **Cooking: 15 minutes**   **Servings: 8**

Ingredients

- *1 large head cauliflower, coarsely chopped (about 8 cups)*
- *2 tablespoons extra virgin olive oil*
- *1/2 small white onion, chopped*
- *2 large cloves garlic, chopped*
- *1 cup chopped carrot*
- *1 quart low-sodium vegetable broth*
- *1/2 teaspoon sea salt*
- *1/2 teaspoon cracked black pepper*
- *1/8 teaspoon chili pepper flakes*
- *1/8 teaspoon dried basil*

Directions

1. Load a large saucepan with water and bring it to a boil. Delete from this the cauliflower head's outer leaves, and then cut out the heart. Chop the cauliflower coarsely and add it to the boiling broth.
2. Cover the pot and simmer for 6 to 8 minutes, or until the cauliflower parts are quickly pierced by a fork. Strain and discard the water from the cauliflower. In the same kettle, heat the oil over a medium heat.
3. Add the carrot, onion, and garlic, and sauté until the onion is translucent. You add the cauliflower. Switch the veggie ladle to a blender.

4. Add 1 cup of broth and mix to blend on low heat, then on high until smooth. To another big jar, move the blended veggies and repeat the process until all the veggies are blended.
5. Heat and season the blended veggies over medium-high heat and with salt, vinegar, flakes of chili pepper, and basil. Get them to a boil, Serve hot.

Nutrition: Calories: 290, Fat: 6g, Sodium: 103mg, Carbohydrates: 17g, Protein: 10g.

185. Mom's Bean Soup

Preparation:10 minutes   **Cooking: 30 minutes**   **Servings: 6**

Ingredients

- 6 cups pinto beans in broth
- 1/4 cup chopped white onion
- 1/2 cup chopped Roma tomato
- 2 large avocados, peeled, pitted, and cubed
- 4 tablespoons chopped fresh cilantro
- 4 tablespoons shredded low-fat Monterey Jack cheese
- 4tea spoons canned chipotle pepper sauce

Directions

1. Get the beans to a boil in a medium to medium-sized kettle. Elevated heat. Turn off the sun. 1 and 1/2 cups of beans with a ladle Broth into a cup of four.
2. Place the raw, diced onion, tomato, avocado, cilantro, shredded cheese, and chipotle sauce on top of each cup. Immediately serve.

Nutrition: Calories: 300, Fat: 14g, Carbohydrates: 18g, Protein: 16g. Sodium: 113mg

186. Chicken And Spring Vegetable Soup

Preparation: 15 minutes   **Cooking: 50 minutes**   **Serve: 8**

Ingredients

- 1 tablespoon olive oil
- 1 1/2 pounds boneless, skinless chicken thighs, excess fat trimmed, cut into bite-sized pieces
- 1 large leek, white and pale green parts only, chopped (1 cup)
- 1-quart Homemade Chicken Broth (here) or canned low-sodium chicken broth
- 1-quart water
- 2 large red-skinned potatoes, scrubbed but unpeeled, cut into 1/2-inch pieces
- 1 teaspoon kosher salt
- 1/2 teaspoon freshly ground black pepper
- 1 pound asparagus, woody stems discarded, cut into 1-inch lengths1 cup thawed frozen peas
- 8 tablespoons light sour cream, for serving

Directions:

1. Heat oil over medium-high heat in a kettle. Add the chicken and cook in two batches, occasionally stirring, until lightly browned, for around 6 minutes. Transfer to a dish.
2. Add the leek to the pot and cook for about 3 minutes, occasionally stirring, until it is softened. Add the broth and stir, loosening the brown bits with a wooden spoon at the bottom of the jar. Then stir in the water, potatoes, salt, and pepper and bring to a boil over high heat, skimming off any foam that rises to the top.
3. Decrease the heat to a medium-low level. Simmer for about 40 minutes, until the chicken is soft and opaque when pierced with the tip of a sharp knife. Stir in the asparagus and peas for the final 5 minutes.
4. Ladle into soup cups, add 1 tablespoon of sour cream to each serving, and serve hot

Nutrition: Calories: 140, Fat: 1g, Fiber: 12g, Carbohydrates: 15g, Protein: 7g. Sodium: 92mg

187. Sweet Potato, Collard, And Black-Eyed Pea Soup

Preparation: 10 Minutes **Cooking: 30 minutes** **Serve: 8**
Ingredients

- *1 tablespoon canola oil*
- *1 (7-ounce) ham steak, cut into bite-sized pieces*
- *1 large yellow onion, chopped*
- *2 cloves garlic, minced*
- *1-quart Homemade Chicken Broth*
- *3 cups of water*
- *1-pound sweet potatoes (yams), peeled and cut into 1/2-inch dice*
- *1/2 teaspoon salt*
- *1/2 teaspoon crushed hot red pepper*
- *4 packed cups thinly sliced collard greens (wash well and remove thick stems before slicing)*
- *1 cup frozen black-eyed peas*

Directions:
1. Over medium heat, heat the oil in a large pot. Add the ham and cook, stirring periodically, until lightly browned, around 3 minutes. Add the onion and garlic and cook, stirring, until the onion softens, around 5minutes.
2. Bring to a boil over high heat and add broth, water, sweet potatoes, salt, and hot pepper. Return the heat to medium and cook at a low boil until the sweet potatoes begin to soften about 10 minutes. Stir in the collards and black-eyed peas and cook until the greens and sweet potatoes are tender, about 10 minutes longer. Ladle it into bowls of soup and serve it sweet.

Nutrition: Calories: 224, Fat: 12g, Carbohydrates: 12g, Protein: 14g. Sodium: 102mg

188. Green Beans Soup

Preparation: 20 minutes **Cooking: 40 minutes** **Serve: 3**
Ingredients

- *1/2 onion, diced*
- *1/3 cup green beans, soaked*
- *3 cups of water*
- *1/2 sweet pepper, chopped*
- *2 potatoes, chopped*
- *1 tablespoon fresh cilantro, chopped*
- *1 teaspoon chili flakes*

Directions:
1. In the saucepan, put all the ingredients and close the lid.
2. On medium heat, cook the soup for 40 minutes or until the ingredients are all tender.

Nutrition: Calories: 253, Fat: 6g, Carbohydrates: 26g, Protein: 22g Sodium: 112mg

189. Turkey Soup

Preparation: 20 minutes **Cooking: 30 minutes** **Serve: 3**
Ingredients

- *1 potato, diced*
- *1 cup ground turkey*
- *1 teaspoon cayenne pepper*
- *1 onion, diced*
- *1 tablespoon olive oil*
- *1/4 carrot, diced*
- *2 cups of water*

Directions:
1. In a saucepan, heat the olive oil and add the diced onion and carrot.
2. For 3 minutes, prepare the vegetables. Then stir them well and add the cayenne pepper and ground turkey.
3. Attach the diced potato and stir well with the spices. Cook them for an extra 2 minutes.
4. Add water, too. Check if all the ingredients have been put in.
5. Cover the lid and simmer for 20 minutes to make the broth.
6. Lower the heat to a low level. Attach the parsley, peppercorns, bay leaf, and thyme. Simmer, uncovered, for at least 2 hours and up to 4 hours, until the stock is well flavored.
7. In a very large heatproof bowl, position a colander. In the bowl, strain the broth, discarding the solids.

Nutrition: Calories: 288, Fat: 23g, Carbohydrates: 10g, Protein: 15g. Sodium: 102mg

190. Potato and Carrot "Impeccable" Soup

Preparation: 15 minutes   **Cooking: 10 minutes**   **Servings: 2**

Ingredients:

- *5 medium sized chopped and peeled potatoes*
- *8 peeled and chopped carrots*
- *1/2 of a chopped yellow onion*
- *3 minced garlic cloves*
- *2 cups of finely chopped fresh kale*
- *1 tablespoon of curry powder*
- *1 teaspoon of cayenne pepper*
- *4 cups of water*
- *2 cups of vegetable broth*

Directions:

1. Mince up garlic and chop up the onions
2. Add 1/4 cup of water to the pot and set the pot to Sauté mode
3. Add onions and garlic and Sauté for 5 minutes
4. Add vegetable broth, cayenne, powdered peanut butter and curry powder
5. Stir everything well. Add water and Sauté for 2 minutes
6. Add the remaining ingredients (except kale) and seal the lid
7. Cook on HIGH pressure for 8 minutes. Release the pressure naturally
8. Open the lid and take an immersion blender to puree the soup
9. Add chopped up kale and mix well. Serve and enjoy!

Nutrition: Calories: 128, Fat: 4g, Carbohydrates: 20g, Protein: 3g Sodium: 112mg

191. Meticulous Butternut Squash Soup

Preparation: 5 minutes   **Cooking: 30 minutes**   **Servings: 4**

Ingredients:

For Soup

- *1 teaspoon of extra virgin olive oil*
- *1 large sized chopped up onion*
- *2 minced garlic cloves*
- *1 tablespoon of curry powder*
- *3 pound of butternut squash, cut up into 1-inch cubes and peeled*
- *3 cups of water*
- *1/2 a cup of coconut milk*

For Extra Toppings

- *Hulled up pumpkin seeds*
- *Dried up cranberries*

Directions:

1. Set the pot to Sauté mode and add olive oil, allow the oil to heat up
2. Add onions and Sauté for 8 minutes
3. Add garlic and curry powder and Sauté for 1 minute
4. Cancel the Sauté mode and add butternut squash, water and flavored vinegar
5. Lock up the lid and cook on HIGH pressure for 30 minutes
6. Release the pressure naturally over 10 minutes
7. Open the lid and blend using an immersion blender
8. Stir in coconut milk and season
9. Serve topped with cranberries/pumpkin seeds.

Nutrition: Calories: 124 Fat: 6g Carbohydrates: 18g Protein: 2g Sodium: 101mg

192. Omnipotent Organic Chicken Thigh Soup

Preparation: 5 minutes   **Cooking: 45 minutes**   **Servings: 4**

Ingredients:

- *2 pound of organic chicken thigh*
- *1 cup of fresh pineapple chunks*
- *1/2 a cup of coconut cream*
- *1 teaspoon of cinnamon*
- *1/8 teaspoon of flavored vinegar*
- *2 tablespoon of coconut aminos*

- *1/2 a cup of chopped up green onion*

Directions:
1. Set your pot to Sauté mode and add ghee
2. Allow the ghee to melt and add diced up onion, cook for about 5 minutes until the onions are caramelized. Add pressed garlic, ham, broth and simmer for 2-3 minutes
3. Add thyme and asparagus and lock up the lid
4. Cook on SOUP mode for 45 minutes. Release the pressure naturally and enjoy!

Nutrition: Calories: 161, Fat: 8g, Carbohydrates: 16g, Protein: 6g , Sodium: 102mg

193. Very Low Carb Ham and Cabbage Bowl

Preparation: 15 minutes   **Cooking: 15 minutes**   **Servings: 6**

Ingredients:
- *1 chopped cabbage head*
- *1 finely chopped onion*
- *1 finely chopped red bell pepper*
- *2 small carrots cut up into rounds*
- *2 cups of diced lean ham*
- *2 pieces of bay leaves*
- *1 teaspoon of all-purpose seasoning*
- *1 teaspoon of granulated garlic*
- *1 tablespoon of dried parsley*
- *1 teaspoon of seasoning flavored vinegar*
- *6 cups of chicken stock*
- *Parmesan cheese for serving*

Directions:
1. Chop up the cabbage, red bell pepper, onion, ham and carrots
2. Add the onion, cabbage and red bell pepper to the Instant Pot
3. Add chopped ham, carrots alongside bay leaves
4. Sprinkle seasoning flavored vinegar on top, all-purpose seasoning, dried parsley and granulated garlic. Lock up the lid and cook on HIGH pressure for 15 minutes
5. Release the pressure naturally over 10 minutes
6. Serve hot with grated parmesan on top. Enjoy!

Nutrition: Calories: 296, Fat: 25g, Carbohydrates: 2g, Protein: 17g, Sodium: 122mg

194. Cabbage and Leek Soup

Preparation: 10 minutes   **Cooking: 25 minutes**   **Servings: 4**

Ingredients:
- *2 tablespoon of coconut oil*
- *1/2 a head of chopped up cabbage*
- *3-4 diced ribs of celery*
- *2-3 carefully cleaned and chopped leeks*
- *1 diced bell pepper*
- *2-3 diced carrots*
- *2/3 cloves of minced garlic*
- *4 cups of chicken broth*
- *1 teaspoon of Italian seasoning*
- *1 teaspoon of Creole seasoning*
- *Black pepper as needed*
- *2-3 cups of mixed salad greens*

Directions:
1. Set your pot to Sauté mode and add coconut oil
2. Allow the oil to heat up
3. Add the veggies (except salad greens) starting from the carrot, making sure to stir it well after each vegetable addition
4. Make sure to add the garlic last
5. Season with Italian seasoning, black pepper and Creole seasoning
6. Add broth and lock up the lid
7. Cook on SOUP mode for 20 minutes
8. Release the pressure naturally and add salad greens, stir well and allow it to sit for a while
9. Allow for a few minutes to wilt the veggies
10. Season with a bit of flavored vinegar and pepper and enjoy!

Nutrition: Calories: 32, Fat: 2g, Carbohydrates: 4g, Protein: 2g, Sodium: 113mg

195. Moroccan Sweet Potato Soup

Preparation: 15 minutes   **Cooking: 25 minutes**   **Servings: 6**

Ingredients:

- *1 tablespoon olive oil*
- *2 diced carrots*
- *1 zested lemon*
- *2 teaspoons cumin*
- *2 diced yellow onions*
- *1 can drained chickpeas*
- *2 diced yellow onions*
- *1 tablespoon turmeric*
- *1/2 teaspoon coriander*
- *2 tablespoons harissa*
- *6 cups vegetable stock*
- *Parsley, mint, harissa, labneh, and lemon wedges to garnish*

Directions:

1. Turn the pot on to sauté and put oil in there, then dice the onion and sauté till golden.
2. Add in the carrots, sweet potatoes, zest, spices, stock, and chickpeas, and then seal the vent, manually cooking for 20 minutes.
3. Get garnish ready while it cooks.
4. Once finished, let it depressurize naturally, then pop off lid.
5. Take the soup and use a stick blender to puree it, or blend it in blender
6. Season to taste.
7. Serve it with garnishees, or even a swirl of coconut cream.

Nutrition: Calories: 260, Fat: 2g, Carbohydrates: 15g, Protein: 1g, Sodium: 92mg

196. Potato Soup

Preparation: 10 minutes   **Cooking: 12 minutes**   **Servings: 6**

Ingredients:

- *6 cups cubed gold potatoes*
- *1/2 chopped yellow onion*
- *black pepper for taste*
- *a pinch of crushed red pepper flakes*
- *2 cups coconut cream*
- *1 cup corn*
- *1 cup fat-free shredded cheddar cheese*
- *3 oz. Cream cheese, cubed*
- *2 tablespoons avocado oil*
- *28 oz. Chicken stock, low sodium*
- *2 tablespoons dried parsley*

Directions:

1. Turn IP to sauté mode, then add oil, onion, and then cook for 5 minutes.
2. Put the pepper, pepper flakes, parsley, and half the stock in, and then stir.
3. Put potatoes in steamer basket, and cook on high for 5 minutes, and then put them in bowl. Add cream cheese and cheese and sauté in instant pot, and the rest of the ingredients, stirring it, and then ladle it to bowls to serve this!

Nutrition: Calories: 200, Fat: 7g, Carbohydrates: 20g, Protein: 8g, Sodium: 112mg

197. Split Pea Cream Soup

Preparation: 10 minutes   **Cooking: 15 minutes**   **Servings: 6**

Ingredients:

- *2 tablespoons olive oil*
- *1 chopped yellow onion*
- *1/2 cup chopped celery*
- *18 oz, low-salt chicken stock*
- *2 cups water*
- *1/2 cup coconut cream*
- *1-pound chicken sausage, ground*
- *1/2 cup chopped carrots*
- *2 minced garlic cloves*
- *black pepper for taste*
- *16 oz, split peas, rinsed*
- *1/4 teaspoon dried pepper flakes*

Directions:

1. Press sauté mode and add sausage, browning for 2-3 minutes then transferring to plate.

2. Add oil to IP, then add celery, onions, carrots, water, garlic, stock, pepper flakes, and peas, stirring, and cooking on manual for 10 minutes.
3. Blend with an immersion blender and then sauté once more, and add the pepper, sausage, and corn, simmering and mix it all together.

Nutrition: Calories: 281, Fat: 7g, Carbohydrates: 19g, Protein: 16g Sodium: 102mg

198. Italian Veggie Soup

Preparation: 10 minutes   **Cooking: 15 minutes**   **Servings: 8**

Ingredients:

- *1 tablespoon olive oil*
- *2 chopped carrots*
- *1 cup corn*
- *3 pounds peeled and chopped tomatoes*
- *1 chopped celery stalk*
- *1 chopped onion*
- *1 chopped zucchini*
- *4 minced garlic cloves*
- *28 oz. Chicken stock*
- *1 teaspoon Italian seasoning*
- *15 oz. Kidney beans, canned, rinsed and drained*
- *black pepper for taste*
- *2 cups baby spinach*
- *2 tablespoons chopped basil*

Directions:

1. Within instant pot, press sauté, heat it up and add the onion, cooking for 5 minutes.
2. Add the veggies and stir for 5 more minutes.
3. Then add spices and cook on high for 4 minutes on manual.
4. Add the spinach and beans, stirring and serving.

Nutrition: Calories: 210, Fat: 6g, Carbohydrates: 18g, Sodium: 82mg, Protein: 98g,

199. Carrot Ginger Soup with Spinach and Chicken

Preparation: 10 minutes   **Cooking: 5 minutes**   **Servings: 6**

Ingredients:

- *1 tablespoon cooking fat*
- *2 diced garlic cloves*
- *1-pound organic carrots, cut into small pieces*
- *1 teaspoon ground coriander*
- *3 cups vegetable broth*
- *1 lemon*
- *4 handfuls of spinach*
- *1 diced onion*
- *2 tablespoons minced ginger*
- *1 teaspoon ground cumin*
- *1/2 teaspoon ground turmeric*
- *1 cup coconut milk*
- *1-pound cooked chicken, cut into cubes*

Directions:

1. Sauté instant pot, and add the ghee, and the onions, cooking till they soften.
2. Add in garlic, ginger, stirring till fragrant, then add carrots, and spices, and stir well.
3. Add broth, close lid, and then manually cook for 5 minutes.
4. Add coconut milk to this, and then let it cook, and then season it with salt, pepper, and lemon after putting it through immersion blender to puree it.
5. Stir spinach into the soup, and then serve!

Nutrition: Calories: 150, Fat: 4g, Carbohydrates: 10g, Sodium: 102mg, Protein: 12g

200. Taco Soup

Preparation: 10 minutes   **Cooking: 10 minutes**   **Servings: 4**

 Ingredients:

- *1 cup ground beef, cooked*
- *1/4 teaspoons alt*
- *3 teaspoons ranch dressing mix*
- *6 oz. Diced tomatoes*
- *1 cup canned pinto beans*
- *1/2 cup diced onion*
- *1/4 teaspoon black pepper*
- *2 teaspoons taco seasoning*

- *1 can of canned kernel corn*
- *4 oz. Diced tomatoes with chiles*

Directions:
1. Turn on IP to sauté, and then put the beef in there, cooking till browned.
2. Put the ingredients in there.
3. Lock it, and then cook on high pressure for 10 minutes, then natural pressure release.

Nutrition: Calories: 200, Fat: 5g, Carbohydrates: 12g, Protein: 15g Sodium: 120mg

201. Ground Beef Soup with Tomatoes

Preparation time: 15 minutes
Cooking time: 30 minutes
Servings: 4-6
Ingredients:
- *1 teaspoon olive oil*
- *1 chopped medium onion*
- *1 teaspoon dried thyme*
- *1/2-pound fresh green beans*
- *2 cans beef broth*
- *salt and pepper for taste*
- *1-pound ground beef,*
- *1 tablespoon minced garlic*
- *1 teaspoon oregano*
- *2 cans diced tomatoes with juice*
- *Parmesan for serving*

Directions:
1. Turn on IP and then sauté the beef until browned, and add in the onion, thyme, garlic, and oregano, and cook for 3 minutes once beef is browned.
2. Add the tomatoes, and the beef broth, and let this all heat.
3. Trim the beans to cut into pieces about an inch long, and then add to pressure cooker.
4. Put it on soup function, and from there, use quick release for this, seasoning to taste, and serve hot with parmesan.

Nutrition: calories: 220, Fat: 6g, Carbohydrates: 7g, Protein: 15g, Sodium: 92mg

202. Chipotle Squash Soup

Preparation: 15 minutes   **Cooking: 4 hours**   **Servings: 6**
Ingredients:
- *6 cups Butternut Squash (cubed)*
- *1/2 cup chopped Onion*
- *2 tsp. Adobo Chipotle 2 cups Chicken Broth*
- *1 tbsp. Brown Sugar*
- *1/4 cup Tart Apple (chopped)*
- *1 cup Yogurt (Greek style)*
- *2 tbsp. Chives (chopped)*

Directions:
1. Except for yogurt, chives, and apple, place all the ingredients in the slow cooker. Cook on "low" for 4 hrs. Now, in a blender or food processer, puree the cooked ingredients. Transfer puree to slow cooker.
2. Put the yogurt and cook on "Low" within 20 more mins. Garnish with chives and apples. Serve hot in heated bowls.

Nutrition: Calories 102 Fat 11 g Carbohydrates 22 g Protein 4 g Sodium 142 mg

203. Kale Verde

Preparation: 15 minutes   **Cooking: 6 hours**   **Servings: 6**
Ingredients:
- *1/4 cup Olive Oil (extra virgin)*
- *1 Yellow Onion (large)*
- *2 cloves Garlic*
- *2 ounces Tomatoes, dried*
- *2 cups Yellow Potatoes (diced)*
- *14-ounce Tomatoes (diced)*
- *6 cups Chicken broth White pepper (ground)*
- *1-pound o chopped Kale*

Directions:

1. Sauté onion for 5 minutes in oil. Add the garlic and sauté again for 1 minute. Transfer the sautéed mixture to the slow cooker. Put the rest of the fixing except pepper into the slow cooker. Cook on "low" for 6 hrs. Season with white pepper to taste. Serve hot in heated bowls

Nutrition: Calories 257 Fat 22g Carbohydrates 27g Protein 14g Sodium 239 mg

204. Escarole with Bean Soup

Preparation: 15 minutes   **Cooking**: 6 hours   **Servings**: 6

Ingredients:

- *1 tbsp. Olive Oil*
- *8 crushed cloves Garlic*
- *1 cup chopped Onions*
- *1 diced Carrot*
- *3 tsp. Basil (dried)*
- *3 tsp. Oregano (dried)*
- *4 cups Chicken Broth*
- *3 cups chopped Escarole*
- *1 cup of Northern Beans (dried)*
- *Parmesan Cheese (grated)*
- *14 ounces o Tomatoes (diced)*

Directions:

1. Sauté garlic for 2 minutes in oil using a large soup pot. Except for the cheese, broth, and beans, add the rest of the ingredients and cook for 5 mins. Transfer the cooked ingredients to the slow cooker.
2. Mix in the broth and beans. Cook on "low" for 6 hrs. Garnish with cheese. Serve hot in heated bowls.

Nutrition: Calories 98, Fat 33 g, Carbohydrates 14g, Protein 8g, Sodium 115 mg

205. Roasted Garlic Soup

Preparation: 15 minutes   **Cooking**: 60 minutes   **Servings**: 10

Ingredients:

- *1 tablespoon olive oil*
- *2 bulbs garlic, peeled*
- *3 shallots, chopped*
- *1 large head cauliflower, chopped*
- *6 cups vegetable broth*
- *Sunflower seeds and pepper to taste*

Directions:

1. Warm your oven to 400 degrees F. Slice 1/4-inch top of the garlic bulb and place it in aluminum foil. Oiled it using olive oil and roast in the oven for 35 minutes. Squeeze flesh out of the roasted garlic.
2. Heat-up oil in a saucepan and add shallots, sauté for 6 minutes. Add garlic and remaining ingredients. Adjust heat to low. Let it cook for 15- 20 minutes.
3. Puree the mixture using an immersion blender. Season soup with sunflower seeds and pepper. Serve and enjoy!

Nutrition: Calories: 142 Fat: 8g Carbohydrates: 3.4g Protein: 4g Sodium: 548 mg

206. Roasted Carrot Soup

Preparation: 15 minutes   **Cooking**: 50 minutes   **Servings**: 4

Ingredients:

- *8 large carrots, washed and peeled*
- *6 tablespoons olive oil*
- *1-quart broth*
- *Cayenne pepper to taste*
- *Sunflower seeds and pepper to taste*

Directions:

1. Warm your oven to 425 degrees F. Take a baking sheet, add carrots, drizzle olive oil, and roast for 30- 45 minutes. Put roasted carrots into a blender and add broth, puree. Pour into saucepan and heat soup. Season with sunflower seeds, pepper and cayenne. Drizzle olive oil. Serve and enjoy!

Nutrition: Calories: 222 Fat: 18g Net Carbohydrates: 7g Protein: 5g Sodium: 266 mg

207. Golden Mushroom Soup

Preparation: 15 minutes   **Cooking: 8 hours**   **Servings: 6**

Ingredients:

- 1 onion, finely chopped
- 1 carrot, peeled and finely chopped
- 1 fennel bulb, finely chopped
- 1-pound fresh mushrooms, quartered
- 8 cups Vegetable Broth, Poultry Broth, or store-bought

- 1/4 cup dry sherry
- teaspoon dried thyme
- 1 teaspoon garlic powder
- 1/2 teaspoon of sea salt
- 1/8 teaspoon freshly ground black pepper

Directions:

1. In your slow cooker, combine all the ingredients, mixing to combine.
2. Cover and set on low. Cook for 8 hours.

Nutrition: Calories: 71 Fat: 1g, Carbohydrates: 15g, Protein: 3g, Sodium: 650 mg

208. Butternut Squash Soup

Preparation: 15 minutes   **Cooking: 8 hours**   **Servings: 6**

Ingredients:

- 1 butternut squash, peeled, seeded, and diced
- 1 onion, chopped
- 1 sweet-tart apple (such as Braeburn), peeled, cored, and chopped
- 3 cups Vegetable Broth or store-bought
- 1 teaspoon garlic powder

- 1/2 teaspoon ground sage
- 1/4 teaspoon of sea salt
- 1/4 teaspoon freshly ground black pepper
- Pinch cayenne pepper
- Pinch nutmeg
- 1/2 cup fat-free half-and-half

Directions:

1. In your slow cooker, combine the squash, onion, apple, broth, garlic powder, sage, salt, black pepper, cayenne, and nutmeg. Cook on low within 8 hours.
2. Using an immersion blender, counter-top blender, or food processor, purée the soup, adding the half-and-half as you do. Stir to combine and serve.

Nutrition: Calories: 106 Fat: 2g Carbohydrates: 26g, Protein: 3g Sodium: 550 mg

209. Black Bean Soup

Preparation: 15 minutes   **Cooking: 8 hours**   **Servings: 6**

Ingredients:

- 1-pound dried black beans, soaked overnight and rinsed
- 1 onion, chopped
- carrot, peeled and chopped
- jalapeño peppers, seeded and diced
- 6 cups Vegetable Broth or store-bought
- 1 teaspoon ground cumin
- 1 teaspoon ground coriander
- 1 teaspoon chili powder

- 1/2 teaspoon ground chipotle pepper
- 1/2 teaspoon of sea salt
- 1/4 teaspoon freshly ground black pepper Pinch cayenne pepper
- 1/4 cup fat-free sour cream, for garnish (optional)
- 1/4 cup grated low-fat Cheddar cheese, for garnish (optional)

Directions:

1. In your slow cooker, combine all the fixing listed, then cook on low for 8 hours. If you'd like, mash the beans with a potato masher, or purée using an immersion blender, blender, or food processor. Serve topped with the optional garnishes, if desired.

Nutrition: Calories: 320 Fat: 3g, Carbohydrates: 57g, Protein: 18g Sodium: 430 mg

210. Chicken & Rice Soup

Preparation: 15 minutes   **Cooking: 8 hours**   **Servings: 6**

Ingredients:

- *1-pound boneless, skinless chicken thighs, cut into 1-inch pieces*
- *1 onion, chopped*
- *3 carrots, peeled and sliced*
- *2 celery stalks, sliced*
- *6 cup Poultry Broth or store-bought*
- *1 teaspoon garlic powder*
- *teaspoon dried rosemary*
- *1/4 teaspoon of sea salt*
- *1/4 teaspoon freshly ground black pepper*
- *3 cups cooked Brown Rice*

Directions:

1. In your slow cooker, combine the chicken, onion, carrots, celery, broth, garlic powder, rosemary, salt, and pepper. Cover and cook on low within 8 hours. Stir in the rice about 10 minutes before serving and allow the broth to warm it.

Nutrition: Calories: 354 Fat: 7g Carbohydrates: 43g Protein: 28g Sodium: 610 mg

211. Tom Kha Gai

Preparation 15 minutes   **Cooking: 8 hours**   **Servings: 6**

Ingredients:

- *1-pound boneless, skinless chicken thighs, cut into 1-inch pieces*
- *1-pound fresh shiitake mushrooms halved*
- *tablespoons grated fresh ginger*
- *cups canned light coconut milk*
- *3 cups Poultry Broth or store-bought 1 tablespoon Asian fish sauce*
- *teaspoon garlic powder*
- *1/4 teaspoon freshly ground black pepper Juice of 1 lime*
- *tablespoons chopped fresh cilantro*

Directions:

1. In your slow cooker, combine the chicken thighs, mushrooms, ginger, coconut milk, broth, fish sauce, garlic powder, and pepper. Cover and cook on low within 8 hours. Stir in the lime juice and cilantro just before serving.

Nutrition: Calories: 481 Fat: 35g Carbohydrates: 19g Protein: 28g Sodium: 160 mg

212. Chicken Corn Chowder

Preparation: 15 minutes   **Cooking: 8 hours**   **Servings: 6**

Ingredients:

- 1-pound boneless, skinless chicken thighs, cut into 1-inch pieces
- 2 onions, chopped
- jalapeño peppers, seeded and minced
- 2 red bell peppers, seeded and chopped
- 1 1/2 cups fresh or frozen corn
- 6 cups Poultry Broth or store-bought
- 1 teaspoon garlic powder
- 1/2 teaspoon of sea salt
- 1/4 teaspoon freshly ground black pepper
- 1 cup skim milk

Directions:

1. In your slow cooker, combine the chicken, onions, jalapeños, red bell peppers, corn, broth, garlic powder, salt, and pepper. Cover and cook on low within 8 hours. Stir in the skim milk just before serving.

Nutrition: Calories: 236 Fat: 6g Carbohydrates: 17g Protein: 27g Sodium: 790 mg

213. Turkey Ginger Soup

Preparation: 15 minutes   **Cooking: 8 hours**   **Servings: 6**

Ingredients:

- *1-pound boneless, skinless turkey thighs, cut into 1-inch pieces*
- *1-pound fresh shiitake mushrooms halved*
- *3 carrots, peeled and sliced*
- *2 cups frozen peas*
- *1 tablespoon grated fresh ginger*

- *6 cups Poultry Broth or store-bought*
- *1 tablespoon low-sodium soy sauce*
- *1 teaspoon toasted sesame oil*
- *2 teaspoons garlic powder*
- *1 1/2 cups cooked Brown Rice*

Directions:

1. In your slow cooker, combine the turkey, mushrooms, carrots, peas, ginger, broth, soy sauce, sesame oil, and garlic powder. Cover and cook on low within 8 hours. About 30 minutes before serving, stir in the rice to warm it through.

Nutrition: Calories: 318 Fat: 7g Carbohydrates: 42g, Protein: 24g Sodium: 690 mg

POULTRY

214. Parmesan and Chicken Spaghetti Squash

Preparation: 15 minutes **Cooking: 20 minutes** **Servings: 6**
Ingredients:
- 16 oz. mozzarella
- 1 spaghetti squash piece
- 1 lb. cooked cube chicken
- 1 c. Marinara sauce

Directions:
1. *Split up the squash in halves and remove the seeds. Arrange or put one cup of water in your pot, then put a trivet on top.*
2. *Add the squash halves to the trivet. Cook within 20 minutes at HIGH pressure. Remove the squashes and shred them using a fork into spaghetti portions*
3. *Pour sauce over the squash and give it a nice mix. Top them up with the cubed-up chicken and top with mozzarella. Broil for 1-2 minutes and broil until the cheese has melted*

Nutrition: Calories: 237 Fat:10 g Carbohydrates:32 g Protein:11 g Sodium: 500 mg

215. Apricot Chicken

Preparation: 15 minutes **Cooking: 6 minutes** **Servings: 4**
Ingredients:
- *1 bottle creamy French dressing*
- *1/4 c. flavorless oil*
- *White cooked rice*
- *1 large jar Apricot preserve*
- *4 lbs. boneless and skinless chicken*
- *1 package onion soup mix*

Directions:
1. Rinse and pat dry the chicken. Dice into bite-size pieces. In a large bowl, mix the apricot preserve, creamy dressing, and onion soup mix. Stir until thoroughly combined. Place the chicken in the bowl. Mix until coated.
2. In a large skillet, heat the oil. Place the chicken in the oil gently. Cook 4 – 6 minutes on each side, until golden brown. Serve over rice.

Nutrition: Calories: 202 Fat:12g Carbohydrates:75g Protein:20g Sodium: 630 mg

216. Oven-Fried Chicken Breasts

Preparation: 15 minutes **Cooking: 30 minutes** **Servings: 8**
Ingredients:
- *1/2 pack Ritz crackers*
- *1 c. plain non-fat yogurt*
- *8 boneless, skinless, and halved chicken breasts*

Directions:
1. Preheat the oven to 350 0F. Rinse and pat dry the chicken breasts. Pour the yogurt into a shallow bowl. Dip the chicken pieces in the yogurt, then roll in the cracker crumbs. Place the chicken in a single layer in a baking dish. Bake within 15 minutes per side. Serve.

Nutrition: Calories: 200 Fat:13g Carbohydrates:98g Protein:19g Sodium:217 mg

217. Rosemary Roasted Chicken

Preparation: 15 minutes **Cooking: 20 minutes** **Servings: 8**
Ingredients:
- *8 rosemary springs*
- *1 minced garlic clove*
- *Black pepper*
- *1 tbsp. chopped rosemary*
- *1 chicken*
- *1 tbsp. organic olive oil*

Directions:

1. In a bowl, mix garlic with rosemary, rub the chicken with black pepper, the oil and rosemary mix, place it inside roasting pan, introduce inside the oven at 350 0F, and roast for sixty minutes and 20 min.
2. Carve chicken, divide between plates and serve using a side dish. Enjoy!

Nutrition: Calories: 325 Fat:5g Carbohydrates:15g Protein:14g Sodium: 950 mg

218. Artichoke and Spinach Chicken

Preparation: 15 minutes   **Cooking: 5 minutes**   **Servings: 4**

Ingredients:

- *10 oz baby spinach*
- *1/2 tsp. crushed red pepper flakes*
- *14 oz. chopped artichoke hearts*
- *28 oz. no-salt-added tomato sauce*
- *2 tbsps. Essential olive oil*
- *4 boneless and skinless chicken breasts*

Directions:

1. Heat-up a pan with the oil over medium-high heat, add chicken and red pepper flakes and cook for 5 minutes on them. Add spinach, artichokes, and tomato sauce, toss, cook for ten minutes more, divide between plates and serve. Enjoy!

Nutrition: Calories: 212 Fat:3g Carbohydrates:16g Protein:20g Sodium:418 mg

219. Pumpkin and Black Beans Chicken

Preparation: 15 minutes   **Cooking: 25 minutes**   **Servings: 4**

Ingredients:

- *1 tbsp. essential olive oil*
- *1 tbsp. Chopped cilantro*
- *1 c. coconut milk*
- *15 oz canned black beans, drained*
- *1 lb. skinless and boneless chicken breasts*
- *2 c. water*
- *1/2 c. pumpkin flesh*

Directions:

1. Heat a pan when using oil over medium-high heat, add the chicken and cook for 5 minutes. Add the river, milk, pumpkin, and black beans toss, cover the pan, reduce heat to medium and cook for 20 mins. Add cilantro, toss, divide between plates and serve. Enjoy!

Nutrition: Calories: 254 Fat:6 g Carbohydrates:16 g Protein:22 g Sodium:92 mg

220. Chicken Thighs and Apples Mix

Preparation: 15 minutes   **Cooking: 60 minutes**   **Servings: 4**

Ingredients:

- *3 cored and sliced apples*
- *1 tbsp apple cider vinegar treatment*
- *3/4 c. natural apple juice*
- *1/4 tsp. pepper and salt*
- *1 tbsp. grated ginger*
- *8 chicken thighs*
- *3 tbsps. Chopped onion*

Directions:

1. In a bowl, mix chicken with salt, pepper, vinegar, onion, ginger, and apple juice, toss well, cover, keep within the fridge for ten minutes, transfer with a baking dish, and include apples. Introduce inside the oven at 400 0F for just 1 hour. Divide between plates and serve. Enjoy!

Nutrition: Calories: 214 Fat:3g Carbohydrates:14g Protein:15g Sodium:405 mg

221. Thai Chicken Thighs

Preparation: 15 minutes   **Cooking time: 1 hour**   **Servings: 6**

Ingredients:

- *1/2 c. Thai chili sauce*
- *1 chopped green onions bunch*
- *4 lbs. chicken thighs*

Directions:
1. Heat a pan over medium-high heat. Add chicken thighs, brown them for 5 minutes on both sides Transfer to some baking dish, then add chili sauce and green onions and toss.
2. Introduce within the oven and bake at 4000F for 60 minutes. Divide everything between plates and serve. Enjoy!

Nutrition: Calories: 220 Fat:4g Carbohydrates:12g Protein:10g Sodium: 870 mg

222. Falling "Off" The Bone Chicken

Preparation: 15 minutes   **Cooking: 40 minutes**   **Servings: 4**

Ingredients:
- *6 peeled garlic cloves*
- *1 tbsp. organic extra virgin coconut oil*
- *2 tbsps. Lemon juice*
- *1 1/2 c. pacific organic bone chicken broth*
- *1/4 tsp freshly ground black pepper*
- *1/2 tsp. sea flavored vinegar*
- *1 whole organic chicken piece*
- *1 tsp. paprika*
- *1 tsp. dried thyme*

Directions:
1. Take a small bowl and toss in the thyme, paprika, pepper, and flavored vinegar and mix them. Use the mixture to season the chicken properly. Pour down the oil in your instant pot and heat it to shimmering; toss in the chicken with breast downward and let it cook for about 6-7 minutes
2. After the 7 minutes, flip over the chicken pour down the broth, garlic cloves, and lemon juice. Cook within 25 minutes on a high setting. Remove the dish from the cooker and let it stand for about 5 minutes before serving.

Nutrition: Calories: 664 Fat:44g Carbohydrates:44g Protein:27g Sodium: 800mg

223. Feisty Chicken Porridge

Preparation: 15 minutes   **Cooking: 30 minutes**   **Servings: 4**

Ingredients:
- *1 1/2 c. fresh ginger*
- *1 lb. cooked chicken legs*
- *Green onions*
- *Toasted cashew nuts*
- *5 c. chicken broth*
- *1 cup jasmine rice*
- *4 c. water*

Directions:
1. Place the rice in your fridge and allow it to chill 1 hour before cooking. Take the rice out and add them to your Instant Pot. Pour broth and water. Lock up the lid and cook on Porridge mode.
2. Separate the meat from the chicken legs and add the meat to your soup. Stir well over sauté mode. Season with a bit of flavored vinegar and enjoy with a garnish of nuts and onion

Nutrition: Calories: 206 Fat:8 g Carbohydrates:8 g Protein:23 g Sodium:950 mg

224. The Ultimate Faux-Tisserie Chicken

Preparation: 15 minutes   **Cooking: 35 minutes**   **Servings: 5**

Ingredients:
- *1 c. low sodium broth*
- *2 tbsps. Olive oil*
- *1/2 quartered medium onion*
- *2 tbsps. Favorite seasoning*
- *2 1/2 lbs. whole chicken*
- *Black pepper*
- *5 large fresh garlic cloves*

Directions:
1. Massage the chicken with 1 tablespoon of olive oil and sprinkle pepper on top. Place onion wedges and garlic cloves inside the chicken. Take a butcher's twin and secure the legs

2. Set your pot to Sauté mode. Put olive oil in your pan on medium heat, allow the oil to heat up. Add chicken and sear both sides for 4 minutes per side. Sprinkle your seasoning over the chicken, remove the chicken and place a trivet at the bottom of your pot
3. Sprinkle seasoning over the chicken, making sure to rub it. Transfer the chicken to the trivet with the breast side facing up, lock up the lid. Cook on HIGH pressure for 25 minutes.
4. Allow it to rest and serve!

Nutrition: Calories: 1010 Fat:64 g Carbohydrates:47 g Protein:60 g Sodium:209 mg

225. Oregano Chicken Thighs

Preparation: 15 minutes   **Cooking: 20 minutes**   **Servings: 6**

Ingredients:
- *12 chicken thighs*
- *1 tsp dried parsley*
- *1/4 tsp. pepper and salt.*
- *1/2 c. extra virgin essential olive oil*
- *4 minced garlic cloves*
- *1 c. chopped oregano*
- *1/4 c. low-sodium veggie stock*

Directions:
1. In your food processor, mix parsley with oregano, garlic, salt, pepper, and stock and pulse. Put chicken thighs within the bowl, add oregano paste, toss, cover, and then leave aside within the fridge for 10 minutes.
2. Heat the kitchen grill over medium heat, add chicken pieces, close the lid and cook for twenty or so minutes with them. Divide between plates and serve!

Nutrition: Calories: 254 Fat:3 g Carbohydrates:7 g Protein:17 g Sodium:730 mg

226. Pesto Chicken Breasts with Summer Squash

Preparation: 15 minutes   **Cooking: 10 minutes**   **Servings: 4**

Ingredients:
- *4 medium boneless, skinless chicken breast halves*
- *1 tbsp. olive oil*
- *2 tbsps. Homemade pesto*
- *2 c. finely chopped zucchini*
- *2 tbsps. Finely shredded Asiago*

Directions:
1. Cook your chicken in hot oil on medium heat within 4 minutes in a large nonstick skillet. Flip the chicken then put the zucchini.
2. Cook within 4 to 6 minutes more or until the chicken is tender and no longer pink (170 F), and squash is crisp-tender, stirring squash gently once or twice. Transfer chicken and squash to 4 dinner plates. Spread pesto over chicken, sprinkle with Asiago.

Nutrition: Calories: 230 Fat:9 g Carbohydrates:8 g Protein:30 g Sodium:578 mg

227. Chicken, Tomato and Green Beans

Preparation: 15 minutes   **Cooking: 25 minutes**   **Servings: 4**

Ingredients:
- *6 oz. low-sodium canned tomato paste*
- *2 tbsps. Olive oil*
- *1/4 tsp. black pepper*
- *2 lbs. trimmed green beans*
- *2 tbsps. Chopped parsley*
- *1 1/2 lbs. boneless, skinless, and cubed chicken breasts*
- *25 oz. no-salt-added canned tomato sauce*

Directions:
1. Heat a pan with 50 % with the oil over medium heat, add chicken, stir, cover, cook within 5 minutes on both sides and transfer to a bowl. Heat inside the same pan while using rest through the oil over medium heat, add green beans, stir and cook for 10 minutes.
2. Return chicken for that pan, add black pepper, tomato sauce, tomato paste, and parsley, stir, cover, cook for 10 minutes more, divide between plates and serve. Enjoy!

Nutrition: Calories: 190 Fat:4 g Carbohydrates:12 g Protein:9 g Sodium:168 mg

228. Chicken Tortillas

Preparation: 15 minutes   **Cooking: 5 minutes**   **Servings: 4**

Ingredients:

- 6 oz. boneless, skinless, and cooked chicken breasts
- Black pepper
- 1/3 c. fat-free yogurt
- 4 heated up whole-wheat tortillas
- 2 chopped tomatoes

Directions:

1. Heat-up a pan over medium heat, add one tortilla during those times, heat up, and hang them on the working surface. Spread yogurt on each tortilla, add chicken and tomatoes, roll, divide between plates and serve. Enjoy!

Nutrition: Calories:190 Fat:2 g Carbohydrates:12 g Protein:6 g Sodium:300 mg

229. Chicken Tikka

Preparation :15minutes   **Cooking :20minutes**   **Servings: 6**

Ingredients:

- 4 chicken breasts, skinless, boneless; cubed
- 2 large onions, cubed
- 10 Cherry tomatoes
- 1/3 cup plain non-fat yogurt
- 4 garlic cloves, crushed
- 1 1/2-inch fresh ginger, peeled and chopped
- 1 small onion, grated
- 1 1/2 teaspoon chili powder
- 1 tablespoon ground coriander
- 1 teaspoon salt
- 2 tablespoons coriander leaves

Directions:

1. In a large bowl, combine the non-fat yogurt, crushed garlic, ginger, chili powder, coriander, salt, and pepper. Add the cubed chicken, stir until the chicken is coated. Cover with plastic film, place in the fridge. Marinate 2–4 hours. Heat the broiler or barbecue.
2. After marinating the chicken, get some skewers ready. Alternate pieces of chicken cubes, cherry tomatoes, and cubed onions onto the skewers.
3. Grill within 6–8 minutes on each side. Once the chicken is cooked through, pull the meat and vegetables off the skewers onto plates. Garnish with coriander.
4. Serve immediately.

Nutrition: Calories: 117 Protein: 19 g Carbohydrates: 59 g Fat: 19 g Sodium: 203 mg

230. Honey Spiced Cajun Chicken

Preparation: 15 minutes   **Cooking: 20 minutes**   **Servings: 4**

Ingredients:

- 2 chicken breasts, skinless, boneless
- 1 tablespoon butter or margarine
- 1 pound linguini
- 3 large mushrooms, sliced
- 1 large tomato, diced
- 2 tablespoons regular mustard
- 4 tablespoons honey
- 3 oz. low-fat table cream
- Parsley, roughly chopped

Directions:

1. Wash and dry the chicken breasts. Warm 1 tablespoon of butter or margarine in a large pan. Add the chicken breasts. Season with salt and pepper. Cook on each side for 6–10 minutes, until cooked thoroughly. Pull the chicken breasts from the pan. Set aside.
2. Cook the linguine as stated to instructions on the package in a large pot. Save 1 cup of the pasta water. Drain the linguine. Add the mushrooms, tomatoes to the pan from cooking the chicken. Heat until they are tender.

3. Add the honey, mustard, and cream. Combine thoroughly. Add the chicken and linguine to the pan. Stir until coated. Garnish with parsley and serve.

Nutrition: Calories: 112 Protein: 12 g Carbohydrates: 56 g Fat: 20 g Sodium: 158mg

231. Italian Chicken

Preparation: 15 minutes   **Cooking : 35 minutes**   **Servings: 4**

Ingredients:

- *4 chicken breasts, skinless boneless*
- *1 large jar pasta sauce, low sodium*
- *1 tablespoon flavorless oil (olive, canola, or sunflower)*
- *1 large onion, diced*
- *1 large green pepper, diced*
- *1/2 teaspoon garlic salt*
- *Salt and pepper to taste*
- *1 cup low-fat mozzarella cheese, grated*
- *Spinach leaves, washed, dried, rough chop*

Directions:

1. Wash the chicken breasts, pat dry. In a large pot, heat the oil. Add the onion, cook, until it sweats and becomes translucent. Add the chicken. Season with salt, pepper, and garlic salt. Cook the chicken. 6–10 minutes on each side.
2. Add the peppers. Cook for 2 minutes. Pour the pasta sauce over the chicken. Mix well. Simmer on low for 20 minutes.
3. Serve on plates, sprinkle the cheese over each piece and garnish with spinach.

Nutrition: Calories: 142 Protein: 17 g Carbohydrates: 51 g Fat: 15 g Sodium: 225 mg

232. Lemon-Parsley Chicken Breast

Preparation: 15minutes   **Cooking:15minutes**   **Servings: 2**

Ingredients:

- *2 chicken breasts, skinless, boneless*
- *1/3 cup white wine*
- *1/3 cup lemon juice*
- *2 garlic cloves, minced*
- *3 tablespoons breadcrumbs*
- *2 tablespoons flavorless oil (olive, canola, or sunflower)*
- *1/4 cup fresh parsley*

Directions:

1. Mix the wine, lemon juice, plus garlic in a measuring cup. Pound each chicken breast until they are 1/4 inch thick. Coat the chicken with breadcrumbs and heat the oil in a large skillet.
2. Fry the chicken within 6 minutes on each side until they turn brown. Stir in the wine mixture over the chicken.
3. Simmer for 5 minutes.
4. Pour any extra juices over the chicken. Garnish with parsley.

Nutrition: Calories: 117 Protein: 14 g Carbohydrates: 74 g Fat: 12 g Sodium: 189 mg

233. Chicken Rolls with Pesto

Preparation: 20 minutes   **Cooking : 30 minutes**   **Servings: 1**

Ingredients:

- *Tablespoon pine nuts*
- *Yeast tablets*
- *Garlic cloves (chopped)*
- *Fresh basil*
- *Olive oil*
- *Chicken breast ready to slice:*
- *Preheat the oven to 175 ° C.*
- *Place the pine nuts in a dry pan and heat to a golden brown over medium heat for 3 minutes. Place on a plate and set aside.*
- *Place pine nuts, yeast flakes, and garlic in a food processor and grind finely.*
- *Add basil and oil and mix briefly until you get pesto.*

Directions

1. Season with salt and pepper.

2. Place each piece of the chicken breast between 2 pieces of plastic wrap. 7 Roll in a frying pan or pasta until the chicken breasts grow out.
3. 0.6 cm thick.
4. Remove the plastic wrap, then apply pesto to the chicken.
5. Roll up the chicken breast and tie it with the cocktail skewers.
6. Season with salt and pepper.
7. Dissolve the coconut oil in the pan and use a high temperature to brown all sides of the chicken skin.
8. Place the chicken rolls on a baking sheet, place in the oven, and bake for 15 to 20 minutes, until cooked.
9. Slice it diagonally and serve it with other pesto sauce.
10. It was served with tomato salad.

Nutrition: Calories: 150 Fat: 4.3g Carbohydrates: 15.4g Protein: 1.6g Sodium: 33mg

234. Epic Mango Chicken

Preparation: 25 minutes   **Cooking: 10 minutes**   **Servings: 4**

Ingredients:
- *2 medium mangoes, peeled and sliced*
- *10-ounce coconut almond milk*
- *4 teaspoons vegetable oil*
- *4 teaspoons spicy curry paste*
- *14-ounce chicken breast halves, skinless and boneless, cut into cubes*
- *4 medium shallots*
- *1 large English cucumber, sliced and seeded*

Directions:
1. Slice half of the mangoes and add the halves to a bowl.
2. Add mangoes and coconut almond milk to a blender and blend until you have a smooth puree.
3. Keep the mixture on the side.
4. Take a large-sized pot and place it over medium heat, add oil and allow the oil to heat up.
5. Add curry paste and cook for 1 minute until you have a nice fragrance, add shallots and chicken to the pot, and cook for 5 minutes.
6. Pour mango puree into the mix and allow it to heat up.
7. Serve the cooked chicken with mango puree and cucumbers.

Nutrition: Calories: 398; Fat: 20g; Carbohydrates: 32g; Protein: 26g Sodium: 132mg

235. Chicken and Cabbage Platter

Preparation: 9 minutes   **Cooking: 14 minutes**   **Servings: 2**

Ingredients:
- *1/2 cup sliced onion*
- *1 tablespoon sesame garlic-flavored oil*
- *2 cups shredded Bok-Choy*
- *1/2 cups fresh bean sprouts*
- *1 1/2 celery stalks, chopped*
- *1 1/2 teaspoons minced garlic*
- *1/2 teaspoon stevia*
- *1/2 cup chicken broth*
- *1 tablespoon coconut aminos*
- *1/2 tablespoon freshly minced ginger*
- *1/2 teaspoon arrowroot*
- *2 boneless chicken breasts, cooked and sliced thinly*

Directions:
1. Shred the cabbage with a knife.
2. Slice onion and add to your platter alongside the rotisserie chicken.
3. Add a dollop of mayonnaise on top and drizzle olive oil over the cabbage.
4. Season with sunflower seeds and pepper according to your taste.

Nutrition: Calories: 368; Fat: 18g; Protein: 42g; Sodium: 72mg; Carbohydrates: 11g

236. Hearty Chicken Liver Stew

Preparation: 10 minutes   **Cooking: 20 minutes**   **Servings: 2**

Ingredients:

- *10 ounces chicken livers*
- *1-ounce onion, chopped*
- *2 ounces sour cream*
- *1 tablespoon olive oil*
- *Sunflower seeds to taste*

Directions:

1. Take a pan and place it over medium heat.
2. Add oil and let it heat up.
3. Add onions and fry until just browned.
4. Add livers and season with sunflower seeds.
5. Cook until livers are half cooked.
6. Transfer the mix to a stew pot.
7. Add sour cream and cook for 20 minutes and serve.

Nutrition: Calories: 146; Fat: 9g; Carbohydrates: 2g; Protein: 15g Sodium: 82mg

237. Chicken Quesadilla

Preparation: 10 minutes   **Cooking: 35 minutes**   **Servings: 2**

Ingredients:

- *1/4 cup ranch dressing*
- *1/2 cup cheddar cheese, shredded*
- *20 slices bacon, center-cut*
- *2 cups grilled chicken, sliced*

Directions:

1. Re-heat your oven to 400°F.
2. Line baking sheet using parchment paper.
3. Weave bacon into two rectangles and bake for 30 minutes.
4. Lay grilled chicken over bacon square, drizzling ranch dressing on top.
5. Sprinkle cheddar cheese and top with another bacon square.
6. Bake for 5 minutes more.
7. Slice and serve.

Nutrition: Calories: 619; Fat: 35g; Carbohydrates: 2g; Protein: 79g , Sodium: 112mg

238. Mustard Chicken

Preparation: 10 minutes   **Cooking: 40 minutes**   **Servings: 2**

Ingredients:

- *2 chicken breasts*
- *1/4 cup chicken broth*
- *2 tablespoons mustard*
- *1 1/2 tablespoon olive oil*
- *1/2 teaspoon paprika*
- *1/2 teaspoon chili powder*
- *1/2 teaspoon garlic powder*

Directions:

1. Take a small bowl and mix mustard, olive oil, paprika, chicken broth, garlic powder, chicken broth, and chili.
2. Add chicken breast and marinate for 30 minutes.
3. Take a lined baking sheet and arrange the chicken.
4. Bake for 35 minutes at 375°F and serve.

Nutrition: Calories: 531; Fat: 23g; Carbohydrates: 10g; Protein: 64g, Sodium: 92mg

239. Chicken and Carrot Stew

Preparation: 15 minutes   **Cooking: 6 minutes**   **Servings: 4**

Ingredients:

- *4 boneless chicken breasts, cubed*
- *3 cups of carrots, peeled and cubed*

- *1 cup onion, chopped*
- *1 cup tomatoes, chopped*
- *1 teaspoon of dried thyme*
- *2 cups of chicken broth*
- *2 garlic cloves, minced*
- *Sunflower seeds and pepper as needed*

Directions:
1. Add all of the listed ingredients to a Slow Cooker.
2. Stir and close the lid.
3. Cook for 6 hours and serve hot.

Nutrition: Calories: 182; Fat: 3g; Carbohydrates: 10g; Protein: 39g, Sodium: 112mg

240. The Delish Turkey Wrap

Preparation: 10 minutes   **Cooking: 10 minutes**   **Servings: 6**

Ingredients:
- *1 1/4 pounds ground turkey, lean*
- *4 green onions, minced*
- *1 tablespoon olive oil*
- *1 garlic clove, minced*
- *2 teaspoons chili paste*
- *8-ounce water chestnut, diced*
- *3 tablespoons hoisin sauce*
- *2 tablespoon coconut aminos*
- *1 tablespoon rice vinegar*
- *12 almond butter lettuce leaves*
- *1/8 teaspoon sunflower seeds*

Directions:
1. Take a pan and place it over medium heat, add turkey and garlic to the pan.
2. Heat for 6 minutes until cooked.
3. Take a bowl and transfer turkey to the bowl.
4. Add onions and water chestnuts.
5. Stir in hoisin sauce, coconut aminos, and vinegar, and chili paste.
6. Toss well and transfer the mix to lettuce leaves. Serve.

Nutrition: Calories: 162; Fat: 4g; Carbohydrates: 7g; Protein: 23g Sodium: 121mg

241. Zucchini Zoodles with Chicken and Basil

Preparation: 10 minutes   **Cooking: 10 minutes**   **Servings: 3**

Ingredients:
- *2 chicken fillets, cubed*
- *2 tablespoons ghee*
- *1-pound tomatoes, diced*
- *1/2 cup basil, chopped*
- *1/4 cup almond milk*
- *1 garlic clove, peeled, minced*
- *1 zucchini, shredded*

Directions:
1. Sauté cubed chicken in ghee until no longer pink.
2. Add tomatoes and season with sunflower seeds.
3. Simmer and reduce the liquid.
4. Prepare your zucchini Zoodles by shredding zucchini in a food processor.
5. Add basil, garlic, coconut almond milk to the chicken and cook for a few minutes.
6. Add half of the zucchini Zoodles to a bowl and top with creamy tomato basil chicken and serve!

Nutrition: Calories: 540; Fat: 27g; Carbohydrates: 13g; Protein: 59g Sodium: 116mg

242. Duck with Cucumber and Carrots

Preparation: 10 minutes   **Cooking: 40 minutes**   **Servings: 8**

Ingredients:
- *1 duck, cut up into medium pieces*
- *1 cucumber, chopped*
- *1 tablespoon low sodium vegetable stock*
- *2 carrots, chopped*
- *2 cups of water*
- *Black pepper as needed*
- *1-inch ginger piece, grated*

Directions:
1. Add duck pieces to your Instant Pot.
2. Add cucumber, stock, carrots, water, ginger, pepper, and stir.
3. Lock up the lid and cook on LOW pressure for 40 minutes.
4. Release the pressure naturally.
5. Serve and enjoy!

Nutrition: Calories: 206; Fats: 7g; Carbohydrates: 28g; Protein: 16g Sodium: 102mg

243. Parmesan Baked Chicken

Preparation: 5 minutes　　　　**Cooking: 20 minutes**　　　　**Servings: 2**

Ingredients:
- 2 tablespoons ghee
- 2 boneless chicken breasts, skinless
- Pink sunflower seeds
- Freshly ground black pepper
- 1/2 cup mayonnaise, low fat
- 1/4 cup parmesan cheese, grated
- 1 tablespoon dried Italian seasoning, low fat, low sodium
- 1/4 cup crushed pork rinds

Directions:
1. Preheat your oven to 425°F.
2. Take a large baking dish and coat it with ghee.
3. Pat chicken breasts dry and wrap with a towel.
4. Season with sunflower seeds and pepper.
5. Place in baking dish.
6. Take a small bowl and add mayonnaise, parmesan cheese, Italian seasoning.
7. Slather mayo mix evenly over chicken breast.
8. Sprinkle crushed pork rinds on top.
9. Bake for 20 minutes until topping is browned and serve!

Nutrition: Calories: 850; Fat: 67g; Carbohydrates: 2g; Protein: 60g Sodium: 89mg

244. Buffalo Chicken Lettuce Wraps

Preparation: 35 minutes　　　　**Cooking: 10 minutes**　　　　**Servings: 2**

Ingredients:
- 3 chicken breasts, boneless and cubed
- 20 slices of almond butter lettuce leaves
- 3/4 cup cherry tomatoes halved
- 1 avocado, chopped
- 1/4 cup green onions, diced
- 1/2 cup ranch dressing
- 3/4 cup hot sauce

Directions:
1. Take a mixing bowl and add chicken cubes and hot sauce, mix.
2. Place in the fridge and let it marinate for 30 minutes.
3. Preheat your oven to 400°F.
4. Place coated chicken on a cookie pan and bake for 9 minutes.
5. Assemble lettuce serving cups with equal amounts of lettuce, green onions, tomatoes, ranch dressing, and cubed chicken. Serve.

Nutrition: Calories: 106; Fat: 6g; Net Carbohydrates: 2g; Protein: 5g Sodium: 76mg

245. Thai Chicken Pasta

Preparation: 10 minutes　　　　**Cooking: 10 minutes**　　　　**Servings: 6**

Ingredients:
- 2 cups chicken, cooked, shredded.
- 6 oz. whole-wheat spaghetti, uncooked.
- 10 oz. sugar snap peas, trimmed and cut into strips.
- 1 cucumber, sliced.
- 2 cups carrots, julienned.
- 1 cup of Thai peanut sauce.
- 2 teaspoons canola oil.

- *Fresh cilantro, chopped, for serving*

Directions:
1. Bring a saucepan of water to a boil and add pasta. Cook according to package instructions until al dente. Drain.
2. Preheat canola oil in a skillet over medium heat and add peas and carrots, cook for about 6-8 minutes.
3. Add cooked chicken, spaghetti, and peanut sauce, toss well to combine and cook for 1-2 minutes more.
4. Serve topped with fresh cilantro.

Nutrition: 192 calories; 5.3 g fat; 181/2 g carbohydrate; 18.3 g protein; 120 mg sodium.

246. Paprika Baked Chicken Breasts

Preparation: 10 minutes   **Cooking: 10 minutes**   **Servings: 4-6**

Ingredients:
- *4-6 chicken breasts, boneless.*
- *1 tablespoon olive oil.*
- *1 tablespoon paprika;*
- *1/4 cup brown sugar;*
- *1 teaspoon ground coriander;*
- *1/2 teaspoon garlic powder;*
- *1/4 teaspoon cayenne pepper;*
- *1/2 teaspoon ground black pepper.*

Directions:
1. Preheat the oven to 400 °F. Prepare a baking sheet and line it with parchment paper.
2. Mix coriander, paprika, salt, sugar, black pepper, garlic powder, and cayenne pepper in a bowl.
3. Drizzle chicken breasts with oil and rub with the spice mixture and refrigerate for about 15 minutes.
4. Place on the baking sheet and cook for 30 minutes. Let cool before serving.

Nutrition: Calories 315, Carbohydrates 10g, Protein 42g, Fat 15g, Sodium 129mg

247. Chicken Lettuce Wraps

Preparation: 10 minutes   **Cooking: 10 minutes**   **Servings: 4**

Ingredients:
- *8 lettuce leaves;*
- *3/4 lb. chicken breasts, boneless, skinless, cubed;*
- *cups carrots, shredded;*
- *1/3 cup almonds, chopped;*
- *2 tablespoons rice vinegar;*
- *2 tablespoons low-sodium teriyaki sauce;*
- *4 green onions, chopped;*
- *cups fresh sweet cherries, pitted, chopped;*
- *2 teaspoons olive oil;*
- *1 tablespoon honey;*
- *1 teaspoon ground ginger;*
- *1/4 teaspoon ground black pepper.*

Directions:
1. Season chicken with ginger and pepper.
2. Preheat olive oil in a skillet over medium heat and add chicken, cook for about 4-5 minutes until meat is no longer pink. Transfer to a plate.
3. Add carrots, green onions, almonds, and cherries to the same skillet, stir well and cook for 1-2 minutes. Add vinegar, honey, and teriyaki sauce, stir well. Add chicken and toss to combine.
4. Top each lettuce leaf with the chicken mixture and serve.

Nutrition: Calories 257, Carbohydrates 22g, Protein 21g, Fat 10g, Sodium 181mg

248. White Wine Garlic Chicken

Preparation: 10 minutes   **Cooking: 25 minutes**   **Servings: 4**

Ingredients:
- *4 chicken breast, boneless, skinless, pounded;*
- *6 oz. baby portobello mushrooms, sliced;*
- *1 onion, chopped;*
- *2 garlic cloves, minced;*
- *1/2 cup dry white wine;*
- *1 tablespoon olive oil;*
- *1/4 teaspoon black pepper.*

Directions:

1. Season chicken with pepper.
2. Preheat olive oil in a skillet over medium heat. Add chicken and cook for about 6 minutes per side. Transfer to a plate.
3. Add onion and mushrooms to the same skillet, cook for 2-3 minutes.
4. Add garlic and cook for 1 minute.
5. Add wine and bring everything to a boil, stir well to combine everything. Cook for 1-2 minutes and serve.

Nutrition: 243 calories; 7.2 g fat; 5.1 g carbohydrate; 36.3 g protein; 381 mg sodium.

249. Turkey Medallions

Preparation: 30 minutes   **Cooking: 15 minutes**   **Servings: 6**

Ingredients:

- *20 oz. turkey tenderloins, sliced;*
- *1 egg;*
- *3 tablespoons olive oil;*
- *2 tablespoons lemon juice;*
- *1 cup panko breadcrumbs.*
- *1/2 cup Parmesan cheese, grated;*
- *1/2 cup walnuts, chopped;*
- *1 teaspoon lemon pepper seasoning;*
- *1/4 teaspoon pepper;*
- *fresh basil, chopped.*

Directions:

1. Mix egg and lemon juice in a bowl.
2. In a separate bowl, mix breadcrumbs, nuts, lemon pepper seasoning, and cheese.
3. Season turkey with pepper.
4. Preheat oil in a skillet over medium heat.
5. . Dip each turkey piece first into the egg mixture and then into the breadcrumb mixture. Add to the skillet and cook for about 2-3 minutes per side. Serve topped with basil.

Nutrition: Calories 351, Carbohydrates 13g, Protein 29g, Fat 13g, Sodium 458mg

250. Walnut Pesto Chicken Penne

Preparation: 20 minutes   **Cooking: 30 minutes**   **Servings: 4**

Ingredients:

- *cups chicken meat, cooked, shredded;*
- *6 oz. whole-wheat penne pasta;*
- *8 oz. green beans, trimmed and halved;*
- *3/4 cup walnuts, chopped, toasted;*
- *2 cups cauliflower florets;*
- *1 cup fresh parsley leaves, chopped;*
- *2 garlic cloves, crushed;*
- *1/3 cup Parmesan cheese, grated;*
- *2 tablespoons olive oil;*
- *a pinch of ground pepper.*

Directions:

1. Bring a pot of water to a boil and add pasta and cook for about 4 minutes.
2. Add cauliflower and green beans, cook for 5-6 minutes more.
3. Mix walnuts, parsley, garlic, and pepper in a blender and blitz until the mixture is ground. Add Parmesan and process to combine. Mix chicken with the mixture.
4. Drain pasta with vegetables and top with cheese and chicken mixture. Toss well to combine and serve.

Nutrition: Calories 514, Carbohydrates 43g, Protein 31g, Fat 27g, Sodium 514mg

251. Green Chicken and Rice Bowl

Preparation: 10 minutes   **Cooking: 32 minutes**   **Servings: 4**

Ingredients:

- *1 cup chicken broth*
- *3 cups water*
- *1/2 teaspoon cumin, paprika, thyme, and turmeric*
- *4 tablespoons hummus*
- *1/2 cup Kalamata olives*
- *2 chicken breasts, skinless*
- *2 cups basmati rice*

- *1/2 teaspoon red pepper*
- *salt and pepper for taste*
- *4 tablespoons tzatziki sauce*
- *4 tablespoons feta cheese*

Directions:
1. Season chicken with spices.
2. Add chicken to instant pot with the broth.
3. Cook on manual high pressure, then release naturally for 10 minutes.
4. Remove chicken and then shred chicken.
5. Rinse rice and then add it to instant pot, cooking for 22 minutes on high pressure, then natural pressure release.
6. Add the rice, chicken, and the rest of the ingredients to make rice bowl.

Nutrition: Calories: 426, Fat: 10g, Carbohydrates: 12g, Protein: 25g, Sodium: 132mg

252. Creamy Turkey Mix

Preparation: 5 minutes   **Cooking: 25 minutes**   **Servings: 4**

Ingredients:
- *2 tablespoons olive oil*
- *1 turkey breast, skinless, boneless and sliced*
- *A pinch of black pepper*
- *1 tablespoon basil, chopped*
- *3 garlic cloves, minced*
- *14 ounces canned artichokes, no-salt-added, chopped*
- *1 cup coconut cream*
- *3/4 cup low-fat mozzarella, shredded*

Directions:
1. Heat the oil to the pot over medium heat, add the meat, garlic and black pepper, mix well and cook for 5 minutes.
2. Add the rest of the ingredients except the cheese, toss and cook over medium heat for 15 minutes.
3. Sprinkle the cheese, cook everything for 5 minutes more, divide between plates and serve.

Nutrition: 268 calories, 8.8g protein, 15g carbohydrates, 211/2g fat 225mg sodium,

Nutrition: Calories 268, Carbohydrates 15g, Protein 9g, Fat 21g, Sodium 225mg

253. Turkey and Onion Mix

Preparation: 10 minutes   **Cooking: 30 minutes**   **Servings: 4**

Ingredients:
- *2 tablespoons avocado oil*
- *1 red onion, chopped*
- *2 garlic cloves, minced*
- *A pinch of black pepper*
- *1 tablespoon oregano, chopped*
- *1 big turkey breast, skinless, boneless and cubed*
- *1 and 1/2 cups low-sodium beef stock*
- *1 tablespoon chives, chopped*

Directions:
1. Heat the oil to the pot over medium heat, add the onions, stir and fry for 3 minutes.
2. Add the garlic and the meat, toss and cook for 3 minutes more.
3. Add the rest of the ingredients, throw them away, boil everything on medium heat for 25 minutes, separate between plates, and serve.

Nutrition: 32 calories, 1.4g protein, 4.6g carbohydrates, 1.1g fat, 154mg sodium.

254. Balsamic Chicken

Preparation: 10 minutes   **Cooking: 35 minutes**   **Servings: 4**

Ingredients:
- 1 tablespoon avocado oil
- 1-pound chicken breast, skinless, boneless
- 2 garlic cloves, minced
- 2 shallots, chopped
- 1/2 cup orange juice
- 1 tablespoon orange zest, grated
- 3 tablespoons balsamic vinegar

- 1 teaspoon rosemary.
- chopped

Directions:
1. Heat oil pan over medium heat, add green onion and garlic, stir fry for 2 minutes.
2. Add the meat, toss gently and cook for 3 minutes more.
3. Mix the rest of the ingredients, toss, introduce the pan in the oven and bake at 340 degrees F for 30 minutes.
4. Divide between plates and serve.

Nutrition: 159 calories, 24.6g protein, 5.4g carbohydrates, 3.4g fat, 60mg sodium,

255. Coconut Chicken and Olives

Preparation: 10 minutes   **Cooking: 25 minutes**   **Servings: 4**

Ingredients:
- *1-pound chicken breasts, skinless, boneless and roughly cubed*
- *A pinch of black pepper*
- *1 tablespoon avocado oil*
- *1 red onion, chopped*
- *1 cup coconut milk*
- *1 tablespoon lemon juice*
- *1 cup kalamata olives, pitted and sliced*
- *1/4 cup cilantro, chopped*

Directions:
1. Heat a frying pan over medium heat, add the onion, meat and brown, for 5 minutes.
2. Add the ingredients, toss, bring to a simmer and cook over medium heat for 20 minutes more.
3. Divide between plates and serve.

Nutrition: Calories 409, Carbohydrates 27g, Protein 35g, Fat 18g, Sodium 402mg

256. Turkey and Peach

Preparation: 10 minutes   **Cooking: 25 minutes**   **Servings: 4**

Ingredients:
- *1 tablespoon avocado oil*
- *1 turkey breast, skinless, boneless and sliced*
- *A pinch of black pepper*
- *1 yellow onion, chopped*
- *4 peaches, stones removed and cut into wedges*
- *1/4 cup balsamic vinegar*
- *2 tablespoons chives, chopped*

Directions:
1. Add the ingredients except the chives, toss gently and bake at   390 degrees F for 20 minutes.
2. Divide everything between plates and serve with the chives sprinkled on top.

Nutrition: Calories 79, Carbohydrates 17g, Protein 2g, Fat 1g, Sodium 115mg

257. Paprika Chicken and Spinach

Preparation: 10 minutes   **Cooking: 25 minutes**   **Servings: 4**

Ingredients:
- *1 tablespoon avocado oil*
- *1-pound chicken breast, skinless, boneless and cubed*
- *1/2 teaspoon basil, dried*
- *A pinch of black pepper*
- *1/4 cup low-sodium vegetable stock*
- *2 cups baby spinach*
- *2 shallots, chopped*
- *2 garlic cloves, minced*
- *1/2 teaspoon sweet paprika*
- *2/3 cup coconut cream*
- *2 tablespoons cilantro, chopped*

Directions:
1. Heat a frying pan over medium heat and add the meat, basil, black pepper and brown for 5 minutes.
2. Add the shallots and the garlic and cook for another 5 minutes.

3. Add the rest of the ingredients, toss, bring to a simmer and cook over medium heat from 15 minutes more.
4. Divide between plates and serve hot.

Nutrition: Calories 237, Carbohydrates 4g, Protein 26g, Fat 13g, Sodium 81mg

258. Chicken and Tomatoes Mix

Preparation: 10 minutes   **Cooking: 25 minutes**   **Servings: 4**

Ingredients:

- *2 chicken breasts, skinless, boneless and cubed*
- *2 tablespoons avocado oil*
- *2 spring onions, chopped*
- *1 bunch asparagus, trimmed and halved*
- *1/2 teaspoon sweet paprika*
- *A pinch of black pepper*
- *8 ounces canned tomatoes, no-salt-added, drained and chopped*

Directions:

1. Heat oil pan over medium heat, add meat and green onions, stir and cook for 5 minutes.
2. Add the asparagus and the other ingredients, toss, cover the pan and cook over medium heat for 20 minutes.
3. Divide everything between plates and serve.

Nutrition: Calories 238, Carbohydrates 6g, Protein 2g, Fat 2g , Sodium 108mg

259. Basil Turkey and Broccoli

Preparation: 10 minutes   **Cooking: 25 minutes**   **Servings: 4**

Ingredients:

- *1 tablespoon olive oil*
- *1 big turkey breast, skinless, boneless and cubed*
- *2 cups broccoli florets*
- *2 shallots, chopped*
- *2 garlic cloves, minced*
- *1 tablespoon basil, chopped*
- *1 tablespoon cilantro, chopped*
- *1/2 cup coconut cream*

Directions:

1. Heat the oil to the pot over medium heat, add the meat, shallots and garlic, mix well and cook for 5 minutes.
2. Add the broccoli and the other ingredients, toss everything, cook for 20 minutes over medium heat, divide between plates and serve.

Nutrition: Calories 121, Carbohydrates 6g, Protein 23g, Fat 3g, Sodium 111mg

260. Chicken with Green Beans and Sauce

Preparation: 10 minutes   **Cooking: 25 minutes**   **Servings: 4**

Ingredients:

- *2 tablespoons olive oil*
- *10 ounces green beans, trimmed and halved*
- *1 yellow onion, chopped*
- *1 tablespoon dill, chopped*
- *2 chicken breasts, skinless, boneless and halved*
- *2 cups tomato sauce, no-salt-added*
- *1/2 teaspoon red pepper flakes, crushed*

Directions:

1. Heat the oil to the pan on medium heat, add the onion and meat, and roast on each side for 2 minutes.
2. Add the green beans and the other ingredients, toss, introduce in the oven and bake at 380 degrees F for 20 minutes.
3. Divide between plates and serve right away.

Nutrition: Calories 126, Carbohydrates 14g, Protein 26g, Fat 4g, Sodium 249mg

261. Turkey and Garlic Sauce

Preparation: 10 minutes   **Cooking: 40 minutes**   **Servings: 4**

Ingredients:

- 1 turkey breast, boneless, skinless and cubed
- 1/2-pound white mushrooms, halved
- 1/3 cup coconut aminos
- 2 garlic cloves, minced
- 2 tablespoons olive oil
- A pinch of black pepper
- 2 green onions, chopped
- 3 tablespoons garlic sauce
- 1 tablespoon rosemary, chopped

Directions:

1. Heat oil in a pan over medium heat, add in shallots, garlic paste and garlic, and fry for 5 minutes.
2. Add the meat and brown it for 5 minutes more.
3. Add the rest of the ingredients, introduce in the oven and bake at 390 degrees F for 30 minutes.
4. Divide the mix between plates and serve.

Nutrition: Calories 100, Carbohydrates 7g, Protein 21 g, Fat 6g, Sodium 216mg

262. Chicken with Zucchini

Preparation: 5 minutes   **Cooking: 25 minutes**   **Servings: 4**

Ingredients:

- 1-pound chicken breasts, skinless, boneless and cubed
- 1 cup low-sodium chicken stock
- 2 zucchinis, roughly cubed
- 1 tablespoon olive oil
- 1 cup canned tomatoes, no-salt-added, chopped
- 1 yellow onion, chopped
- 1 teaspoon chili powder
- 1 tablespoon cilantro, chopped

Directions:

1. Warm up the oil to the pan over medium heat, add the meat and onions, and sprinkle with brown, for 5 minutes.
2. Add the zucchinis and the rest of the ingredients, toss gently, reduce the heat to medium and cook for 20 minutes.
3. Divide everything between plates and serve.

Nutrition: Calories 284, Carbohydrates 15g, Protein 32g, Fat 8g, Sodium 151mg

263. Lemon Chicken Mix

Preparation time: 10 minutes   **Cooking time: 20 minutes**
                                          Servings: 4

Ingredients:

- 2 chicken breasts, skinless, boneless and halved
- Juice of 1/2 lemon
- 2 tablespoons olive oil
- 2 garlic cloves, minced
- 1/2 cup low-sodium vegetable stock
- 1 avocado, peeled, pitted and cut into wedges
- A pinch of black pepper

Directions:

1. Heat up a pan with the oil over medium heat, add the garlic and the meat and brown for 2 minutes on each side.
2. Add the lemon juice and the other ingredients, bring to a simmer and cook over medium heat for 15 minutes.
3. Divide the whole mix between plates and serve.

Nutrition: Calories 170, Carbohydrates 7g, Protein 18g, Fat 2g, Sodium 180mg

264. Ravaging Beef Pot Roast

Preparation: 10 minutes   **Cooking: 75 minutes**   **Servings: 4**
Ingredients:

- *3 and 1/2 pounds beef roast*
- *4 ounces mushrooms, sliced*
- *12 ounces beef stock*
- *1 onion soup mix*
- *1/2 cup Italian dressing, low sodium, and low fat*

Directions:
1. Take a bowl and add the stock, onion soup mix, and Italian dressing.
2. Stir.
3. Put beef roast in a pan.
4. Add mushrooms, stock mix to the pan, and cover with foil.
5. Preheat your oven to 300 degrees F.
6. Bake for 1 hour and 15 minutes.
7. Let the roast cool.
8. Slice and serve and with the gravy on top!

Nutrition: Calories: 700 Fat: 56g Carbohydrates: 10g Protein: 70g Sodium: 350mg

265. Beef Stroganoff

Preparation: 15 minutes   **Cooking: 25 minutes**   **Servings: 4**
Ingredients:

- *Boneless beef round steak (1/2 lb. or 230 g)*
- *Onion (1/2 cup)*
- *Yolkless egg noodles (4 cups - uncooked)*
- *Paprika (1/2 tsp.)*
- *All-purpose flour (1 tbsp.)*
- *Water (1/2 cup)*
- *Undiluted cream of mushroom soup - fat-free (half of 1 small can)*
- *Fat-free sour cream (1/2 cup)*

Directions:
1. Trim the fat from the steak and slice it into 3/4-inch-thick slices.
2. Chop the onions and measure the rest of the fixings.
3. On the stovetop, using the medium-temperature setting, place a skillet with a spritz of cooking oil spray, adding the onions to sauté (5 min.).
4. Fold in the beef - sautéing till the beef is done (5 min.). Drain and set it to the side.
5. Prepare a big pot of water (3/4 full of water).
6. After it's boiling, toss in the noodles and let them cook (10-12 min.). At that point, toss the pasta into a colander to drain.
7. Use another saucepan, mix the water with the soup and flour using the medium-temperature setting. Add the paprika and soup mixture to the beef in the frying pan.
8. Stir till they are thoroughly warmed. Take the pan from the burner and mix in the sour cream and serve as desired.

Nutrition: Calories: 273 Protein: 20 g Carbohydrates: 27 g Fat: 5 g Sodium: 193 mg

266. Low-Sodium Dash Meatloaf

Preparation: 10 minutes   **Cooking: 1 hour**   **Servings: 10**
Ingredients:

- *Lean ground beef (680 g/11/2 lb.)*
- *Panko breadcrumbs (.75 cup)*
- *No-salt-added ketchup - divided (1/2 cup)*
- *Onion powder (1 tbsp.)*
- *Parsley flakes (11/2 tbsp.)*
- *Fresh oregano (2 tbsp.)*
- *Black pepper (1 tsp.)*
- *Garlic powder (.75 tsp.)*
- *Egg (1 large)*

Directions:
1. Set the oven temperature to reach 350° Fahrenheit/177° Celsius.
2. Combine all of the fixings in a mixing container (omit 1/4 cup of the ketchup).
3. Shape the meat mixture and scoop it into a greased loaf pan.
4. Set a timer to bake it for 45 minutes. Brush the rest of the ketchup over meatloaf and bake another 15 minutes for a total of one hour. Its internal temp when done should be 165° Fahrenheit/74° Celsius.
5. Serve with your favorite DASH sides.

Nutrition: Calories: 170 Protein: 13 g Total Carbohydrates: 5 g Fat: 11 g Sodium: 255 mg

267. Philly Cheesesteak Stuffed Peppers

Preparation: 10 minutes   **Cooking: 40 minutes**   **Servings: 4**

Ingredients:
- Bell peppers (2 large)
- Olive oil (1 tbsp.)
- Onion (1 large)
- Mushrooms (8 oz. or 230 g pkg.)
- Top round steak (12 oz. or 340 g)
-
- Italian seasoning (1 tbsp.)
- Salt (.25 tsp.)
- Black pepper (1/2 tsp.)
- Worcestershire sauce (1 tbsp.)
- Provolone cheese (4 slices)

Directions:
1. Preheat the oven temperature to 375° Fahrenheit/191° Celsius.
2. Slice the peppers into halves - lengthwise and discard its seeds.
3. Arrange the halves on the baking tray - baking till they're tender - yet holding their shape (1/2 hour).
4. Meanwhile, warm oil in a big skillet using the medium-temperature setting.
5. Cut the onion in half and slice it - toss it in the pan. Sauté it tills it starts browning (4-5 min.).
6. Slice the mushrooms into halves, toss in the pan, and sauté them till they're softened (5 min.).
7. Thinly slice and add the steak, pepper, Italian seasoning, and salt. Simmer till the steak is just cooked through (3-4 min.).
8. Transfer the pan onto a cool burner and stir in Worcestershire.
9. Warm the oven broiler to high.
10. Portion the filling into the pepper halves and add a cheese slice.
11. Pop it in the oven and broil it about five inches from the heat till the cheese is lightly browned (2-3 min.).

Nutrition: Calories: 308 Protein: 29g Carbohydrates: 12 g Fat: 7 g Sodium: 301mg

268. Skillet Steak with Mushroom Sauce

Preparation: 5 minutes   **Cooking: 20 minutes**   **Servings: 4**

Ingredients:
- Canola oil (2 tsp.)
- Beef top sirloin steak (340 g/12 oz. - 1-inch thick)
- Salt-free steak grilling seasoning (2 tsp.)
- Broccoli rabe (170 g/6 oz.)
- Sliced fresh mushrooms (3 cups)
- Frozen peas (2 cups)
- Unsalted beef broth (1 cup)
- Whole-grain mustard (1 tbsp.)
- Salt (.25 tsp.)
- Cornstarch (2 tsp.)

Directions:
1. Warm the oven temperature setting in advance to reach 350° Fahrenheit/177° Celsius.
2. Trim all bones from the steak.
3. Sprinkle the meat with steak seasoning.
4. In a skillet, warm the oil using a medium-high temperature setting.
5. When heated, add the meat and trimmed broccoli rabe. Let it cook for four minutes, turning the broccoli once (don't turn the meat).
6. Sprinkle the peas around the meat and pop the skillet into the oven.

7. Set a timer to bake for eight minutes or until meat is medium-rare at 145° Fahrenheit/63° Celsius.
8. Transfer the veggies and meat from the pan. Tent them using a sheet of aluminum foil to keep them warm. Make the sauce by adding the mushrooms to the pan's drippings. Sauté them using the med-high setting for three minutes, stirring intermittently.
9. Whisk the beef broth with cornstarch, salt, and mustard - mix into the mushrooms.
10. Simmer till it's thickened and piping hot (1 min.). Serve the veggies and meat with sauce.

Nutrition: Calories 226, Carbohydrates 16g, Protein 26g, Fat 6g, Sodium 355 mg

269. Spaghetti & Quick Meat Sauce

Preparation: 10 minutes   **Cooking: 25 minutes**   **Servings: 8**

Ingredients:
- Whole-wheat spaghetti (450 g or 1 lb.)
- Olive oil (2 tsp.)
- Onion (1 large)
- Celery (1 stalk)
- Carrot (1 large)
- Garlic (4 cloves)
- Italian seasoning (1 tbsp.)
- Lean ground beef (450 g/1 lb.)
- Crushed tomatoes (790 g/28 oz. can)
- Chopped flat-leaf parsley (.25 cup)
- Salt (1/2 tsp.)
- Parmesan cheese - grated (1/2 cup)

Directions:
1. Prepare a big pot of boiling water. Toss in the pasta and simmer it per its package instructions (8-10 min.). Drain it into a colander.
2. Meantime, warm oil in a big skillet using a medium temperature setting till it's hot.
3. Chop or mince the celery, carrots, and onion - sautéing them as you are mixing - till the onion has started browning (5-8 min.).
4. Mince and add Italian seasoning and garlic - simmer until it's fragrant (30 sec.).
5. Mix in the beef and continue to cook as you break it apart using a spoon till the pink is gone (3-5 min.). Raise the temperature setting to high.
6. Pour in tomatoes, parsley, and salt - simmer till it's thickened (4-6 min.).
7. Serve the sauce over the pasta with a serving of cheese.
8. Meal Prep Tips: Tightly cover the container and pop it into the fridge for up to three days. You can also freeze the sauce for up to three months.

Nutrition: Calories 389, Carbohydrates 54g, Protein 27g, Fat 9g, Sodium 483mg

270. Irish Pork Roast with Roasted Root Vegetables

Preparation: 20 minutes   **Cooking time: 80 minutes**   **Servings: 8**

Ingredients:
- Carrots (1 and 1/2 lb./680 g)
- Parsnips (1 and 1/2 lb.)
- Olive oil (3 tbsp. divided)
- Fresh thyme (2 tsp. leaves - divided)
- Black pepper & salt (.75 tsp. each - divided)
- Boneless pork loin roast (2 lb./910 g)
- Dry hard cider (1 cup)
- Honey (1 tsp.)
- To Serve: Ploughman's chutney/Bramley applesauce

Directions:
1. Warm the oven to 400° Fahrenheit/204° Celsius. Peel and slice the parsnips and carrots, cutting them into one-inch chunks - tossing them into a big mixing container with oil (2 tbsp.), thyme (1 tsp.), and 1/4 teaspoon each of pepper and salt.
2. Spread the veggies in a roasting pan. Rub the pork using the rest of the oil (1 tbsp.) and sprinkle with the remainder of the thyme (1 tsp.) and 1/2 teaspoon each of the pepper and salt.
3. Arrange the pork (fat-side up) over the veggies.
4. Roast - occasionally stir the veggies until the internal temp reaches 145° Fahrenheit/63° Celsius (50-65 min.).

5. Scoop the pork onto a cutting block and layer it using a tent of foil. Wait for it to rest for about 15 minutes. Scoop the veggies into a big mixing container and mix in honey.
6. Put the roasting pan over two burners using a high-temperature setting. Add cider and simmer while you scrape up any browned bits until the mix is reduced by half (3-5 min.).
7. Slice and serve the pork with sauce, vegetables, and chutney to your liking.

Nutrition: Calories 272, Carbohydrates 23g, Protein 23g, Fat 9g, Sodium 122mg

271. Pork & Cherry Tomatoes

Preparation: 5 minutes   **Cooking: 30 minutes**   **Servings: 4**

Ingredients:
- *Rutabaga (1 lb.)*
- *Olive oil (2 tbsp. divided)*
- *Black pepper and salt (.75 tsp. each - divided)*
- *Cherry tomatoes (4 cups - halved)*
- *Pork tenderloin (1.25 lb.)*
- *Ground coriander (1/2 tsp.)*
- *Dried sage (1/2 tsp.)*
- *Balsamic vinegar (3 tbsp.)*

Directions:
1. Warm the oven temperature setting to reach 425° Fahrenheit/218° Celsius.
2. Peel and slice the rutabaga into 1/2-inch wedges. Slice the pork into one-inch-thick medallions.
3. Toss rutabaga with oil (1 tbsp.) and 1/4 teaspoon each of pepper and salt in a big mixing container. Scatter the mixture evenly over a rimmed baking tray.
4. Set a timer and roast for 15 minutes.
5. Combine the tomatoes with the remaining oil (1 tbsp.) and 1/4 teaspoon each of the pepper and salt in a mixing container. Mix it with the rutabaga on the baking tray.
6. Season the pork with sage, coriander, and the remainder of the pepper and salt (1/4 tsp. each). Scatter it over the vegetables.
7. Roast till the pork is cooked, and the veggies are deliciously tender (10-15 min.).
8. Scoop a portion of the pork to a serving plate. Spritz the vinegar over the vegetables and serve with the pork.

Nutrition: Calories: 288 Protein: 30g Carbohydrates: 16 g Fat: 11.2 g Sodium: 102mg

272. Pork Chops with Tomato Curry

Preparation: 15 minutes   **Cooking: 25 minutes**   **Servings: 6**

Ingredients:
- *Butter (4 tsp. - divided)*
- *Boneless pork loin chops (6 @ 6 oz./170 g each)*
- *Onion (1 small)*
- *Apples (3 medium/about 5 cups)*
- *Whole tomatoes - undrained (28 oz./790 g can)*
- *Salt (1/2 tsp.)*
- *Curry powder (2 tsp.)*
- *Sugar (4 tsp.)*
- *Chili powder (1/2 tsp.)*
- *Hot - cooked brown rice (4 cups)*
- *Optional: Toasted slivered almonds (2 tbsp.)*

Directions:
1. Warm butter (2 tsp.) in the stockpot (med-high).
2. Brown the chops in batches. Remove them from the pan.
3. Warm the remainder of the butter using the medium temperature setting.
4. Finely chop and add the onion. Sauté them till tender (2-3 min.).
5. Thinly slice and fold in apples, tomatoes, sugar, curry powder, salt, and chili powder. Wait for it to boil - stir to break up tomatoes.
6. Return the chops to the pan. Lower the temperature setting and simmer with the lid off the pan (5 min.).

7. Flip the chops and simmer till a thermometer inserted in the pork's center reads 145° Fahrenheit/63° Celsius (3-5 min.).
8. Let it rest - standing for about five minutes.
9. Serve the delicious treat with a serving of rice and a sprinkle of almonds.

Nutrition: Calories: 478 Protein: 38g Carbohydrates: 50g Fat: 14g Sodium: 475 mg

273. Beef & Blue Cheese Penne with Pesto

Preparation: 10 minutes   **Cooking: 20 minutes**   **Servings: 4**

Ingredients:
- *Penne pasta - whole-wheat (2 cups - uncooked)*
- *Beef tenderloin steaks (2 @ 170 g/6 oz. each)*
- *Black pepper & salt (.25 tsp. each)*
- *Baby spinach (140 g/5 oz./about 6 cups)*
- *Grape tomatoes (2 cups)*
- *Prepared pesto (.33 cup)*
- *Walnuts (.25 cup)*
- *Crumbled Gorgonzola cheese (.25 cup)*

Directions:
1. Prepare the pasta per its package directions.
2. Sprinkle each of the steaks with a bit of pepper and salt.
3. Grill the steaks with the lid on using the medium-temperature setting.
4. Alternately, you can broil them four inches from the burner till the meat is as desired (5-7 min. per side) or (medium-rare is at 135° F or 57° C; medium will be at 140° F or 60° C; & medium-well will reach 145° F or 63° C).
5. Drain pasta and toss it into a big mixing container. Chop the walnuts into a bowl
6. Coarsely chop and add the spinach. Slice the tomatoes into halves and toss them in with the walnuts and pesto - tossing to cover.
7. Thinly slice the steak than serve with pasta and a dusting of cheese.

Nutrition: Calories: 532 Protein: 35g Carbohydrates: 49g Fat: 22g Sodium: 132mg

274. Pork Roast with Orange Sauce

Preparation: 15 minutes   **Cooking: 80 minutes**   **Servings: 2**

Ingredients:
- *1-pound pork loin roast*
- *1/2 cup carrot, diced*
- *1/2 cup celery stalk, chopped*
- *1/2 cup onion, diced*
- *1 teaspoon Italian seasonings*
- *1 cup of orange juice*
- *1 tablespoon potato starch*

Directions:
1. Rub the pork loin roast with Italian seasonings.
2. Then put the carrot, celery stalk, and diced onion in the tray.
3. Put the meat over the vegetables. Add orange juice.
4. Bake the meat for 75 minutes at 365F.
5. After this, transfer all vegetables and juice to the saucepan and bring it to a boil.
6. Blend the mixture with the help of the blender. Add potato starch and whisk it well.
7. Simmer the sauce for 2 minutes.
8. Slice the cooked meat and sprinkle it with orange sauce.

Nutrition: Calories 292, Carbohydrates 12g, Protein 33g, Fat 11g, Sodium 187mg

275. Southwestern Steak

Preparation: 15 minutes   **Cooking: 16 minutes**   **Servings: 2**

Ingredients:
- *2 beef flank steaks*
- *1 tablespoon lemon juice*
- *1 teaspoon chili flakes*
- *1 teaspoon garlic powder*
- *1 tablespoon avocado oil*

Directions:
1. Preheat the grill to 385F.
2. Then rub the meat with chili flakes and garlic powder.
3. Then sprinkle it with lemon juice and avocado oil.
4. Grill the stakes for 8 minutes per side.

Nutrition: Calories 174, Carbohydrates 2g, Protein 26g, Fat 6g, Sodium 258mg

276. Tender Pork Medallions

Preparation: 10 minutes   **Cooking: 25 minutes**   **Servings: 2**
Ingredients:
- *12 oz pork tenderloin*
- *1 teaspoon dried sage*
- *1 tablespoon margarine*
- *1 teaspoon ground black pepper*
- *1/2 cup low-fat yogurt*

Directions:
1. Cut the pork tenderloin into 3 medallions and sprinkle with sage and ground black pepper.
2. Heat up margarine in the saucepan and add pork medallions.
3. Roast them for 5 minutes per side.
4. Then add yogurt and coat the meat in it well.
5. Close the lid and simmer the medallions for 15 minutes over medium heat.

Nutrition: Calories 289, Carbohydrates 13g, Protein 23g, Fat 18g, Sodium 338mg

277. Garlic Pork Meatballs

Preparation: 10 minutes   **Cooking: 28 minutes**   **Servings: 2**
Ingredients:
- *2 pork medallions*
- *1 teaspoon minced garlic*
- *1/4 cup of coconut milk*
- *1 tablespoon olive oil*
- *1 teaspoon cayenne pepper*

Directions:
1. Sprinkle each pork medallion with cayenne pepper.
2. Heat up olive oil in the skillet and add meat.
3. Roast the pork medallions for 3 minutes from each side.
4. After this, add coconut milk and minced garlic. Close the lid and simmer the meat for 20 minutes on low heat.

Nutrition: Calories 284, Carbohydrates 3g, Protein 20g, Fat 16g, Sodium 362mg

278. Fajita Pork Strips

Preparation: 10 minutes   **Cooking: 35 minutes**   **Servings: 2**
Ingredients:
- *16 oz pork sirloin*
- *1 tablespoon Fajita seasonings*
- *1 tablespoon canola oil*

Directions:
1. Cut the pork sirloin into strips and sprinkle with fajita seasonings and canola oil.
2. Then transfer the meat to the baking tray in one layer.
3. Bake it for 35 minutes at 365F. Stir the meat every 10 minutes during cooking.

Nutrition: Calories 184, Carbohydrates 3g, Protein 19g, Fat 9g, Sodium 157mg

279. Pepper Pork Tenderloins

Preparation: 15 minutes   **Cooking: 60 minutes**   **Servings: 2**
Ingredients:
- *8 oz pork tenderloin*
- *1 tablespoon mustard*
- *1 teaspoon ground black pepper*
- *2 tablespoons olive oil*

Directions:
1. Rub the meat with mustard and sprinkle with ground black pepper.
2. Then brush it with olive oil and wrap it in the foil.
3. Bake the meat for 60 minutes at 375F.
4. Then discard the foil and slice the tenderloin into servings.

Nutrition: Calories 311, Carbohydrates 11g, Protein 31g, Fat 14g, Sodium 258mg

280. Spiced Beef

Preparation: 10 minutes   **Cooking: 80 minutes**   **Servings: 2**

Ingredients:
- *1-pound beef sirloin*
- *1 tablespoon five-spice seasoning*
- *1 bay leaf*
- *2 cups of water*
- *1 teaspoon peppercorn*

Directions:
1. Rub the meat with five-spice seasoning and put it in the saucepan.
2. Add nay leaf, water, and peppercorns.
3. Close the lid and simmer it for 80 minutes on medium heat.
4. Chop the cooked meat and sprinkle it with hot spiced water from the saucepan.

Nutrition: Calories 213, Carbohydrates 7g, Protein 34 g, Fat 9g, Sodium 316mg

281. Tomato Beef

Preparation: 10 minutes   **Cooking: 17 minutes**   **Servings: 2**

Ingredients:
- *2 chuck shoulder steaks*
- *1/4 cup tomato sauce*
- *1 tablespoon olive oil*

Directions:
1. Brush the steaks with tomato sauce and olive oil and transfer to the preheated to 390F grill.
2. Grill the meat for 9 minutes.
3. Then flip it on another side and cook for 8 minutes more.

Nutrition: Calories 247, Carbohydrates 2g, Protein 21g, Fat 17g, Sodium 231mg

282. Hoisin Pork

Preparation: 10 minutes   **Cooking: 14 minutes**   **Servings: 2**

Ingredients:
- *1-pound pork loin steaks*
- *2 tablespoons hoisin sauce*
- *1 tablespoon apple cider vinegar*
- *1 teaspoon olive oil*

Directions:
1. Rub the pork steaks with hoisin sauce, apple cider vinegar, and olive oil.
2. Then preheat the grill to 395F.
3. Put the pork steak in the grill and cook them for 7 minutes per side.

Nutrition: Calories 263, Carbohydrates 4g, Protein 14g, Fat 8g, Sodium 130mg

283. Sage Beef Loin

Preparation: 10 minutes   **Cooking: 18 minutes**   **Servings: 2**

Ingredients:
- *10 oz beef loin, strips*
- *1 garlic clove, diced*
- *2 tablespoons margarine*
- *1 teaspoon dried sage*

Directions:
1. Toss margarine in the skillet.
2. Add garlic and dried sage and roast them for 2 minutes on low heat.

3. Add beef loin strips and roast them for 15 minutes on medium heat. Stir the meat occasionally.
Nutrition: Calories 363, Carbohydrates 13g, Protein 28g, Fat 19g, Sodium 211mg

284. Beef Chili

Preparation: 10 minutes   **Cooking: 30 minutes**   **Servings: 2**
Ingredients:

- *1 cup lean ground beef*
- *1 onion, diced*
- *1 tablespoon olive oil*
- *1 cup crushed tomatoes*
- *1/2 cup red kidney beans, cooked*
- *1/2 cup of water*
- *1 teaspoon chili seasonings*

Directions:
1. Heat up olive oil in the saucepan and add lean ground beef.
2. Cook it for 7 minutes over medium heat.
3. Then add chili seasonings and diced onion. Stir the ingredients and cook them for 10 minutes.
4. After this, add water, crushed tomatoes, red kidney beans, and stir the chili well.
5. Close the lid and simmer the meal for 13 minutes.

Nutrition: Calories 220, Carbohydrates 7g, Protein 18g, Fat 7g, Sodium 177mg

285. Celery Beef Stew

Preparation: 5 minutes   **Cooking: 55 minutes**   **Servings: 2**
Ingredients:

- *1-pound beef loin, chopped*
- *2 cups celery stalk, chopped*
- *1 garlic clove, diced*
- *1 yellow onion, diced*
- *1 tablespoon olive oil*
- *1 tablespoon tomato paste*
- *1 teaspoon chili powder*
- *1 teaspoon dried dill*
- *2 cups of water*

Directions:
1. Roast the beef loin with olive oil in the saucepan for 5 minutes.
2. After this, add all remaining ingredients and close the lid.
3. Cook the stew for 50 minutes on medium heat.

Nutrition: Calories 150, Carbohydrates 8g, Protein 15g, Fat 8g, Sodium 370mg

286. Beef Skillet

Preparation: 10 minutes   **Cooking: 30 minutes**   **Servings: 2**
Ingredients:

- *1 cup lean ground beef*
- *1 cup bell pepper, sliced*
- *2 tomatoes, chopped*
- *1 chili pepper, chopped*
- *1 tablespoon olive oil*
- *1/2 cup of water*

Directions:
1. Heat up olive oil in the skillet and add lean ground beef.
2. Roast it for 10 minutes.
3. Then stir the meat well and add chili pepper and bell pepper. Roast the ingredients for 10 minutes more.
4. Add tomatoes and water.
5. Close the lid and simmer the meal for 10 minutes.

Nutrition: Calories 167, Carbohydrates 6g, Protein 16g, Fat 8g, Sodium 150mg

287. Hot Beef Strips

Preparation: 10 minutes   **Cooking: 15 minutes**   **Servings: 2**

Ingredients:

- 9 oz beef tenders
- 2 tablespoons cayenne pepper
- 1 tablespoon lemon juice
- 2 tablespoons canola oil

Directions:

1. Cut the beef tenders into strips and rub with cayenne pepper.
2. Sprinkle the meat with lemon juice and put it in the hot skillet.
3. Add canola oil and roast the meat for 15 minutes on medium heat. Stir it from time to time to avoid burning.

Nutrition: Calories 231, Carbohydrates 2g, Protein 21g, Fat 14g, Sodium 162mg

288. Sloppy Joe

Preparation: 10 minutes   **Cooking: 35 minutes**   **Servings: 2**

Ingredients:

- 1 cup lean ground beef
- 1 cup onion, diced
- 1/2 cup sweet peppers, diced
- 1 teaspoon minced garlic
- 1 tablespoon canola oil
- 1 teaspoon liquid honey
- 1/2 cup tomato puree
- 1 teaspoon tomato paste

Directions:

1. Mix up canola oil and lean ground beef in the saucepan.
2. Add onion and sweet pepper and stir the ingredient well.
3. Cook them for 10 minutes.
4. Then add honey, tomato puree, and tomato paste. Mix up the mixture well.
5. Close the lid and cook it for 25 minutes on medium heat.

Nutrition: Calories 134, Carbohydrates 8g, Protein 16g, Fat 10g, Sodium 134mg

289. Pork and Greens Salad

Preparation: 10 Minutes   **Cooking: 15 Minutes**   **Servings: 1**

Ingredients:

- 1/4-pound pork chops, boneless and cut into strips
- 2 ounces white mushrooms, sliced
- 1/2 cup Italian dressing
- 2 cups mixed salad greens
- 2 ounces jarred artichoke hearts, drained
- Salt and black pepper to the taste
- 1/2 cup basil, chopped
- 1 tablespoon olive oil

Directions:

1. Heat a pan with the oil over medium-high heat, add the pork and brown for 5 minutes.
2. Add the mushrooms, stir and sauté for 5 minutes more.
3. Add the dressing, artichokes, salad greens, salt, pepper, and basil, cook for 4-5 minutes, divide everything into bowls and serve.

Nutrition: Calories: 235 Proteins: 11 g Fats: 4 g Carbohydrates: 14 g Sodium: 182mg

290. Pork Strips and Rice

Preparation: 10 Minutes   **Cooking: 25 Minutes**   **Servings: 1**

Ingredients:

- 1/2-pound pork loin, cut into strips
- Salt and black pepper to taste
- 1 tablespoons olive oil
- 1 carrot, chopped
- 1 red bell pepper, chopped
- 2 garlic cloves, minced
- 1/2 cups veggie stock
- 1/4 cup basmati rice
- 1/4 cup garbanzo beans
- 2 black olives, pitted and sliced

- *1 tablespoon parsley, chopped*

Directions:
1. Heat a pan with the oil over medium-high heat.
2. Add the pork fillets, stir, cook for 5 minutes and transfer them to a plate.
3. Add the carrots, bell pepper, and garlic, stir and cook for 5 more minutes.
4. Add the rice, the stock, beans, and the olives, stir, cook for 14 minutes, divide between plates, sprinkle the parsley on top and serve.

Nutrition: Calories: 220 Proteins: 11 g Fats: 12 g Carbohydrates: 7 g Sodium: 102mg

291. Herb Roasted Pork

Preparation: 20 Minutes　　　　**Cooking: 2 Hours**　　　　**Servings: 1**

Ingredients:
- *1/2 pounds pork loin roast, trimmed, chine bone removed*
- *Salt and black pepper to taste*
- *2 garlic cloves, minced*
- *1 tablespoons rosemary, chopped*
- *1 teaspoon fennel, ground*
- *1 tablespoon fennel seeds*
- *1 teaspoon red pepper, crushed*
- *1/8 cup olive oil*

Directions:
1. In a food processor mix garlic with fennel seeds, fennel, rosemary, red pepper, some black pepper, and olive oil and blend until you obtain a paste.
2. Place pork roast in a roasting pan spread 2 tablespoons garlic paste all over and rub well.
3. Season with salt and pepper, place in the oven at 400 degrees F and bake for 1 hour.
4. Reduce heat to 325 degrees F and bake for another 35 minutes. Carve roast into chops, divide between plates and serve right away.

Nutrition: Calories: 300 Proteins: 15 g Fats: 4 g Carbohydrates: 6 g Sodium: 123mg

292. Mediterranean Beef Dish

Preparation: 10 Minutes　　　　**Cooking: 15 Minutes**　　　　**Servings: 1**

Ingredients:
- *1/3-pound beef, ground*
- *1/2 cups zucchinis, chopped*
- *1/4 cup yellow onion, chopped*
- *Salt and black pepper to taste*
- *3 ounces canned roasted tomatoes and garlic*
- *1/4 cup of water*
- *1/4 cup cheddar cheese, shredded*

Directions:
1. Heat a pan over medium-high heat, add beef, onion, salt, pepper, and zucchini, stir and cook for 7 minutes.
2. Add water, tomatoes, and garlic, stir and bring to a boil. Add rice, more salt, and pepper, stir, cover, take off the heat and leave aside for 7 minutes.
3. Divide between plates and serve with cheddar cheese on top.

Nutrition: Calories: 278　Proteins: 27 g　Fats: 7 g　Carbohydrates: 28g Sodium: 72mg

293. Yummy Pork Chop

Preparation: 10 Minutes　　　　**Cooking: 15 Minutes**　　　　**Servings: 1**

Ingredients:
- *1 pieces of bone-in pork loin or rib chops, 1/2 inch thick*
- *1/2 tablespoons clarified butter*
- *1/4 cup chicken broth*
- *1/4 cup white grape juice*
- *1/2 tablespoon of minced fresh dill fronds*
- *4 baby carrots*
- *Salt and black pepper to taste*
- *1/2 tablespoon of ghee*

Directions:
1. Set your slow cooker to sauté mode. Season pork chop with salt and pepper. Add the chop to the slow cooker and cook for 4-minutes.
2. Cook chops in batches if needed, transferring them to a plate. Add 1 tablespoon of ghee to the pot along with carrots, dill and cook for 1-minute.
3. Add a 1/2 cup of grape juice and deglaze the pot. Stir in the broth and add in the chops.
4. Shut the lid on the pot, and set it to Manual Mode, on high with a cooking time of 18-minutes.
5. When the cooking time is completed, release the pressure naturally for 10-minutes.
6. Serve by pouring the cooking sauce over the chops.

Nutrition: Calories: 296 Fats:25g Carbohydrates: 2g Proteins: 17 g Sodium: 112mg

294. Pork and Lentil Soup

Preparation: 10 Minutes   **Cooking: 60 Minutes**   **Servings: 1**

Ingredients:
- *1 small yellow onion, chopped*
- *1 tablespoon olive oil*
- *1/2 teaspoons basil, chopped*
- *1/2 teaspoons ginger, grated*
- *2 garlic cloves, chopped*
- *Salt and black pepper to taste*
- *1/2 teaspoon cumin, ground*
- *1 carrot, chopped*
- *1/4-pound pork chops, bone-in 3 ounces brown lentils, rinsed*
- *1 cups chicken stock*
- *1/2 tablespoons tomato paste*
- *1/2 tablespoons lime juice*
- *1/2 teaspoon red chili flakes, crushed*

Directions:
1. Heat a saucepan with the oil over medium heat, add garlic, onion, basil, ginger, salt, pepper and cumin, stir well and cook for 6 minutes.
2. Add carrots, stir and cook 5 more minutes. Add pork and brown for a few minutes.
3. Add lentils, tomato paste and stock, stir, bring to a boil, cover pan and simmer for 50 minutes.
4. Transfer pork to a plate, discard bones, shred it and return to pan.
5. Add chili flakes and lime juice, stir, ladle into bowls and serve.

Nutrition: Calories: 263 Proteins: 20g Fats: 14 g Carbohydrates: 8 g Sodium: 102mg

295. Simple Braised Pork

Preparation: 40 Minutes   **Cooking: 60 Minutes**   **Servings: 1**

Ingredients:
- *1/4 pounds pork loin roast, boneless and cubed*
- *1 tablespoons butter*
- *Salt and black pepper to taste*
- *1/4 cups chicken stock*
- *1/8 cup dry white wine*
- *2 garlic cloves, minced*
- *1 teaspoon thyme, chopped*
- *1 thyme spring*
- *1 bay leaf*
- *1/2 yellow onion, chopped*
- *1 tablespoon white flour*
- *1/4-pound pearl onions*
- *1/4-pound red grapes*

Directions:
1. Heat a pan with 2 tablespoons butter over high heat, add pork loin, some salt, and pepper, stir, brown for 10 minutes and transfer to a plate.
2. Add wine to the pan, bring to a boil over high heat and cook for 3 minutes.
3. Add stock, garlic, thyme spring, bay leaf, yellow onion and return meat to the pan, bring to a boil, cover, reduce heat to low, cook for 1 hour, strain liquid into another saucepan and transfer pork to a plate.
4. Put pearl onions in a small saucepan, add water to cover, bring to a boil over medium-high heat, boil them for 5 minutes, drain, peel them and leave aside for now.
5. In a bowl, mix 2 tablespoons butter with flour and stir well. Add 1/2 cup of the strained cooking liquid and whisk well.

6. Pour this into cooking liquid, bring to a simmer over medium heat and cook for 5 minutes.
7. Add salt and pepper, chopped thyme, pork and pearl onions, cover and simmer for a few minutes.
8. Meanwhile, heat a pan with 1 tablespoon butter, add grapes, stir and cook them for 1-2 minutes.
9. Divide pork meat on plates, drizzle the sauce all over and serve with onions and grapes on the side.

Nutrition: Calories: 320 Proteins: 18 g Fats: 14 g Carbohydrates: 9 g Sodium: 112mg

296. Fennel Sauce Tenderloin

Preparation: 10 Minutes   **Cooking: 25 minutes**   **Servings: 4**

Ingredients:

- *1 Fennel Bulb, Cored & Sliced*
- *1 Sweet Onion, Sliced*
- *1/2 Cup Dry White Wine*
- *1 Teaspoon Fennel Seeds*
- *4 Pork Tenderloin Fillets*
- *2 Tablespoons Olive Oil*
- *12 Ounces Chicken Broth, Low Sodium*
- *Fennel Fronds for Garnish*
- *Orange Slices for Garnish*

Directions:

1. Thin your pork tenderloin by spreading them between parchment sheets and pounding with a mallet.
2. Heat a skillet, and add in your oil. Place it over medium heat, and cook your fennel seeds for three minutes.
3. Add the pork to the pan, cooking for an additional three minutes per side.
4. Transfer your pork to a platter before setting it to the side, and add in your fennel and onion.
5. Cook for five minutes, and then place the vegetables to the side.
6. Pour in your broth and wine, and bring it to a boil over high heat. Cook until the liquid has reduced by half.
7. Return your pork to the skillet, and cook for another five minutes.
8. Stir in your onion mixture, covering again. Cook for two more minutes, and serve warm.

Nutrition: Calories: 276 Protein: 23.4g, Fat: 24g, Carbohydrates:14g , Sodium: 647 mg

297. Beefy Fennel Stew

Preparation: 20 Minutes   **Cooking: 80 minutes**   **Servings: 4**

Ingredients:

- *1 lb. Lean Beef, Boneless & Cubed*
- *2 Tablespoons Olive Oil*
- *1/2 Fennel Bulb, Sliced*
- *3 Tablespoons All Purpose Flour*
- *3 Shallots, Large & Chopped*
- *3/4 Teaspoon Black Pepper, Divided*
- *2 Thyme Sprigs, Fresh*
- *1 Bay Leaf*
- *1/2 Cup Red Wine*
- *3 Cups Vegetable Stock*
- *4 Carrots, Peeled & Sliced into 1 Inch Pieces*
- *4 White Potatoes, Large & Cubed*
- *18 Small Boiling Onions, Halved*
- *1/3 Cup Flat Leaf Parsley, Fresh & Chopped*
- *3 Portobello Mushrooms, Chopped*

Directions:

1. Get out a shallow container and add in your flour. Dredge the beef cubes through it, shaking off the excess flour.
2. Get out a saucepan and add in your oil, heating it over medium heat.
3. Add your beef, and cook for five minutes.
4. Add in your fennel and shallots, cooking for seven minutes. Stir in your pepper, bay leaf and thyme. Cook for a minute more.
5. Add your beef to the pan with your stock and wine.
6. Boil it and reduce it to a simmer. Cover, cooking for forty-five minutes.
7. Add in your onions, potatoes, carrots and mushrooms. Cook for another half hour, which should leave your vegetables tender.
8. Remove the thyme sprigs and bay leaf before serving warm. Garnish with parsley.

Nutrition: Calories:244 Protein:21g Fat: 8g Carbohydrates: 22g Sodium: 587 mg

298. Currant Pork Chops

Preparation: 10 Minutes   **Cooking: 20 minutes**   **Servings: 6**

Ingredients:

- 2 Tablespoons Dijon Mustard
- 6 Pork Loin Chops, Center Cut
- 2 Teaspoons Olive Oil
- 1/3 Cup Wine Vinegar
- 1/4 Cup Black Currant Jam
- 6 Orange Slices
- 1/8 Teaspoon Black Pepper

Directions:

1. Start by mixing your mustard and jam together in a bowl.
2. Get out a nonstick skillet, and grease it with olive oil before placing it over medium heat. Cook your chops for five minutes per side, and then top with a tablespoon of the jam mixture. Cover, and allow it to cook for two minutes. Transfer them to a serving plate.
3. Pour your wine vinegar in the same skillet, and scape the bits up to deglaze the pan, mixing well. Drizzle this over your pork chops.
4. Garnish with pepper and orange slices before serving warm.

Nutrition: Calories 265, Carbohydrates 11g, Protein 25g, Fat 6g, Sodium 12mg

299. Easy Beef Brisket

Preparation: 10 Minutes   **Cooking: 3 Hours**   **Servings: 4**

Ingredients:

- 1 Teaspoon Thyme
- 4 Cloves Garlic, Peeled & Smashed
- 1 and ½ Cups Onion, chopped
- 2 and 1/2 lbs. Beef Brisket, Chopped
- 1 Tablespoons Olive Oil
- 1/4 Teaspoon Black Pepper
- 14 Ounces Tomatoes & Liquid, Canned
- 1/4 Cup Red Wine Vinegar
- 1 Cup Beef Stock, Low Sodium

Directions:

1. Turn the oven to 350, and then grease an oven using a tablespoon of oil. Place it over medium heat.
2. Add in your pepper and brisket. Cook until it browns, and then place your brisket on a plate.
3. Put your onions in the pot, and cook until golden brown. Stir in your garlic and thyme, cooking for another full minute before adding in the stock, vinegar and tomatoes.
4. Cook until it comes to a boil and add in your brisket again.
5. Reduce to a simmer, and cook for three hours in the oven until tender.

Nutrition: Calories 299, Carbohydrates 21g, Protein 10g, Fat 9g, Sodium 372mg

300. Pork with Mushrooms Bowls

Preparation: 10 minutes   **Cooking: 23 minutes**   **Servings: 6**

Ingredients:

- Juice of 1 lime
- 1- and ½ pounds pork steak, cut into strips
- 1/2 teaspoon chili powder
- Black pepper to the taste
- 1 teaspoon sweet paprika
- 1/2 teaspoon oregano, dried
- 2 tablespoons olive oil
- 2 red bell peppers, chopped
- 1 yellow onion, sliced
- 5 ounces mushrooms, chopped
- 1 garlic clove, minced
- 2 green onions, chopped
- 1 jalapeno, chopped
- 1 cup low-sodium veggie stock
- 1/4 cup parsley, chopped

Directions:

1. In a bowl, mix lime juice with black pepper, chili powder, paprika, oregano and meat strips and toss well.

2. Heat up a pan with the oil over medium-high heat, add the meat, cook for 4 minutes on each side and transfer to a plate.
3. Heat up the same pan over medium heat, add bell peppers, mushrooms, garlic and onions, stir and cook for 5 minutes.
4. Add stock, green onion, lime juice, jalapeno, return the meat, stir and cook for 10 minutes more.
5. Divide everything between plates and serve with parsley on top.

Nutrition: Calories 250, Carbohydrates 7g, Protein 14g, Fat 12g, Sodium 182mg

301. Tarragon Pork Steak with Tomatoes

Preparation: 10 minutes   **Cooking: 22 minutes**   **Servings: 4**

Ingredients:
- 4 medium pork steaks
- Black pepper to the taste
- 1 tablespoon olive oil
- 8 cherry tomatoes, halved
- A handful tarragon, chopped

Directions:
1. Heat up a pan with the oil over medium-high heat, add steaks, season with black pepper, cook them for 6 minutes on each side and divide between plates.
2. Heat up the same pan over medium heat, add the tomatoes and the tarragon, cook for 10 minutes, divide next to the pork and serve.

Nutrition: Calories 263, Carbohydrates 12g, Protein 16g, Fat 4g, Sodium 112mg

302. Pork Meatballs

Preparation: 10 minutes   **Cooking: 10 minutes**   **Servings: 4**

Ingredients:
- 1 pound pork, ground
- 1/3 cup cilantro, chopped
- 1 cup red onion, chopped
- 4 garlic cloves, minced
- 1 tablespoon ginger, grated
- 1 Thai chili, chopped
- 2 tablespoons olive oil

Directions:
1. In a bowl, combine the meat with cilantro, onion, garlic, ginger and chili, stir well and shape medium meatballs out of this mix.
2. Heat up a pan with the oil over medium-high heat, add the meatballs, cook them for 5 minutes on each side, divide them between plates and serve with a side salad.

Nutrition: Calories 220, Carbohydrates 8, Protein 14g, Fat 4g, Sodium 202mg

303. Pork with Scallions and Peanuts

Preparation: 10 minutes   **Cooking: 16 minutes**   **Servings: 4**

Ingredients:
- 2 tablespoons lime juice
- 2 tablespoons coconut aminos
- 1 and 1/2 tablespoons brown sugar
- 5 garlic cloves, minced
- 3 tablespoons olive oil
- Black pepper to the taste
- 1 yellow onion, cut into wedges
- 1- and 1/2-pound pork tenderloin, cubed
- 3 tablespoons peanuts, chopped
- 2 scallions, chopped

Directions:
1. In a bowl, mix lime juice with aminos and sugar and stir very well.
2. In another bowl, mix garlic with 1 and 1/2 teaspoon oil and some black pepper and stir.
3. Heat up a pan with the rest of the oil over medium-high heat, add meat, cook for 3 minutes on each side and transfer to a bowl.
4. Heat up the same pan over medium-high heat, add onion, stir and cook for 3 minutes.

5. Add the garlic mix, return the pork, also add the aminos mix, toss, cook for 6 minutes, divide between plates, sprinkle scallions and peanuts on top and serve.

Nutrition: Calories 273, Carbohydrates 12g, Protein 18g, Fat 4g, Sodium 162mg

304. Pork And Veggies Mix

Preparation: 15 minutes **Cooking: 1 hour** **Servings: 6**

Ingredients:

- *4 eggplants, cut into halves lengthwise*
- *4 ounces olive oil*
- *2 yellow onions, chopped*
- *4 ounces pork meat, ground*
- *2 green bell peppers, chopped*
- *1-pound tomatoes, chopped*
- *4 tomato slices*
- *2 tablespoons low-sodium tomato paste*
- *1/2 cup parsley, chopped*
- *4 garlic cloves, minced*
- *1/2 cup hot water*
- *Black pepper to the taste*

Directions:

1. Heat up a pan with the olive oil over medium-high heat, add eggplant halves, cook for 5 minutes and transfer to a plate.
2. Heat up the same pan over medium-high heat, add onion, stir and cook for 3 minutes.
3. Add bell peppers, pork, tomato paste, pepper, parsley and chopped tomatoes, stir and cook for 7 minutes.
4. Arrange the eggplant halves in a baking tray, divide garlic in each, spoon meat filling and top with a tomato slice.
5. Pour the water over them, cover tray with foil, bake in the oven at 350 degrees F for 40 minutes, divide between plates and serve.

Nutrition: Calories 253, Carbohydrates 12g, Protein 16g, Fat 3g, Sodium 162mg

305. Pork Chili

Preparation: 10 minutes **Cooking: 75 minutes** **Servings: 6**

Ingredients:

- *1 green bell pepper, chopped*
- *1 pound pork, cubed*
- *1 yellow onion, chopped*
- *4 carrots, chopped*
- *Black pepper to the taste*
- *26 ounces canned tomatoes, no-salt-added and chopped*
- *1 teaspoon onion powder*
- *1 tablespoon parsley, chopped*
- *4 teaspoons chili powder*
- *1 teaspoon garlic powder*
- *1 teaspoon sweet paprika*

Directions:

1. Heat up a pot over medium-high heat, add the meat and brown for 5 minutes.
2. Add bell pepper, carrots, onions, tomatoes, black pepper, onion powder, chili powder, paprika and garlic powder, toss, bring to a simmer, reduce heat to medium, cover the pot and cook for 1 hour.
3. Add parsley, toss, divide into bowls and serve.

Nutrition: calories 284, fat 6, fiber 6, Carbohydrates 12, protein 24 Sodium: 301 mg

306. Pork And Sweet Potatoes with Chili

Preparation: 10 minutes **Cooking time: 80 minutes** **Servings: 8**

Ingredients:

- *2 pounds sweet potatoes, chopped*
- *A drizzle of olive oil*
- *1 yellow onion, chopped*
- *2 pounds pork meat, ground*
- *1 tablespoon chili powder*
- *Black pepper to the taste*
- *1 teaspoon cumin, ground*
- *1/2 teaspoon garlic powder*
- *1/2 teaspoon oregano, chopped*
- *1/2 teaspoon cinnamon powder*

- *1 cup low-sodium veggie stock*
- *1/2 cup cilantro, chopped*

Directions:
1. Heat up a pan with the oil over medium-high heat, add sweet potatoes and onion, stir, cook for 15 minutes and transfer to a bowl.
2. Heat up the pan again over medium-high heat, add pork, stir and brown for 5 minutes.
3. Add black pepper, cumin, garlic powder, oregano, chili powder, cinnamon, stock, return potatoes and onion, stir and cook for 1 hour over medium heat.
4. Add the cilantro, toss, divide into bowls and serve.

Nutrition: Calories 320, Carbohydrates 12g, Protein 22g, Fat 7g, Sodium 112 mg

307. Pork And Pumpkin Chili

Preparation: 10 minutes   **Cooking: 90 minutes**   **Servings: 6**

Ingredients:
- *1 green bell pepper, chopped*
- *2 cups yellow onion, chopped*
- *1 tablespoon olive oil*
- *6 garlic cloves, minced*
- *28 ounces canned tomatoes, no-salt-added and chopped*
- *1- and 1/2-pounds pork, ground*
- *6 ounces low-sodium tomato paste*
- *14 ounces pumpkin puree*
- *1 cup low-sodium chicken stock*
- *2 and 1/2 teaspoons oregano, dried*
- *1 and 1/2 teaspoon cinnamon, ground*
- *1 and 1/2 tablespoon chili powder*
- *Black pepper to the taste*

Directions:
1. Heat up a pot with the oil over medium-high heat, add bell peppers and onion, stir and cook for 7 minutes.
2. Add garlic and the pork, toss and cook for 10 minutes.
3. Add tomatoes, tomato paste, pumpkin puree, stock, oregano, cinnamon, chili powder and pepper, stir, cover, cook over medium heat for 1 hour and 10 minutes, divide into bowls and serve.

Nutrition: Calories 289, Carbohydrates 12g, Protein 20g, Fat 11g, Sodium 102mg

308. Spiced Pork Soup

Preparation: 10 minutes   **Cooking: 90 minutes**   **Servings: 6**

Ingredients:
- *3 carrots, chopped*
- *1 pound pork meat, cubed*
- *1 tomato, chopped*
- *3 mushrooms, sliced*
- *6-star anise*
- *4 bay leaves*
- *5 ginger slices*
- *2 tablespoons Sichuan peppercorns*
- *1 and 1/2 tablespoons fennel powder*
- *1 teaspoon coriander, ground*
- *1 tablespoon cumin powder*
- *1/4 teaspoon five spice powder*
- *Black pepper to the taste*
- *A bunch of scallions, chopped*
- *8 cups water*
- *1/3 cup coconut aminos*

Directions:
1. Put the water in a pot and heat up over medium heat.
2. Add carrots, pork, tomato, mushrooms, star anise, bay leaves, ginger, peppercorns, fennel, coriander, cumin, five spice, black pepper, aminos and scallions, stir, bring to a boil and cook for 1 hour and 30 minutes.
3. Discard star anise, ginger, bay leaves and peppercorns, ladle the soup into bowls and serve.

Nutrition: Calories 250, Fat 2, Carbohydrates 14, Protein 14 Sodium: 112mg

309. Ground Pork and Kale Soup

Preparation: 10 minutes **Cooking: 30 minutes** **Servings: 4**

Ingredients:

- 1 pound pork, ground
- 3 carrots, chopped
- 4 potatoes, chopped
- 1 yellow onion, chopped
- 1/2 bunch kale, chopped
- 4 garlic cloves, minced
- 2 cups squash, cooked and pureed
- 2 quarts low-sodium veggie stock
- Black pepper to the taste
- 3 teaspoons Italian seasoning

Directions:

1. Heat up a pot over medium-high heat, add pork, stir, brown for 5 minutes and transfer to a bowl.
2. Heat up the pot again over medium heat, add potatoes, onion, carrots, kale, garlic and pepper, stir and cook for 10 minutes.
3. Return beef, also add stock, squash puree and Italian seasoning, stir, simmer over medium heat for 15 minutes, ladle into bowls and serve.

Nutrition: Calories 270, Carbohydrates 12g, Protein 23g, Fat 12g, Sodium 115mg

310. Peaches and Kale Steak Salad

Preparation: 10 minutes **Cooking: 12 minutes** **Servings: 2**

Ingredients:

- 2 peaches, chopped
- 3 handfuls kale, chopped
- 8 ounces pork steak, cut into strips
- 1 tablespoon avocado oil
- A drizzle of olive oil
- 1 tablespoon balsamic vinegar

Directions:

1. Heat up a pan with the avocado oil over medium-high heat, add steak strips, cook them for 6 minutes on each side and transfer to a salad bowl.
2. Add peaches, kale, olive oil and vinegar, toss and serve.

Nutrition: Calories 240, Carbohydrates 8g, Protein 15g, Fat 5g, Sodium 160mg

311. Spiced Winter Pork Roast

Preparation: 10 minutes **Cooking: 3 hours and 20 minutes** **Servings: 6**

Ingredients:

- 2- and 1/2-pounds pork roast
- Black pepper to the taste
- 1 teaspoon chili powder
- 1/2 teaspoon onion powder
- 1/4 teaspoon cumin, ground
- 1 teaspoon cocoa powder

Directions:

1. In a roasting pan, combine the roast with black pepper, chili powder, onion powder, cumin and cocoa, rub, cover the pan, introduce in the oven and bake at 325 degrees F for 3 hours and 20 minutes.
2. Slice, divide between plates and serve with a side salad.

Nutrition: Calories 288, Carbohydrates 12g, Protein 23g, Fat 5g, Sodium 82mg

312. Creamy Smoky Pork Chops

Preparation: 10 minutes **Cooking: 20 minutes** **Servings: 4**

Ingredients:

- 2 tablespoons olive oil
- 4 pork chops
- 1 tablespoon chili powder
- Black pepper to the taste
- 1 teaspoon sweet paprika
- 1 garlic clove, minced
- 1 cup coconut milk
- 1 teaspoon liquid smoke
- 1/4 cup cilantro, chopped
- Juice of 1 lemon

Directions:

1. In a bowl, mix pork chops with pepper, chili powder, paprika and garlic and rub well.
2. Heat up a pan with the oil over medium-high heat, add pork chops and cook for 5 minutes on each side.
3. In a blender, mix coconut milk with liquid smoke, lemon juice and cilantro, blend well, pour over the chops, cook for 10 minutes more, divide everything between plates and serve.

Nutrition: Calories 240, Carbohydrates 10g, Protein 22g, Fat 8g, Sodium 132mg

313. Pork with Dates Sauce

Preparation: 10 minutes   **Cooking: 40 minutes**   **Servings: 6**

Ingredients:

- *1- and 1/2-pounds pork tenderloin*
- *2 tablespoons water*
- *1/3 cup dates, pitted*
- *1/4 teaspoon onion powder*
- *1/4 teaspoon smoked paprika*
- *2 tablespoons mustard*
- *1/4 cup coconut aminos*
- *Black pepper to the taste*

Directions:

1. In your food processor, mix dates with water, coconut aminos, mustard, paprika, pepper and onion powder and blend well.
2. Put pork tenderloin in a roasting pan, add the dates sauce, toss to coat very well, introduce everything in the oven at 400 degrees F, bake for 40 minutes, slice the meat, divide it and the sauce between plates and serve.

Nutrition: calories 240, fat 8, fiber 4, Carbohydrates 13, protein 24 Sodium: 92mg

314. Pork Chops and Apples

Preparation: 10 minutes   **Cooking: 1 hour**   **Servings: 4**

Ingredients:

- *1 and 1/2 cups low-sodium chicken stock*
- *Black pepper to the taste*
- *4 pork chops*
- *1 yellow onion, chopped*
- *1 tablespoon olive oil*
- *2 garlic cloves, minced*
- *3 apples, cored and sliced*
- *1 tablespoon thyme, chopped*

Directions:

1. Heat up a pan with the oil over medium-high heat, add pork chops, season with black pepper and cook for 5 minutes on each side.
2. Add onion, garlic, apples, thyme and stock, toss, introduce in the oven and bake at 350 degrees F for 50 minutes.
3. Divide everything between plates and serve.
4. Enjoy!

Nutrition: Calories 340, Carbohydrates 14g, Protein 27g, Fat 9g, Sodium 123mg

315. Steamed Salmon Teriyaki

Preparation: 10 minutes   **Cooking: 15 minutes**   **Servings: 2**

Ingredients

- *3 green onions, minced*
- *2 packets of Stevia*
- *1 tablespoon of freshly grated ginger*
- *1 clove of garlic, minced*
- *2 teaspoon of sesame seeds*
- *1 tablespoon of sesame oil*
- *1/4 cup of mirin*
- *2 tablespoons of low sodium soy sauce*
- *1/2-lb. of salmon filet*

Directions

1. Place a large saucepan on the medium-high fire. Place a trivet inside the saucepan and fill the pan halfway with water. Cover and bring to a boil.
2. Meanwhile, in a heatproof dish that fits inside the saucepan, mix well stevia, ginger, garlic, oil, mirin, and soy sauce. Add salmon and cover well with the sauce.
3. Top the salmon with sesame seeds and green onions. Cover dish with foil.
4. Place on top of the trivet. Cover and steam for 15 minutes.
5. Let it rest for 5 minutes in the pan and serve.

Nutrition: Calories: 242.7 Carbohydrates: 1.2 g Protein: 35.4 g Fat 10.7 g Sodium: 285 mg

316. Dill And Lemon Cod Packets

Preparation: 10 minutes   **Cooking: 10 minutes**   **Servings: 2**

Ingredients

- *2 teaspoon of olive oil, divided*
- *4 slices of lemon, divided*
- *2 sprigs of fresh dill, divided*
- *1/2 teaspoon of garlic powder, divided*
- *Pepper to taste*
- *1/2-lb. of cod filets*

Directions

1. Place a large saucepan on the medium-high fire. Place a trivet inside the saucepan and fill the pan halfway with water. Cover and bring to a boil.
2. Cut 2 pieces of 15-inch length foil.
3. In one foil, place one filet in the middle. Season with pepper to taste. Sprinkle 1/4
1. teaspoon of garlic. Add a teaspoon of oil on top of the filet. Top with 2 slices of lemon and a sprig of dill. Fold over the foil and seal the filet inside. Repeat the process for the remaining fish.
4. Place the packet on the trivet. Cover and steam for 10 minutes and serve.

Nutrition: Calories: 164.8 Carbohydrates: 9.4 g Protein: 18.3 g Fat: 6 g Sodium: 105mg

317. Steamed Fish Mediterranean Style

Preparation: 10 minutes   **Cooking: 15 minutes**   **Servings: 2**

Ingredients

- *Pepper to taste*
- *1 clove of garlic, smashed*
- *2 teaspoon of olive oil*
- *1 bunch of fresh thyme*
- *2 tablespoons of pickled capers*
- *1 cup of black salt-cured olives*
- *1-lb. of cherry tomatoes halved*
- *1 1/2-lbs. of cod filets*
- *Capers and olives for garnish*

Directions

1. Place a large saucepan on a medium-high fire. Place a trivet inside the saucepan and fill the pan halfway with water. Cover and bring to a boil.
2. Meanwhile, in a heatproof dish that fits inside the saucepan, layer half of the halved cherry tomatoes. Season with pepper.

3. Add the filets on top of the tomatoes and season with pepper. Drizzle oil. Sprinkle 3/4s of thyme on top and the smashed garlic.
4. Cover the top of fish with the remaining cherry tomatoes plus the capers and olives then place the dish on the trivet. Cover the dish with foil.
5. Cover the pan and steam for 15 minutes and serve.

Nutrition: Calories: 263.2 Carbohydrates: 21.8 g Protein: 27.8 g Fat 7.2g Sodium: 99mg

318. Steamed Veggie and Lemon Pepper Salmon

Preparation: 10 minutes   **Cooking: 15 minutes**   **Servings: 2**

Ingredients
- *1 carrot, peeled and julienned*
- *1 red bell pepper, julienned*
- *1 zucchini, julienned*
- *1/2 lemon, sliced thinly*
- *1 teaspoon of pepper*
- *1/2 teaspoon of salt*
- *1/2-lb. of salmon filet with skin on*
- *A dash of tarragon*

Directions
1. Place a large saucepan on the medium-high fire. Place a trivet inside the saucepan and fill the pan halfway with water. Cover and bring to a boil.
2. Meanwhile, in a heatproof dish that fits inside the saucepan, add the salmon with the skin side down. Season with pepper. Add slices of lemon on top.
3. Place the julienned vegetables on top of the salmon and season with tarragon.
4. Cover dish with foil.
5. Cover pan and steam for 15 minutes and serve.

Nutrition: Calories: 216.2 Carbohydrates: 4.1 g Protein: 35.1 g Fat: 6.6 g Sodium: 87mg

319. Steamed Fish with Scallions and Ginger

Preparation: 10 minutes   **Cooking: 15 minutes**   **Servings: 2**

Ingredients
- *1-lb. of Tilapia filets*
- *1 teaspoon of garlic*
- *1 teaspoon of minced ginger*
- *2 tablespoon of rice wine*
- *1 tablespoon of low sodium soy sauce*

Directions
1. In a heatproof dish that fits inside the saucepan, add garlic, minced ginger, rice wine, and soy sauce. Mix well. Add the Tilapia filet and marinate for half an hour while turning it over at a half time.
2. Place a large saucepan on the medium-high fire. Place a trivet inside the saucepan and fill the pan halfway with water. Cover and bring to a boil.
3. Cover the dish of fish with foil and place on trivet.
4. Cover the pan and steam for 15 minutes.
5. Serve and enjoy.

Nutrition: Calories: 219 Carbohydrates: 4g Protein: 31.8g Fat: 8.2g Sodium: 252 Mg

320. Stewed Cod Filet with Tomatoes

Preparation: 10 minutes   **Cooking: 15 minutes**   **Servings: 2**

Ingredients
- *1 tablespoon of olive oil*
- *1 onion, sliced*
- *1 and 1/2 pound of fresh cod fillets*
- *Pepper*
- *1 lemon juice, freshly squeezed*
- *1 can of diced tomatoes*

Directions
1. Place a heavy bottomed pot on medium-high fire and heat pot for 3 minutes.
2. Once hot, add oil and stir around to coat the pot with oil.
3. Sauté the onion for 2 minutes. Stir in diced tomatoes and cook for 5 minutes.
4. Add the cod filet and season with pepper.

5. Cover, bring to a boil, lower the fire to a simmer, and simmer for 5 minutes.
6. Serve and enjoy with freshly squeezed lemon juice.

Nutrition: Calories: 106.4 Carbohydrates: 2g Protein: 17.8 g Fat: 2.8 g Sodium: 76mg

321. Lemony Parmesan Shrimps

Preparation: 10 minutes   **Cooking: 15 minutes**   **Servings: 2**

Ingredients

- *1 tablespoon of olive oil*
- *1/2 cup of onion, chopped*
- *3 cloves of garlic, minced*
- *1-pound of shrimps, peeled and deveined*
- *1/2 cup of parmesan cheese, low fat*
- *1 cup of spinach, shredded*
- *1/2 cup of chicken broth, low sodium*
- *1/4 cup of water*
- *Pepper*

Directions

1. Place a heavy bottomed pot on medium-high fire and heat pot for 3 minutes.
2. Once hot, add oil and stir around to coat the pot with oil.
3. Sauté the onion and garlic for 5 minutes. Stir in shrimps and cook for 2 minutes.
4. Add the remaining ingredients, except for the parmesan.
5. Cover, bring to a boil, lower the fire to a simmer, and simmer for 5 minutes.
6. Serve and enjoy with a sprinkle of parmesan.

Nutrition: Calories: 252 Carbohydrates: 5g Protein:33.9g Fat: 10.6g Sodium: 344 mg

322. Tuna 'N Carrots Casserole

Preparation: 10 minutes   **Cooking: 12 minutes**   **Servings: 2**

Ingredients

- *2 carrots, peeled and chopped*
- *1/4 cup of diced onions*
- *1 cup of frozen peas*
- *3/4 cup of milk*
- *2 cans of tuna in water, drained*
- *1 can of cream of celery soup*
- *1 tablespoon of olive oil*
- *1/2 cup of water*
- *2 eggs beaten*
- *Pepper*

Directions

1. Place a heavy bottomed pot on medium-high fire and heat pot for 3 minutes.
2. Once hot, add the oil and stir around to coat the pot with oil.
3. Sauté the onion and carrots for 3 minutes.
4. Add the remaining ingredients and mix well.
5. Bring to a boil while constantly stirring, cook until thickened around 5 minutes and serve.

Nutrition: Calories: 281 Carbohydrates: 14g Protein: 24g Fat: 14g Sodium: 112mg

323. Garlic 'N Tomatoes on Mussels

Preparation: 10 minutes   **Cooking: 15 minutes**   **Servings: 2**

Ingredients

- *1/4 cup of white wine*
- *1/2 cup of water*
- *3 Roma tomatoes, chopped*
- *2 cloves of garlic, minced*
- *1 bay leaf*
- *2 pounds of mussels, scrubbed*
- *1/2 cup of fresh parsley, chopped*
- *1 tablespoon of oil*
- *Pepper*

Directions

1. Place a heavy bottomed pot on medium-high fire and heat pot for 3 minutes.
2. Once hot, add oil and stir around to coat the pot with oil.
3. Sauté the garlic, bay leaf, and tomatoes for 5 minutes.
4. Add the remaining ingredients, except for parsley and mussels. Mix well.

5. Add the mussels.
6. Cover and bring to a boil for 5 minutes.
7. Serve and enjoy with a sprinkle of parsley and discard any unopened mussels.

Nutrition: Calories: 172 Carbohydrates: 10.2g Protein: 19g Fat: 6g Sodium: 261mg

324. Tasty Corn and Clam Stew

Preparation: 10 minutes　　　　**Cooking: 25 minutes**　　　　**Servings: 2**

Ingredients

- *1-lb. of clam*
- *1 cup of frozen corn*
- *1/2 cup of water*
- *4 cloves of garlic*
- *1 teaspoon of oil*
- *1 teaspoon of celery seeds*
- *1 teaspoon of Cajun seasoning*

Directions

1. Place a nonstick saucepan on medium-high fire and heat pot for 3 minutes.
2. Once hot, add oil and stir around to coat the pot with oil.
3. Sauté the garlic for a minute.
4. Add the remaining ingredients, except for the clams, and mix well. Cook for 3 minutes.
5. Stir in clams.
6. Cover, bring to a boil, lower the fire to a simmer, and simmer for 5 minutes.
7. Serve and enjoy. Discard any unopened clam.

Nutrition: Calories: 120 Carbohydrates: 23g Protein: 22g Fat: 2 g Sodium: 466 mg

325. Generous Stuffed Salmon Avocado

Preparation: 10 minutes　　　　**Cooking: 30 minutes**　　　　**Servings: 2**

Ingredients:

- *1 ripe organic avocado*
- *2 oz. wild-caught smoked salmon*
- *2 oz. cashew cheese*
- *2 tablespoons extra virgin olive oil*
- *Sunflower seeds as needed*

Directions:

1. Cut avocado in half and deseed.
2. Add the rest of the ingredients to a food processor and process until coarsely chopped.
3. Place mixture into the avocado and serve.

Nutrition: Calories: 525 Fat: 48g Carbohydrates: 4g Protein: 19g Sodium: 122mg

326. Spanish Mussels

Preparation: 10 minutes　　　　**Cooking: 23 minutes**　　　　**Servings: 4**

Ingredients:

- *3 tablespoons olive oil*
- *2 pounds mussels, scrubbed*
- *Pepper to taste*
- *3 cups canned tomatoes, crushed*
- *1 shallot, chopped*
- *1 garlic clove, minced*
- *2 cups low sodium vegetable stock*
- *1/3 cup cilantro, chopped*

Directions:

1. Take a pan and place it over medium-high heat, add shallot, and stir-cook for 3 minutes.
2. Add garlic, stock, tomatoes and pepper; stir and reduce heat; simmer for 10 minutes.
3. Add mussels, cilantro, and toss.
4. Cover and cook for 10 minutes more and serve.

Nutrition: Calories: 210, Fat: 2g, Carbohydrates: 5g, Protein: 8g Sodium: 105mg

327. Tilapia Broccoli Platter

Preparation: 4 minutes   **Cooking: 14 minutes**   **Servings: 2**

Ingredients:

- 6-oz. tilapia, frozen
- 1 tablespoon almond butter
- 1 tablespoon garlic, minced
- 1 teaspoon lemon pepper seasoning
- 1 cup broccoli florets, fresh

Directions:

1. Preheat your oven to 350° F.
2. Add fish in aluminum foil packets.
3. Arrange broccoli around fish.
4. Sprinkle lemon pepper on top.
5. Close the packets and seal.
6. Bake for 14 minutes.
7. Take a bowl and add garlic and almond butter, mix well and keep the mixture on the side.
8. Remove the packet from the oven and transfer it to a platter.
9. Place almond butter on top of the fish and broccoli, serve and enjoy!

Nutrition: Calories: 362 Fat: 25 g Carbohydrates: 2 g Protein: 29 g Sodium: 104mg

328. Mackerel and Orange Medley

Preparation: 10 minutes   **Cooking: 10 minutes**   **Servings: 4**

Ingredients:

- 4 mackerel fillets, skinless and boneless
- 4 spring onion, chopped
- teaspoon olive oil
- 1-inch ginger piece, grated
- Black pepper as needed
- Juice and zest 1 whole orange
- 1 cup low Sodium: fish stock

Directions:

1. Season the fillets with black pepper and rub olive oil.
2. Add stock, orange juice, ginger, orange zest, and onion to Instant Pot.
3. Place a steamer basket and add the fillets.
4. Lock the lid and cook on HIGH pressure for 10 minutes.
5. Release the pressure naturally over 10 minutes.
6. Divide the fillets amongst plates and drizzle the orange sauce from the pot over the fish and enjoy!

Nutrition: Calories: 200 Fat: 4 g Carbohydrates: 19 g Protein: 14 g Sodium: 134mg

329. Spicy Chili Salmon

Preparation: 10 minutes   **Cooking: 7 minutes**   **Servings: 4**

Ingredients:

- 4 salmon fillets, boneless and skin-on
- 2 tablespoons assorted chili peppers, chopped
- Juice 1 lemon
- 1 lemon, sliced
- 1 cup water
- Black pepper to taste

Directions:

1. Add water to the Instant Pot.
2. Add steamer basket and add salmon fillets; season the fillets with salt and pepper.
3. Drizzle lemon juice on top.
4. Top with lemon slices.
5. Lock the lid and cook on HIGH pressure for 7 minutes.
6. Release the pressure naturally over 10 minutes.
7. Divide the salmon and lemon slices between serving plates and enjoy!

Nutrition: Calories: 281 Fat: 8 g Carbohydrates: 19 g Protein: 7 g Sodium: 116mg

330. Simple One-Pot Mussels

Preparation: 10 minutes   **Cooking: 5 minutes**   **Servings: 4**

Ingredients:

- 2 tablespoons butter
- 2 chopped shallots
- 4 minced garlic cloves
- 1/2 cup broth
- 1/2 cup white wine
- 2 pounds cleaned mussels
- Lemon and parsley for serving

Directions:

1. Clean the mussels and remove the beard.
2. Discard any mussels that do not close when tapped against a hard surface.
3. Set your pot to Sauté mode and add chopped onion and butter.
4. Stir and sauté onions.
5. Add garlic and cook for 1 minute. Add broth and wine.
6. Lock the lid and cook for 5 minutes on HIGH pressure.
7. Release the pressure naturally over 10 minutes.
8. Serve with a sprinkle of parsley and enjoy!

Nutrition: Calories: 286 Fat: 14 g Carbohydrates: 12 g Protein: 28 g Sodium: 302mg

331. Lemon Pepper and Salmon

Preparation: 5 minutes   **Cooking 6 minutes**   **Servings: 3**

Ingredients:

- 3/4 cup water
- Few sprigs parsley, basil, tarragon, basil
- 1 pound salmon, skin on
- 2 teaspoons ghee
- 1/4 teaspoon salt
- 1/2 teaspoon pepper
- 1/2 lemon, thinly sliced
- 1 whole carrot, julienned

Directions:

1. Set your pot to Sauté mode and water and herbs.
2. Place a steamer rack inside your pot and place salmon.
3. Drizzle the ghee on top of the salmon and season with salt and pepper.
4. Cover lemon slices.
5. Lock the lid and cook on HIGH pressure for 3 minutes.
6. Release the pressure naturally over 10 minutes.
7. Transfer the salmon to a serving platter.
8. Set your pot to Sauté mode and add vegetables.
9. Cook for 1-2 minutes and serve with veggies and salmon.

Nutrition: Calories: 464 Fat: 34 g Carbohydrates: 3 g Protein: 34 g Sodium: 68mg

332. Simple Sautéed Garlic and Parsley Scallops

Preparation: 5 minutes   **Cooking: 25 minutes**   **Servings: 4**

Ingredients:

- 8 tablespoons almond butter
- 2 garlic cloves, minced
- 16 large sea scallops
- Sunflower seeds and pepper to taste
- 1/2 tablespoons olive oil

Directions:

1. Seasons scallops with sunflower seeds and pepper.
2. Take a skillet, place it over medium heat, add oil and let it heat up.
3. Sauté scallops for 2 minutes per side, repeat until all scallops are cooked.
4. Add almond butter to the skillet and let it melt.
5. Stir in garlic and cook for 15 minutes.
6. Return scallops to skillet and stir to coat. Serve.

Nutrition: Calories: 417 Fat: 31 g Carbohydrates: 5 g Protein: 29 g Sodium: 72mg

333. Ginger Salmon Delight

Preparation: *15 minutes*   **Cooking:** *20 minutes*   **Servings:** *6*

Ingredients:
- 2 untreated cedar planks
- 1/3 cup vegetable oil
- 1 and 1/2 tablespoons rice vinegar
- 1/3 cup low sodium soy sauce
- 1 teaspoon sesame oil
- 1/4 cup green onions, chopped
- 1 teaspoon garlic, minced
- 1 tablespoon ginger, grated
- 2 salmon fillets, skinless and boneless

Directions:
1. Place cedar planks in a dish, cover with warm water and soak for about 1 hour.
2. Meanwhile, in another dish mix vegetable oil with vinegar, soy sauce, sesame oil, ginger, green onions and garlic and whisk well
3. Add salmon to this mix, cover and leave aside for 15 minutes.
4. Heat up your grill over medium heat, place planks on it and add salmon fillets when planks begin to smoke.
5. Cover grill and cook for 20 minutes.
6. Divide between plates and serve right away!

Nutrition: Calories: 240; Fat: 3g; Carbohydrates: 20g; Protein: 5g; Sodium: 321mg

334. Scallops and Jalapeno Vinaigrette

Preparation: *5 minutes*   **Cooking:** *6 minutes*   **Servings:** *4*

Ingredients:
- 1 jalapeno pepper, seedless and minced
- 1/4 cup extra virgin olive oil
- 1/4 cup rice vinegar
- 1/4 teaspoon mustard
- Black pepper to the taste
- A pinch cayenne peppers
- 1 tablespoon vegetable oil
- 12 big sea scallops
- 2 oranges, sliced

Directions:
1. In your blender, mix jalapeno with olive oil, mustard, black and vinegar and pulse well.
2. Season scallops with cayenne pepper.
3. Heat up a pan with the vegetable oil over high temperature, add scallops and cook them for 3 minutes on each side.
4. Divide scallops on plates, place orange slices on top and drizzle the jalapeno vinaigrette.

Nutrition: Calories: 467; Fat: 19g; Carbohydrates: 33g; Protein: 30g ; Sodium: 125mg

335. Tuna and Orange Salsa

Preparation: 10 minutes   **Cooking:** 5 minutes   **Servings:** 4

Ingredients:
- 2 oranges, sliced
- 1/2 cup red onion, chopped
- 1 red bell pepper, chopped
- 1/4 cup mint, chopped
- 1 tablespoon red wine vinegar
- 1 tablespoon vegetable oil
- Black pepper to the taste
- 4 tuna steaks
- 1 teaspoon coriander, dried

Directions:
1. In a bowl, mix oranges with onion, bell pepper, mint, vinegar, salt and pepper, stir and leave aside for now. Heat up your kitchen grill over medium high heat, rub tuna steaks with oil, pepper and coriander and grill for about 5 minutes.
2. Divide on plates, top with the orange salsa you've prepared and serve.

Nutrition: Calories: 150; Fat: 19g; Carbohydrates: 9g; Protein: 4g   Sodium: 595mg

336. White Steamed Fish

Preparation: 10 minutes   **Coooking:10 minute**   **Servings: 4**

Ingredients:

- 4 white fish fillets
- 1 tablespoon olive oil
- 1 teaspoon thyme, dried
- 1 pound cherry tomatoes, halved
- A pinch of sea salt and black pepper
- 1 garlic clove, minced
- 1 cup black olives, pitted and chopped, soaked for 5 hours
- 1 cup water

Directions:

1. Put the water in your instant pot, place the steamer basket on top and arrange fish inside.
2. Season with salt, pepper, thyme and garlic.
3. Add oil, olives and tomatoes, rub gently, cover your instant pot and cook on Low for 10 minutes.
4. Release the pressure fast, divide fish and all veggies between plates and serve hot.

Nutrition: Calories 267;Fat 5 g; Carbohydrates 29g; Protein 2g Sodium 90 mg

337. Shrimp Umani

Preparation: 10 minutes   **Cooking: 3 minutes**   **Servings: 2**

Ingredients:

- 8 big shrimps
- 1 tablespoon ginger, grated
- 3 tablespoons low sodium soy sauce
- 1/3 cup's sake
- 1 cup dashi
- 3 tablespoons mirin
- 1 tablespoon sugar

Directions:

1. Heat up a pan with the dashi over medium heat, add sugar, ginger, soy sauce, mirin and sake, stir and bring to a boil.
2. Add shrimp, cook for 3 minutes, take off heat, leave aside to cool down completely, divide between 2 plates and serve.

Nutrition: Calories 155, Carbohydrates 12g, Protein 15g, Fat 2g, Sodium 126mg

338. Mexican Shrimp Salad

Preparation: 10 minutes   **Cooking: 20 minutes**   **Servings: 6**

Ingredients:

- 1 pound shrimp, deveined and peeled
- 2 cups cherry tomatoes, halved
- 2 romaine lettuce hearts, shredded
- 1 cucumber, chopped
- 1 avocado, pitted, peeled and chopped
- 1/2 cup cilantro leaves, chopped
- Black pepper to the taste
- 4 cups tortilla chips
- 2 tablespoons low fat sour cream
- 2 tablespoons lime juice
- 1/2 teaspoon lime zest, grated

Directions:

1. Put water in a pot, bring to a boil over medium high heat, add shrimp, cook for 3 minutes, transfer them to a bowl filled with ice water, drain, pat dry them and put in a salad bowl.
2. Add lettuce, cucumber, tomatoes, avocado, cilantro and tortilla chips.
3. In a bowl, mix sour cream with lime juice, lime zest, and black pepper to the taste and whisk well.
4. Pour this over salad, toss to coat and serve right away.

Nutrition: Calories: 204; Fat: 8g; Carbohydrates: 21g; Protein: 27g; Sodium: 584mg

339. Ginger Tuna Kabobs

Preparation: 30 minutes   **Cooking: 10 minutes**   **Servings: 8**

Ingredients:

- 1/4 cup low sodium soy sauce
- 1 pound tuna steaks, cubed in 16 pieces
- 2 tablespoons rice vinegar
- Black pepper to the taste
- 1 tablespoon sesame seeds
- 2 tablespoons canola oil
- 16 pieces pickled ginger
- 1 bunch watercress

Directions:

1. In a bowl, mix soy sauce with vinegar and tuna, toss to coat, cover bowl and keep in the fridge for 30 minutes.
2. Discard marinade, pat dry tuna and sprinkle it with black pepper and sesame seeds.
3. Heat up a pan with the oil over medium heat, add tuna pieces, cook them until they are pink in the center and browned on the outside, take them off heat and transfer them to a plate.
4. Thread one ginger slice on 16 skewers.
5. Thread one tuna cube on each of the 16 skewers.
6. Arrange watercress on a platter, arrange tuna kabobs on top and serve.

Nutrition: Calories: 432; Fat: 2g; Carbohydrates: 21g; Protein: 20g; Sodium: 214mg

340. Roasted Salmon

Preparation: 10 minutes   **Cooking: 35 minutes**   **Servings: 6**

Ingredients:

- *2 pounds salmon fillets, boneless*
- *1 garlic clove, minced*
- *1/4 cup maple syrup*
- *1/4 cup balsamic vinegar*
- *A pinch of black pepper*
- *Chopped mint for serving*
- *Cooking spray*

Directions:

1. Heat up a pan over medium low heat, add maple syrup, vinegar and garlic, stir and heat up for 1 minutes.
2. Transfer this to a bowl and leave aside to cool down a bit.
3. Spray a baking sheet with cooking spray, arrange salmon fillets on the sheet, season them with a pinch of black pepper and brush with half of the maple glaze.
4. Introduce in the oven at 450 degrees F and bake for 10 minutes.
5. Brush salmon with the rest of the glaze and bake for 20 minutes more.
6. Divide on plates, sprinkle mint on top and serve.

Nutrition: Calories 317, Carbohydrates 21g, Protein 20g, Fat 8g, Sodium 214mg

341. Easy Roast Salmon with Roasted Asparagus

Preparation: 5 minutes   **Cooking: 15 minutes**   **Servings: 2**

Ingredients:

- *2 (5-ounce) salmon fillets with skin*
- *2 teaspoons olive oil, plus extra for drizzling*
- *Pinch of Salt*
- *Freshly ground black pepper*
- *1 bunch asparagus, trimmed*
- *1 teaspoon dried chives*
- *1 teaspoon dried tarragon*
- *Fresh lemon wedges for serving*

Directions

1. Preheat the oven to 425°F.
2. Rub salmon completely with 1 teaspoon of olive oil per fillet. Season with salt and pepper.
3. Place asparagus spears on a foil lined baking sheet and lay the salmon fillets skin-side down on top. Put pan in upper-third of oven and roast until fish is just cooked through (about 12 minutes). Roasting time will vary depending on the thickness of your salmon. Salmon should flake easily with a fork when it's ready and an instant-read thermometer should register 145°F.

4. When cooked, remove from the oven, cut fillets in half crosswise, then lift flesh from skin with a metal spatula and transfer to a plate. Discard the skin. Drizzle salmon with oil, sprinkle with herbs, and serve with lemon wedges and roasted asparagus spears.

Nutrition: Calories 353, Carbohydrates 5g, Protein 34g, Fat 4g, Sodium 34mg

342. Cilantro-Lime Tilapia Tacos

Preparation: 10 minutes   **Cooking: 10 minutes**   **Servings: 4**

Ingredients

- *1 teaspoon olive oil*
- *1 pound tilapia fillets, rinsed and dried*
- *3 cups diced tomatoes*
- *1/2 cup fresh cilantro, chopped, plus additional for serving*
- *3 tablespoons freshly squeezed lime juice*
- *Freshly ground black pepper*
- *8 (5-inch) white-corn tortillas*
- *1 avocado sliced into 8 wedges*
- *Optional: lime wedges and fat-free sour cream for serving*

Directions

1. Heat the oil in a large skillet, add the tilapia and cook until the flesh starts to flake (about 5 minutes per side).
2. Add the tomatoes, cilantro, and lime juice. Sauté over medium-high heat for about 5 minutes, breaking up the fish and mixing well. Season to taste with salt and pepper.
3. Heat tortillas in a skillet for a few minutes on each side to warm.
4. Serve 1/4 cup of fish mixture on each warmed tortilla with two slices of avocado.
5. Serve immediately with optional toppings.

Nutrition: Calories 286, Carbohydrates 22g, Protein 28g, Fat 12g, Sodium 117mg

343. Pan-Seared Scallops

Preparation:5minutes   **Cooking:6minutes**   **Servings: 4**

Ingredients

- *2 cups chopped tomato*
- *1/2 cup chopped fresh basil*
- *1/4 teaspoon freshly ground black pepper, divided*
- *2 tablespoons olive oil, divided*
- *1- and 1/2-pounds sea scallops*
- *1/8 teaspoon salt*
- *1 cup fresh corn kernels*
- *1 cup zucchini, diced*

Directions

1. In a medium bowl, combine tomato, basil, and 1/8 teaspoon black pepper. Toss gently.
2. Heat a large skillet over high heat. Add 1 tablespoon of olive oil to the pan, swirling to coat. Pat scallops dry with paper towels. Sprinkle with salt and remaining black pepper. Add scallops to the pan, cook for 2 minutes or until browned. Turn scallops and cook for 2 minutes more or until browned. Remove scallops from the pan and keep warm.
3. Heat the remaining olive oil in the pan. Add corn and zucchini to the pan. Sauté for 2 minutes or until lightly browned. Add to tomato mixture and toss gently.
4. Serve scallops with a spinach salad, if desired.

Nutrition: Calories 221, Carbohydrates 17g, Protein 20g, Fat 9g, Sodium 214mg

344. Lemon-Dill Tilapia

Preparation: 5 minutes   **Cooking: 20 minutes**   **Serves 4**

Ingredients:

- *4 (4-ounce) tilapia fillets*
- *1/4 teaspoon salt*
- *1/2 teaspoon freshly ground black pepper*
- *2 tablespoons unsalted butter*
- *2 large lemons, 1 juiced, 1 sliced*
- *1/4 cup chopped fresh dill*

Directions:

1. Preheat the oven to 350°F.

2. Put the tilapia fillets in a glass baking dish. Season with the salt and pepper.
3. Top each fillet with 1/2 tablespoon of butter, the lemon juice, and 1 tablespoon of dill. Once they are coated, place the lemon slices on top.
4. Bake for 15 to 20 minutes, or until the fish flakes with a fork. Divide among 4 storage containers.

Nutrition: Calories: 163; Fat: 8g; Carbohydrates: 6g; Protein: 22g; Sodium: 194mg

345. Sesame-Crusted Ahi Tuna Steaks

Preparation: 5 minutes   **Cooking: 6 minutes**   **Serves 4**

Ingredients:

- *2 tablespoons reduced-sodium soy sauce*
- *1 tablespoon sesame oil*
- *1 tablespoon rice vinegar*
- *1/2 tablespoon honey*
- *4 (4-ounce) ahi tuna steaks*
- *1/4 cup white sesame seeds*
- *1/4 cup black sesame seeds*
- *1 tablespoon extra-virgin olive oil*
- *2 scallions, chopped*

Directions:

1. In a small bowl, mix the soy sauce, sesame oil, vinegar, and honey.
2. Coat the tuna steaks with the mixture.
3. Spread the white and black sesame seeds out on a plate and press both sides of each tuna steak into the seeds to coat.
4. In a skillet or nonstick pan, heat the olive oil over high heat. Sear the tuna steaks for 30 to 45 seconds on each side. You'll know the tuna is done when it has been seared white on the outside but remains pink in the middle. Divide among 4 storage containers. Top with the scallions.

Nutrition: Calories: 302; Fat: 17g; Carbohydrates: 6g; Protein: 32g; Sodium: 345mg

346. Grilled Halibut with Black Bean and Mango Salsa

Preparation: 15 minutes   **Cooking: 10 minutes**   **Serves 4**

Ingredients:

- *1 (15-ounce) can no-salt-added black beans, drained and rinsed*
- *1 (15-ounce) can juice-packed diced mango, drained*
- *1/2 medium red onion, chopped*
- *1/2 medium red bell pepper, diced*
- *3 tablespoons minced fresh cilantro*
- *Juice of 1 large lime*
- *Juice of 1 large lemon*
- *3 tablespoons extra-virgin olive oil*
- *1 teaspoon freshly ground black pepper*
- *1 garlic clove, minced*
- *4 (4-ounce) halibut fillets*

Directions:

1. Preheat the grill to medium-high heat (350°F to 400°F). In a large bowl, mix the beans, mango, onion, bell pepper, cilantro, and lime juice. Divide into 4 storage containers.
2. In a small bowl, mix the lemon juice, oil, black pepper, and garlic.
3. Coat the halibut fillets in the lemon marinade and let rest for 10 minutes.
4. Grill for 2 minutes on each side. Take off the grill and allow it to rest. Divide into 4 storage containers.
5. To serve, reheat and top each fillet with a generous serving of the salsa.

Nutrition: Calories: 340; Fat: 13g; Carbohydrates: 31g; Protein: 26g; Sodium: 94mg

347. Jerk Salmon

Preparation: 5 minutes   **Cooking: 15 minutes**   **Serves 4**

Ingredients:

- *2 tablespoons extra-virgin olive oil, divided*
- *2 1/2 teaspoons dried thyme*
- *2 teaspoons ground allspice*
- *2 teaspoons onion powder*
- *2 teaspoons freshly ground black pepper*
- *1/2 teaspoon ground cinnamon*
- *1/2 teaspoon cayenne pepper*

- *4 (4-ounce) skin-on salmon fillets*

Directions:
1. Preheat the oven to 350°F. Lightly coat a sheet pan with 1/2 tablespoon of oil.
2. In a small bowl, mix the thyme, allspice, onion powder, black pepper, cinnamon, and cayenne pepper. Lightly coat the salmon fillets with the remaining 11/2 tablespoons of oil and season with the rub.
3. Place the salmon, skin-side down, on the prepared sheet pan. Bake for 12 to 15 minutes, or until the salmon is cooked through and flakes easily with a fork. Divide among 4 storage containers.

Nutrition: Calories: 255; Fat: 15g; Carbohydrates: 3g; Protein: 26g; Sodium: 59mg

348. Mediterranean-Herbed Scallops

Preparation: 5 minutes   **Cooking :15 minutes**   **Serves 4**

Ingredients:
- *1/4 cup fresh basil leaves*
- *1/4 cup fresh thyme leaves*
- *1 tablespoon fresh rosemary leaves*
- *1 tablespoon chopped fresh sage*
- *2 teaspoons freshly ground black pepper*
- *1 tablespoon fresh lemon juice*
- *3 tablespoons extra-virgin olive oil, divided*
- *1 garlic clove, minced*
- *12 scallops*
- *4 lemon wedges (optional)*

Directions:
1. In a food processor or blender, combine the basil, thyme, rosemary, sage, pepper, lemon juice, and 11/2 tablespoons of oil. Pulse until mixed. The herbs should still be visible.
2. In a large skillet, heat the remaining 11/2 tablespoons of oil over medium-high heat. Add the garlic and cook, stirring rapidly, for 30 seconds. Working in batches, sear the scallops on each side, for 2 to 3 minutes per side. Remove from the skillet and top with the herbed oil. Place 3 herb-topped scallops in each of 4 storage containers.
3. To serve, after reheating the scallops, place a lemon wedge on the side (if using).

Nutrition: Calories: 158; Fat: 11g; Carbohydrates: 5g; Protein: 11g; Sodium: 335mg

349. Pistachio-Crusted Tilapia

Preparation: 10 minutes   **Cooking: 15 minutes**   **Serves 4**

Ingredients:
- *Nonstick cooking spray*
- *4 (4-ounce) tilapia fillets*
- *1/4 teaspoon salt*
- *1/2 teaspoon freshly ground black pepper*
- *1/2 teaspoon garlic powder*
- *1/4 cup nonfat plain Greek yogurt*
- *1/2 cup dried unseasoned breadcrumbs*
- *1/2 cup raw pistachios, finely chopped*
- *1 teaspoon dried oregano*
- *1 teaspoon dried thyme*

Direction:
1. Preheat the oven to 375°F. Cover a sheet pan with foil and coat with nonstick cooking spray.
2. Season the fillets with the salt, pepper, and garlic powder. Spread 1 tablespoon of yogurt onto each fillet until evenly coated. Set aside.
3. In a shallow dish, mix breadcrumbs, pistachios, oregano, and thyme.
4. Press each fillet in the pistachio and bread crumb mixture on both sides until well coated.
5. Arrange the fillets on the prepared sheet pan and bake for 12 to 15 minutes, or until cooked through. Divide among 4 storage containers.

Nutrition: Calories 348, Carbohydrates 16g, Protein 29g, Fat 21g, Sodium 348mg

350. <u>Shrimp Ceviche</u>

Preparation time: 1 hour   **Cooking time: 10 minutes**   **Servings: 4**

Ingredients:

- *2 pounds medium shrimp, peeled, deveined, and cooked*
- *3/4 cup fresh lime juice*
- *1/4 cup fresh lemon juice*
- *1/3 cup fresh orange juice*
- *1 cup finely chopped red onion*
- *3/4 cup diced cucumber*
- *2 small Roma (plum) tomatoes, seeded and diced*
- *1 cup chopped fresh cilantro*
- *1 avocado, pitted, peeled, and chopped*

Directions:

1. In a large bowl, combine the shrimp, lime juice, lemon juice, and orange juice. Cover and refrigerate for 30 minutes.
2. Add the onion, cucumber, tomatoes, cilantro, and avocado to the bowl. Toss to coat and mix evenly. Divide into 4 storage containers.

Nutrition: Calories 259, Carbohydrates 11g, Protein 41g, Fat 6g, Sodium 243mg

351. <u>Pineapple And Shrimp Skewers</u>

Preparation: 15 minutes   **Cooking: 25 minutes**   **Servings: 8**

Ingredients:

- *1/4 cup honey*
- *Juice of 1/2 medium orange*
- *Juice of 2 limes*
- *1 tablespoon extra-virgin olive oil*
- *2 teaspoons reduced-sodium soy sauce*
- *1 teaspoon freshly ground black pepper*
- *1/4 teaspoon chili powder*
- *1 small green bell pepper, cut into 1-inch squares*
- *1 small red bell pepper, cut into 1-inch squares*
- *1 small red onion, cut into 1-inch chunks*
- *1 pound peeled and deveined shrimp (32 to 40), fresh or (thawed) frozen*
- *2 cups cubed (1-inch) pineapple*

Directions

1. If using wooden skewers, soak them in water for 30 to 60 minutes before grilling. Preheat the grill to medium heat (350°F to 400°F).
2. In a small bowl, whisk together the honey, orange juice, lime juice, oil, soy sauce, black pepper, and chili powder until well mixed. Set aside.
3. Assemble 8 skewers by alternating ingredients: a veggie chunk, a shrimp, a veggie chunk, a pineapple chunk, and another veggie chunk (such as: green bell pepper, a shrimp, an onion chunk, a pineapple chunk, and a red bell pepper), repeating until there is about 1 inch left at the bottom of the skewer and 1/2 inch at the top. Brush the skewers all over with the honey and soy sauce marinade until all sides are fully coated. Let them rest for at least 10 minutes.
4. Put the skewers on the grill and cook, flipping once, for 4 to 5 minutes per side, or until the shrimp are cooked through. While grilling, brush the skewers with more marinade. Place 2 skewers in each of 4 storage containers.

Nutrition: Calories 260, Carbohydrates 35g, Protein 24g, Fat 4g, Sodium 235mg

352. <u>Broccoli and Cod Mash</u>

Preparation: 10 minutes   **Cooking: 20 minutes**   **Servings: 1**

Ingredients:

- *2 cups broccoli, chopped*
- *4 cod fillets, boneless, chopped*
- *1 white onion, chopped*
- *2 tablespoons olive oil*
- *1 cup of water*
- *1 tablespoon low-fat cream cheese*
- *1/2 teaspoon ground black pepper*

Directions:
1. Roast the cod in the saucepan with olive oil for 1 minute per side.
2. Then add all remaining ingredients except cream cheese and boil the meal for 18 minutes.
3. After this, drain water, add cream cheese, and stir the meal well.

Nutrition: Calories 186, Carbohydrates 6g, Protein 22g, Fat 9g, Sodium 105mg

353. Greek Style Salmon

Preparation: 10 minutes   **Cooking: 10 minutes**   **Servings: 2**

Ingredients:
- *4 medium salmon fillets, skinless and boneless*
- *1 tablespoon lemon juice*
- *1 tablespoon dried oregano*
- *1 teaspoon dried thyme*
- *1/4 teaspoon onion powder*
- *1 tablespoon olive oil*

Directions:
1. Heat up olive oil in the skillet.
2. Sprinkle the salmon with dried oregano, thyme, onion powder, and lemon juice.
3. Put the fish in the skillet and cook for 4 minutes per side.

Nutrition: Calories 271, Carbohydrates 1g, Protein 35g, Fat 15g, Sodium 430mg

354. Spicy Ginger Seabass

Preparation: 5 minutes   **Cooking: 10 minutes**   **Servings: 2**

Ingredients:
- *1 tablespoon ginger, grated*
- *2 tablespoons sesame oil*
- *1/4 teaspoon chili powder*
- *4 sea bass fillets, boneless*
- *1 tablespoon margarine*

Directions:
1. Heat up sesame oil and margarine in the skillet.
2. Add chili powder and ginger.
3. Then add seabass and cook the fish for 3 minutes per side.
4. Then close the lid and simmer the fish for 3 minutes over low heat.

Nutrition: Calories 216, Carbohydrates 12g, Protein 24g, Fat 12g, Sodium 123mg

355. Yogurt Shrimps

Preparation: 5 minutes   **Cooking: 10 minutes**   **Servings: 2**

Ingredients:
- *1 pound shrimp, peeled*
- *1 tablespoon margarine*
- *1/4 cup low-fat yogurt*
- *1 teaspoon lemon zest, grated*
- *1 chili pepper, chopped*

Directions:
1. Melt the margarine in the skillet, add chili pepper, and roast it for 1 minute.
2. Then add shrimps and lemon zest.
3. Roast the shrimps for 2 minutes per side.
4. After this, add yogurt, stir the shrimps well and cook for 5 minutes.

Nutrition: Calories 137, Carbohydrates 3g, Protein 21g, Fat 4g, Sodium 257mg

356. Aromatic Salmon with Fennel Seeds

Preparation: 8 minutes   **Cooking: 10 minutes**   **Servings: 2**

Ingredients:
- *4 medium salmon fillets, skinless and boneless*
- *1 tablespoon fennel seeds*

- *2 tablespoons olive oil*
- *1 tablespoon lemon juice*
- *1 tablespoon water*

Directions:
1. Heat up olive oil in the skillet.
2. Add fennel seeds and roast them for 1 minute.
3. Add salmon fillets and sprinkle with lemon juice.
4. Add water and roast the fish for 4 minutes per side over the medium heat.

Nutrition: Calories 301, Carbohydrates 1g, Protein 18g, Fat 5g, Sodium 135 mg

357. Shrimp Quesadillas

Preparation: 16 minutes   **Cooking: 5 minutes**   **Servings: 2**

Ingredients:
- *Two whole wheat tortillas*
- *1/2 tsp. ground cumin*
- *4 cilantro leaves*
- *3 oz. diced cooked shrimp*
- *1 de-seeded plump tomato*
- *3/4 c. grated non-fat mozzarella cheese*
- *1/4 c. diced red onion*

Directions:
1. In medium bowl, combine the grated mozzarella cheese and the warm, cooked shrimp. Add the ground cumin, red onion, and tomato. Mix. Spread the mixture evenly on the tortillas.
2. Heat a non-stick frying pan. Place the tortillas in the pan, then heat until they crisp.
3. Add the cilantro leaves. Fold over the tortillas.
4. Press down for 1 – 2 minutes. Slice the tortillas into wedges and serve immediately!

Nutrition: Calories: 99 Fat: 9 g Carbohydrates: 7.2 g Protein: 59gSodium: 500 mg

358. The OG Tuna Sandwich

Preparation: 15 minutes   **Cooking: 5 minutes**   **Servings: 2**

Ingredients:
- *30 g olive oil*
- *1 peeled and diced medium cucumber*
- *2 and 1/2 g pepper*
- *4 whole wheat bread slices*
- *85 g diced onion*
- *2 and 1/2 g salt*
- *1 can flavored tuna*
- *85 g shredded spinach*

Directions:
1. Grab your blender and add the spinach, tuna, onion, oil, salt and pepper in, and pulse for about 10 to 20 seconds.
2. In the meantime, toast your bread and add your diced cucumber to a bowl, which you can pour your tuna mixture in. Carefully mix and add the mixture to the bread once toasted.
3. Slice in half and serve, while storing the remaining mixture in the fridge.

Nutrition: Calories 302, Carbohydrates 37g, Protein 28g, Fat 6g, Sodium 445mg

359. Easy to Understand Mussels

Preparation: 10 minutes   **Cooking: 10 minutes**   **Servings: 2**

Ingredients:
- *2 lbs. cleaned mussels*
- *4 minced garlic cloves*
- *2 chopped shallots*
- *Lemon and parsley*
- *2 tbsps. Butter*
- *1/2 c. broth*
- *1/2 c. white wine*

Directions:
1. Clean the mussels and remove the beard
2. Discard any mussels that do not close when tapped against a hard surface
3. Set your pot to Sauté mode and add chopped onion and butter

4. Stir and sauté onions
5. Add garlic and cook for 1 minute
6. Add broth and wine
7. Lock up the lid and cook for 5 minutes on HIGH pressure
8. Release the pressure naturally over 10 minutes
9. Serve with a sprinkle of parsley and enjoy!

Nutrition: Calories: 286 Fat: 14g Carbohydrates: 12g Protein: 28g Sodium: 314 mg

360. Cheesy Shrimp Mix

Preparation: 10 minutes   **Cooking: 30 minutes**   **Servings: 10**

Ingredients:

- *1/2-pound shrimp, already peeled and deveined*
- *1 cup avocado mayonnaise*
- *1/2 cup low-fat mozzarella cheese, shredded*
- *3 garlic cloves, minced*
- *1/4 teaspoon hot sauce*
- *1 tablespoon lemon juice*
- *A drizzle of olive oil*
- *1/2 cup scallions, sliced*

Directions:

1. In a bowl, mix mozzarella with mayo, hot sauce, garlic and lemon juice and whisk well.
2. Add scallions and shrimp, toss, pour into a baking dish greased with the olive oil, introduce in the oven at 350 degrees F and bake for 30 minutes.
3. Divide into bowls and serve.

Nutrition: Calories 275, Carbohydrates 8g, Protein 12g, Fat 10g, Sodium 112mg

361. Smoked Salmon with Capers and Radishes

Preparation: 10 minutes   **Servings: 8**

Ingredients:

- *3 tablespoons beet horseradish, prepared*
- *1-pound smoked salmon, skinless, boneless and flaked*
- *2 teaspoons lemon zest, grated*
- *4 radishes, chopped*
- *1/2 cup capers, drained and chopped*
- *1/3 cup red onion, roughly chopped*
- *3 tablespoons chives, chopped*

Directions:

1. In a bowl, combine the salmon with the beet horseradish, lemon zest, radish, capers, onions and chives, toss and serve cold.

Nutrition: Calories 254, Carbohydrates 7g, Protein 17g, Fat 2g, Sodium 115mg

362. Trout Spread

Preparation : 10 minutes   **Servings: 8**

Ingredients:

- *4 ounces smoked trout, skinless, boneless and flaked*
- *1/4 cup coconut cream*
- *1 tablespoon lemon juice*
- *1/3 cup non-fat yogurt*
- *1 and 1/2 tablespoon parsley, chopped*
- *3 tablespoons chives, chopped*
- *Black pepper to the taste*
- *A drizzle of olive oil*

Directions:

1. In a bowl mix trout with yogurt, cream, black pepper, chives, lemon juice and the dill and stir.
2. Drizzle the olive oil at the end and serve.

Nutrition: Calories 204, Carbohydrates 8g, Protein 15g, Fat 2g, Sodium 114mg

363. Easy Shrimp and Mango

Preparation: 10 minutes   **Servings: 4**
Ingredients:

- *3 tablespoons balsamic vinegar*
- *3 tablespoons coconut sugar*
- *6 tablespoons avocado mayonnaise*
- *3 mangos, peeled and cubed*
- *3 tablespoons parsley, finely chopped*
- *1 pound shrimp, peeled, deveined and cooked*

Directions:

1. In a bowl, mix vinegar with sugar and mayo and whisk.
2. In another bowl, combine the mango with the parsley and shrimp, add the mayo mix, toss and serve.

Nutrition: Calories 204, Carbohydrates 8g, Protein 18g, Fat 2g, Sodium 114 mg

364. Acorn Squash with Apples

Preparation: 20 minutes   **Cooking: 15 minutes**   **Servings: 2**

Ingredients

- 1 Granny Smith apple, peeled, cored, and sliced
- 2 tbsp. brown sugar
- 1 small acorn squash, about 6 inches in diameter
- 2 tsp. trans-fat-free margarin

Directions

1. In a small bowl, combine the apple and brown sugar. Set aside.
2. Punch the squash several times with a sharp knife to allow steam to escape during cooking. Microwave over high heat until tender, about 5 minutes. Turn the squash after 3 minutes to ensure even cooking.
3. Place the squash on a cutting board and cut it in half. Scrape the seeds from the center of each half and discard them. Fill the pumpkin with the apple mixture. Return squash to microwave and cook until apples are tender about 2 minutes.
4. Transfer the squash to a serving plate.
5. Top each half with 1 tsp. of margarine and serve immediately.

Nutrition: Calories 204, Protein 12 g, Carbohydrates 40 g, Fat 4 g Sodium 246 mg

365. Asparagus with Hazelnut

Preparation: 10 minutes   **Cooking: 10 minutes**   **Servings: 4**

Ingredients

- 1 pound asparagus, tough ends removed, then peeled if the skin is thick
- 1 clove garlic, minced
- 1 tbsp. chopped fresh flat-leaf (Italian) parsley, plus sprigs for garnish
- 1 tbsp. finely chopped toasted hazelnuts (filberts)
- 1/4 tsp. finely grated lemon zest, plus extra for garnish
- 2 tsp. fresh lemon juice
- 1 tsp. extra-virgin olive oil
- 1/4 tsp. salt

Directions

1. In a big saucepan fitted with a steamer basket, bring about 1 inch of water to a boil. Add the asparagus, cover, and steam until tender, about 4 minutes. Remove from the pot.
2. In a large bowl, combine the asparagus, garlic, chopped parsley, hazelnuts, 1/4 tsp. lemon zest, lemon juice, olive oil, and salt. Stir well to mix and coat.
3. Carefully arrange the asparagus in a serving dish and garnish it with parsley sprigs and lemon zest. Serve immediately.

Nutrition: Calories 150, Protein 8 g, Carbohydrates 15 g, Fat 12 g, Sodium 148mg

366. Baby Minted Carrots

Preparation: 10 minutes   **Cooking: 15 minutes**   **Servings: 4**

Ingredients

- 6 cups of water
- 1 pound baby carrots, rinsed (about 51/2 cups)
- 1/4 cup 100% apple juice
- 1 tbsp. cornstarch
- 1/2 tbsp. chopped fresh mint leaves
- 1/8 tsp. ground cinnamon

Directions

1. Pour the water into a large saucepan. Include carrots and simmer until tender, about 10 minutes. Drain the carrots and set them aside in a serving bowl.
2. In a small saucepan over medium heat, combine the apple juice and cornstarch. Stir until mixture thickens, about 5 minutes. Add the mint and cinnamon.

3. Pour the mixture over the carrots. Serve immediately.

Nutrition: Calories 44, Protein 3 g, Carbohydrates 16 g, Fat 0 g Sodium 51 mg

367. Black Bean Cakes

Preparation: 80 minutes   **Cooking: 1 hour**   **Servings: 8**

Ingredients

- *4 cups of water*
- *2 cups of dried black beans, picked over and rinsed, soaked overnight, and drained*
- *8 cloves garlic, chopped*
- *1/2 tsp. salt*
- *1/2 cup chopped fresh cilantro*
- *2 tbsp. olive oil*

Directions

1. In a big size saucepan over high heat, mix the black beans and water. Bring to a boil.
2. Reduce heat to low, partially cover, and simmer until beans are tender about 60 to 70 minutes. Drain well.
3. In a big bowl, mash the beans and garlic. Add the cilantro and salt.
4. Form 8 cakes with the mixture. Move to a plate and refrigerate for about 1 hour.
5. In a large nonstick skillet, heat olive oil over medium heat. Add cakes and cook, turning once, until lukewarm and outside is slightly crisp, about 5 minutes.
6. Serve immediately.

Nutrition: Calories 196, Protein 10g, Carbohydrates 30g, Fat 4g Sodium 156 mg

368. Braised Kale

Preparation: 15 minutes   **Cooking: 30 minutes**   **Servings: 6**

Ingredients

- *2 tsp. extra-virgin olive oil*
- *4 garlic cloves, thinly sliced*
- *1 pound kale, tough stems removed and leaves coarsely chopped*
- *1/2 cup low-sodium vegetable stock or broth*
- *1 cup cherry tomatoes, halved*
- *1 tbsp. fresh lemon juice*
- *1/4 tsp. salt*
- *1/8 tsp. Freshly ground black pepper*

Directions

1. In a big-size skillet, heat up the olive oil over medium heat. Add garlic and sauté until lightly browned for 1 to 2 minutes. Add the black cabbage and the vegetable broth. Cover, reduce heat to medium-low and cook until cabbage is wilted and some of the liquid has evaporated about 5 minutes.
2. Include the tomatoes and cook, uncovered, until the cabbage is tender, another 5 to 7 minutes.
3. Take it out from the heat and add the lemon juice, salt, and pepper. Serve immediately.

Nutrition: Calories 170, Protein 4 g, Carbohydrates 9g, Fat 4g, Sodium 133 mg

369. Broccoli with Garlic and Lemon

Preparation: 10 minutes   **Cooking: 10 minutes**   **Servings: 4**

Ingredients

- *1 tsp. olive oil*
- *1/4 tsp. ground black pepper*
- *4 cups broccoli florets*
- *1 tbsp. minced garlic*
- *1/4 tsp. kosher salt*
- *1 tsp. lemon zest*

Directions

1. In a portable saucepan, bring one cup of water to a boil. Add up the broccoli to the boiling water and cook, 2 to 3 minutes or until just tender. Drain the broccoli.
2. In a small pan, fry over medium-high heat. Add the garlic and sauté for 30 seconds.
3. Add the broccoli, lemon zest, salt, and pepper. Mix well and serve.

Nutrition: Calories 45, Protein 3 g, Carbohydrates 7 g, Fat 1g, Sodium 153 mg

370. Brown Rice Pilaf

Preparation: 10 minutes   **Cooking: 45 minutes**   **Servings: 8**
Ingredients

- 1 cup dark brown rice, rinsed and drained
- 2 cups of water
- 3/4 tsp. salt, divided
- 1/4 tsp. saffron threads or ground turmeric
- 1/2 tsp. grated orange zest
- 3 tbsp. fresh orange juice
- 1 and 1/2 tbsp. pistachio oil or canola oil
- 1/4 cup chopped pistachio nuts
- 1/4 cup dried apricots, chopped

Directions

1. In a big saucepan over high heat, combine the rice, water, 1/4 tsp. of salt, and saffron. Bring to a boil.
2. Reduce heat to low, cover, and simmer until water is absorbed and rice is tender for about 45 minutes.
3. Transfer to a large bowl and keep warm.
4. In a portable bowl, mix the orange zest and juice, oil, and the remaining 1/2 tsp. of salt. Whisk to mix.
5. Pour the orange mixture over the hot rice. Add the nuts and apricots and toss gently to combine and coat. Serve immediately.

Nutrition: Calories 153, Protein 3g, Carbohydrates 24g, Fat 4g Sodium 222 mg

371. Brussels Sprouts with Shallots

Preparation: 10 minutes   **Cooking: 20 minutes**   **Servings: 4**
Ingredients

- 3 shallots, thinly sliced (about 3 tbsp.)
- 3 tsp. extra-virgin olive oil, divided
- 1/4 tsp. salt, divided
- 1/2 cup no-salt-added vegetable stock or broth
- 1 pound of trimmed Brussels sprouts, cut into quarters
- 1/4 tsp. finely grated lemon zest
- 1/4 tsp. of black pepper (freshly ground)
- 1 tbsp. fresh lemon juice

Directions

1. In a big nonstick skillet, heat 2 tsp. of olive oil over medium heat. Add the shallot and sauté until tender and lightly browned, about 6 minutes. Stir in 1/8 tsp. of salt. Put it in a bowl and set it aside.
2. In the same pan, heat the remaining 1 tsp. of olive oil over medium heat. Add the Brussels sprouts and sauté until just starting to brown for 3-4 minutes. Add the vegetable broth and bring to a boil.
3. Cook, uncovered, until the Brussels sprouts are tender, 5 to 6 minutes.
4. Return the shallots to the pan. Add lemon zest and juice, 1/8 tsp. of salt and pepper and serve.

Nutrition: Calories 104Protein 5 g, Carbohydrates 12 g, Fat 4g, Sodium 191 mg

372. Buttermilk Mashed Potatoes

Preparation: 10 minutes   **Cooking: 25 minutes**   **Servings: 4**
Ingredients

- 1/2 tsp. kosher salt
- 2 pounds russet potatoes
- 2 tbsp. unsalted butter
- 2 tbsp. chopped chives, for garnish (optional)
- 3/4 cup low-fat buttermilk

Directions

1. Fill a large pot halfway with water. Chop the potatoes into medium pieces, as equal in size as possible. Add potatoes to the pot and add more water if needed to cover. Bring to a boil over high heat.
2. Cook until the potatoes are tender (stick a knife into a potato to check), 12 to 15 minutes.
3. Drain the potatoes and transfer them to the pot. Add the salt, butter, and buttermilk.
4. Mash the potatoes until smooth, adding more buttermilk for the desired consistency, if needed.
5. Taste & season with extra salt if needed and garnish with chives if using.

Nutrition: Calories 241, Sodium 353 mg, Protein 6 g, Carbohydrates 44 g, Fat 6 g

373. Cauliflower Mashed 'Potatoes'

Preparation: 10 minutes   **Cooking: 30 minutes**   **Servings: 4**

Ingredients
- 1 head cauliflower
- 1 clove garlic
- 1 leek, white only, split into 4 pieces
- 1 tbsp. soft-tub margarine, nonhydrogenated
- Pepper to taste

Directions
1. Break the cauliflower into small pieces. In a large saucepan, steam the cauliflower, garlic, and leeks in water until completely tender, about 20-30 minutes.
2. Use a food processor to blend the vegetables until the consistency resembles mashed potatoes. Treat only a small portion at a time. If you prefer a softer texture, use a blender.
3. Be sure to hold the blender lid firmly with a kitchen towel.
4. Add a little hot water if the vegetables seem dry.
5. Mix the margarine and pepper to taste and serve.

Nutrition: Calories 67, Protein 2 g, Carbohydrates 40 g, Fat 1g Sodium 60 mg

374. Celery Root and Apple Puree

Preparation: 30 minutes   **Cooking: 1 hour**   **Servings: 4**

Ingredients
- 2 red apples, peeled and sliced
- 2 pounds of peeled celery root, cut into 1-inch pieces
- 2 tbsp. unsalted butter
- 1/4 tsp. kosher salt
- 1/2 cup low-fat milk

Directions
1. Add the celery root to a pot of salted water over high heat. When the water reaches a boil, add the apples and cook until the celery root is easily pierced with a knife, about 12 minutes.
2. Reserving one cup of the cooking water, drain the celery root and apples and place them in a food processor. Add the butter, milk, and salt. Blend until smooth, scraping sides as needed.
3. In case you want a smoother consistency, add the reserved cooking water as needed. Serve at once.

Nutrition: Calories 207, Protein 5 g, Carbohydrates 35g, Fat 7g Sodium 348 mg

375. Chinese-Style Asparagus

Preparation: 10 minutes   **Cooking: 15 minutes**   **Servings: 4**

Ingredients
- 1/2 tsp. sugar
- 1 1/2 pounds fresh asparagus, woody ends removed and cut into 1 1/2-inch length
- 1/2 cup water
- 1 tsp. reduced-sodium soy sauce

Directions
1. In a big saucepan, heat up the water, sugar, and soy sauce over high heat.
2. Cook to the boiling, then add the asparagus.
3. Reduce heat and simmer until asparagus is crisp and tender about 3-4 minutes.
4. Move to a serving plate and serve immediately.

Nutrition: Calories 24, Protein 2g, Carbohydrates 4g, Fat 0g Sodium 76 mg

376. Cilantro Brown Rice

Preparation: 45 minutes   **Servings: 4**

Ingredients
- 1 bunch cilantro leaves, washed
- 1 cup of brown rice
- 1 avocado, chopped
- Juice of 1 lime
- 2 scallions, coarsely chopped
- 1 clove garlic, crushed

- *1 tbsp. extra-virgin olive oil*
- *1/2 tsp. kosher salt*

Directions
1. In a portable pot, cook the brown rice according to the package instructions. When the rice is almost done, puree the cilantro, avocado, scallions, lime juice, garlic, and salt in a food processor.
2. Pour the olive oil through the feed tube and puree until smooth, 1 to 2 minutes. Drain when the rice is tender and return to the pot. Add the cilantro seasoning to the rice and stir to combine.

Nutrition: Calories 288Protein 5 g, Carbohydrates 42 g, Fat 12 g, Sodium 300 mg

377. Tomatoes Side Salad

Preparation: 10 minutes　　　　**Servings: 4**

Ingredients:
- *1/2 bunch mint, chopped*
- *8 plum tomatoes, sliced*
- *1 teaspoon mustard*
- *1 tablespoon rosemary vinegar*
- *A pinch of black pepper*

Directions:
1. In a bowl, mix vinegar with mustard and pepper and whisk.
2. In another bowl, combine the tomatoes with the mint and the vinaigrette, toss, divide between plates and serve as a side dish and enjoy!

Nutrition: Calories 70, Carbohydrates 6g, Protein 4g, Fat 2g, Sodium 67mg

378. Squash Salsa

Preparation: 10 minutes　　　**Cooking: 13 minutes**　　　**Servings: 6**

Ingredients:
- *3 tablespoons olive oil*
- *5 medium squashes, peeled and sliced*
- *1 cup pepitas, toasted*
- *7 tomatillos*
- *A pinch of black pepper*
- *1 small onion, chopped*
- *2 tablespoons fresh lime juice*
- *2 tablespoons cilantro, chopped*

Directions:
1. Heat up a pan over medium heat, add tomatillos, onion and black pepper, stir, cook for 3 minutes, transfer to your food processor and pulse.
2. Add lime juice and cilantro, pulse again and transfer to a bowl.
3. Heat up your kitchen grill over high heat, drizzle the oil over squash slices, grill them for 10 minutes, divide them between plates, add pepitas and tomatillos mix on top and serve as a side dish.

Nutrition: Calories 120, Fat 2g, Carbohydrates 7g, Protein 19g, Sodium 201mg

379. Apples and Fennel Mix

Preparation: 10 minutes　　　　**Servings: 3**

Ingredients:
- *3 big apples, cored and sliced*
- *1 and 1/2 cup fennel, shredded*
- *1/3 cup coconut cream*
- *3 tablespoons apple vinegar*
- *1/2 teaspoon caraway seeds*
- *Black pepper to the taste*

Directions:
1. In a bowl, mix fennel with apples and toss.
2. In another bowl, mix coconut cream with vinegar, black pepper and caraway seeds, whisk well, add over the fennel mix, toss, divide between plates and serve as a side dish.

Nutrition: Calories 130, Carbohydrates 10 g, Protein 3g, Fat 3g, Sodium 112mg

380. Simple Roasted Celery Mix

Preparation: 10 minutes   **Cooking: 25 minutes**   **Servings: 3**

Ingredients:

- 3 celery roots, cubed
- 2 tablespoons olive oil
- A pinch of black pepper
- 2 cups natural and unsweetened apple juice
- 1/4 cup parsley, chopped
- 1/4 cup walnuts, chopped

Directions:

1. In a baking dish, combine the celery with the oil, pepper, parsley, walnuts and apple juice, toss to coat, introduce in the oven at 450 degrees F, bake for 25 minutes, divide between plates and serve as a side dish.

Nutrition: Calories 140, Carbohydrates 7g, Protein 7g, Fat 2g, Sodium 92mg

381. Thyme Spring Onions

Preparation: 10 minutes   **Cooking: 40 minutes**   **Servings: 8**

Ingredients:

- 15 spring onions
- A pinch of black pepper
- 1 teaspoon thyme, chopped
- 1 tablespoon olive oil

Directions:

1. Put onions in a baking dish, add thyme, black pepper and oil, toss, bake in the oven at 350 degrees F for 40 minutes, divide between plates and serve as a side dish.

Nutrition: Calories 120, Carbohydrates 7g, Protein 2g, Fat 2g, Sodium 72mg

382. Carrot Slaw

Preparation: 10 minutes   **Cooking: 10 minutes**   **Servings: 4**

Ingredients:

- 1/4 yellow onion, chopped
- 5 carrots, cut into thin matchsticks
- 1 tablespoon olive oil
- 1 garlic clove, minced
- 1 tablespoon Dijon mustard
- 1 tablespoon red vinegar
- A pinch of black pepper
- 1 tablespoon lemon juice

Directions:

1. In a bowl, mix vinegar with black pepper, mustard and lemon juice and whisk.
2. Heat oil to the pot over medium heat, add onions, stir and cook for 5 minutes.
3. Add garlic and carrots, stir, cook for 5 minutes more, transfer to a salad bowl, cool down, add the vinaigrette, toss, divide between plates and serve as a side dish.

Nutrition: Calories 120, Carbohydrates 7g, Protein 5g, Fat 3g, Sodium 282mg

383. Watermelon Tomato Salsa

Preparation: 10 minutes   **Servings: 16**

Ingredients:

- 4 yellow tomatoes, seedless and chopped
- A pinch of black pepper
- 1 cup watermelon, seedless and chopped
- 1/3 cup red onion, chopped
- 2 jalapeno peppers, chopped
- 1/4 cup cilantro, chopped
- 3 tablespoons lime juice

Directions:

1. In a bowl, mix tomatoes with watermelon, onion and jalapeno.
2. Add cilantro, lime juice and pepper, toss, divide between plates and serve as a side dish.

Nutrition: Calories 87, Fat 1g, Carbohydrates 4g, Protein 7g Sodium: 112mg

384. Sprouts Side Salad

Preparation: 10 minutes   **Servings: 4**
Ingredients:

- 2 zucchinis, cut with a spiralizer
- 2 cups bean sprouts
- 4 green onions, chopped
- 1 red bell pepper, chopped
- Juice of 1 lime
- 1 tablespoon olive oil
- 1/2 cup cilantro, chopped
- 3/4 cup almonds, chopped
- Black pepper to the taste

Directions:

1. In a salad bowl, mix zucchinis with bean sprouts, onions and bell pepper.
2. Add black pepper, lime juice, almonds, cilantro and olive oil, toss everything, divide between plates and serve as a side dish and enjoy!

Nutrition: Calories 120g, fat 4g, fiber 2g, Carbohydrates 7g, protein 12   Sodium: 115mg

385. Cabbage Slaw

Preparation: 10 minutes   **Servings: 4**
Ingredients:

- 1 green cabbage head, shredded
- 1/3 cup coconut, shredded
- 1/4 cup olive oil
- 2 tablespoons lemon juice
- 1/4 cup coconut aminos
- 3 tablespoons sesame seeds
- 1/2 teaspoon curry powder
- 1/3 teaspoon turmeric powder
- 1/2 teaspoon cumin, ground

Directions:

1. In a bowl, mix cabbage with coconut and lemon juice and stir.
2. Add oil, aminos, sesame seeds, curry powder, turmeric and cumin, toss to coat and serve as a side dish and enjoy!

Nutrition: Calories 130, Fat 4g, Carbohydrates 8g, Protein 6g , Sodium: 206mg

386. Cauliflower Risotto

Preparation: 10 minutes   **Cooking: 7 minutes**   **Servings: 4**
Ingredients:

- 2 tablespoons olive oil
- 2 garlic cloves, minced
- 12 ounces cauliflower rice
- 2 tablespoons thyme, chopped
- 1 tablespoon lemon juice
- Zest of 1/2 lemon, grated
- A pinch of black pepper

Directions:

1. Heat oil pan over medium heat, add cauliflower rice and garlic, stir and cook for 5 minutes.
2. Add lemon juice, lemon zest, thyme, salt and pepper, stir, cook for 2 minutes more, divide between plates and serve as a side dish.

Nutrition: Calories 130, Carbohydrates6 g, Protein 8g, Fat 2g, Sodium 112mg

387. Three Beans Mix

Preparation: 10 minutes   **Servings: 4**
Ingredients:

- 15 ounces canned kidney beans, no-salt-added, drained and rinsed
- 15 ounces canned garbanzo beans, no-salt-added and drained
- 15 ounces canned pinto beans, no-salt-added and drained
- 3 tablespoons balsamic vinegar
- 2 tablespoons olive oil
- 2 teaspoon Italian seasoning
- 2 teaspoons garlic powder
- 1 teaspoon onion powder

Directions:
1. In a large salad bowl, combine the beans with vinegar, oil, seasoning, garlic powder and onion powder, toss, divide between plates and serve as a side dish. Enjoy!

Nutrition: Calories 140, Carbohydrates 10g, Protein 7g, Fat 1g, Sodium 78mg

388. Creamy Cucumber Mix

Preparation: 10 minutes   **Servings: 2**

Ingredients:
- 1 big cucumber, peeled and chopped
- 1 small red onion, chopped
- 4 tablespoons non-fat yogurt
- 1 teaspoon balsamic vinegar

Directions:
1. In a bowl, mix onion with cucumber, yogurt and vinegar, toss, divide between plates and serve as a side dish. Enjoy!

Nutrition: Calories 90, Carbohydrates 7g, Protein 5g, Fat 1g, Sodium 38mg

389. Bell Peppers Mix

Preparation: 10 minutes   **Cooking: 10 minutes**   **Servings: 2**

Ingredients:
- 1 tablespoon olive oil
- 2 teaspoons garlic powder
- 2 red bell peppers, chopped
- 2 yellow bell peppers, chopped
- 2 orange bell peppers, chopped
- Black pepper to the taste

Directions:
1. Heat the oil over medium heat, add all the bell peppers, stir and cook for 5 minutes.
2. Add garlic powder and black pepper, stir, cook for 5 minutes, divide between plates and serve as a side dish. Enjoy!

Nutrition: Calories 145, Carbohydrates 5g, Protein 8g, Fat g, Sodium 76mg

390. Spiced Broccoli Florets

Preparation: 10 minutes   **Cooking: 3 hours**   **Servings: 10**

Ingredients:
- 6 cups broccoli florets
- 1 and 1/2 cups low-fat cheddar cheese, shredded
- 1/2 teaspoon cider vinegar
- 1/4 cup yellow onion, chopped
- 10 ounces tomato sauce, sodium-free
- 2 tablespoons olive oil
- A pinch of black pepper

Directions:
1. Grease your slow cooker with the oil, add broccoli, tomato sauce, cider vinegar, onion and black pepper, cover and cook on High for 2 hours and 30 minutes.
2. Sprinkle the cheese all over, cover, cook on High for 30 minutes more, divide between plates and serve as a side dish.

Nutrition: Calories 119, Fat 8.7g, Carbohydrate 5.7g, Protein 6.2g, Sodium 272mg

391. Lima Beans Dish

Preparation: 10 minutes   **Cooking: 5 hours**   **Servings: 10**

Ingredients:
- 1 green bell pepper, chopped
- 1 sweet red pepper, chopped
- 1 and 1/2 cups tomato sauce, salt-free
- 1 yellow onion, chopped
- 1/2 cup water
- 16 ounces canned kidney beans, no-salt-added, drained and rinsed
- 16 ounces canned black-eyed peas, no-salt-added, drained and rinsed
- 15 ounces corn

- *15 ounces canned lima beans, no-salt-added, drained and rinsed*
- *15 ounces canned black beans, no-salt-added, drained and rinsed*
- *2 celery ribs, chopped*
- *2 bay leaves*
- *1 teaspoon ground mustard*
- *1 tablespoon cider vinegar*

Directions:
1. In your slow cooker, mix the tomato sauce with the onion, celery, red pepper, green bell pepper, water, bay leaves, mustard, vinegar, kidney beans, black-eyed peas, corn, lima beans and black beans, cover and cook on Low for 5 hours.
2. Discard bay leaves, divide the whole mix between plates and serve.

Nutrition: Calories 602, Fat 4.8g, , Carbohydrate 117.7g, Protein 33g, Sodium 255mg

392. Soy Sauce Green Beans

Preparation: 10 minutes   **Cooking: 2 hours**   **Servings: 12**
Ingredients:
- *3 tablespoons olive oil*
- *16 ounces green beans*
- *1/2 teaspoon garlic powder*
- *1/2 cup coconut sugar*
- *1 teaspoon low-sodium soy sauce*

Directions:
1. In your slow cooker, mix the green beans with the oil, sugar, soy sauce and garlic powder, cover and cook on Low for 2 hours.
2. Toss the beans, divide them between plates and serve as a side dish.

Nutrition: Calories 46, Fat 3.6g, Carbohydrate 3.6g, Protein 0.8g Sodium 290mg

393. Butter Corn

Preparation: 10 minutes   **Cooking: 4 hours**   **Servings: 12**
Ingredients:
- *20 ounces fat-free cream cheese*
- *10 cups corn*
- *1/2 cup low-fat butter*
- *1/2 cup fat-free milk*
- *A pinch of black pepper*
- *2 tablespoons green onions, chopped*

Directions:
1. In your slow cooker, mix the corn with cream cheese, milk, butter, black pepper and onions, toss, cover and cook on Low for 4 hours.
2. Toss one more time, divide between plates and serve as a side dish.

Nutrition: Calories 279, Fat 18g, Carbohydrate 26g, Protein 8.1g, Sodium 165mg

394. Lemon And Herb Couscous

Preparation: 5 minutes   **Cooking: 15 minutes**   **Serves 6**
Ingredients:
- *2 cups unsalted chicken stock*
- *1 1/2 cups whole wheat couscous*
- *1 tablespoon finely grated lemon zest*
- *2 tablespoons fresh lemon juice*
- *1/4 cup finely chopped fresh parsley*
- *1/4 cup finely chopped fresh basil*
- *1/4 cup slivered almonds*
- *2 tablespoons extra-virgin olive oil*
- *3 garlic cloves, minced*
- *1/3 cup coarsely chopped fresh chives*

Directions:
1. In a medium saucepan, bring the chicken stock to a boil over high heat. Remove from the heat, stir in the couscous, cover, and let sit for 5 minutes, or until all liquid is absorbed.
2. Stir in the lemon zest, lemon juice, parsley, basil, and almonds. Fluff and mix well with a fork. Set aside.
3. In a large skillet, heat the oil over medium heat. Add the garlic and chives and sauté for about 2 minutes. Add to the couscous mixture and combine well. Divide into 6 storage containers.

Nutrition: Calories 248, Carbohydrates 36g, Protein 9g, Fat 7g, Sodium 129mg

395. Roasted Carrots and Beets

Preparation: 10 minutes   **Cooking: 1 hour**   **Serves 4**
Ingredients:

- *Nonstick cooking spray*
- *8 medium carrots, peeled*
- *4 medium beets, peeled*
- *4 tablespoons extra-virgin olive oil, divided*
- *2 tablespoons balsamic vinegar, divided*
- *2 tablespoons chopped fresh parsley, divided*
- *1 teaspoon grated lemon zest*
- *1/8 teaspoon freshly ground black pepper*

Directions:

1. Preheat the oven to 375°F. Line a sheet pan with aluminum foil and coat with nonstick cooking spray.
2. Cut the carrots diagonally into 2-inch lengths on the thin end of the carrot and into 1-inch lengths on the thick end. Cut the beets into 1- to 2-inch cubes.
3. In a large bowl, whisk together 2 tablespoons of oil, 1 tablespoon of vinegar, and 1 tablespoon of parsley. Add the carrots and toss. Place the carrots on half of the prepared sheet pan. Add the remaining 2 tablespoons of oil, 1 tablespoon of vinegar, and 1 tablespoon of parsley to the bowl. Add the beets and toss. Place the beets on the other half of the prepared sheet pan. Sprinkle with the lemon zest and pepper.
4. Bake for about 1 hour, or until the beets turn a dark purple and the carrots a dull orange. They should be soft enough to cut through with a fork. Let cool, then divide into 4 storage containers.

Nutrition: Calories: 238; Fat: 18g; Carbohydrates: 21g; Protein: 2g; Sodium: 151mg

396. Zesty Lemon Brussels Sprouts

Preparation: 10 minutes   **Cooking: 40 minutes**   **Serves 4**
Ingredients:

- *Nonstick cooking spray*
- *1 pound Brussels sprouts, trimmed and halved*
- *2 tablespoons extra-virgin olive oil*
- *2 tablespoons grated lemon zest*
- *1/4 teaspoon freshly ground black pepper*

Direction:

1. Preheat the oven to 400°F. Coat a sheet pan with cooking spray.
2. In a large bowl, toss together the Brussels sprouts, oil, lemon zest, and pepper.
3. Arrange on the prepared sheet pan and roast for 35 to 40 minutes, or until caramelized, shaking the pan every 5 to 7 minutes to ensure they roast evenly. Let cool, then divide into 4 storage containers.

Nutrition: Calories: 162; Fat: 15g; Carbohydrates: 11g; Protein: 4g; Sodium: 29mg

397. Crisp And Sweet Quinoa

Preparation: 20 minutes   **Cooking: 20 minutes**   **Serves 5**
Ingredients:

- *1 cup quinoa*
- *2 cups water*
- *3 cups diced cucumber*
- *1 1/2 cups diced mango*
- *1/4 cup diced onion*
- *1/2 cup chopped fresh parsley*
- *1/2 teaspoon freshly ground black pepper*

Directions:

1. If your brand of quinoa has not been prerinsed and washed, place it in a fine-mesh sieve and rinse under cool water for 30 seconds.
2. In a medium saucepan, combine the quinoa and water and bring to a boil. Cover the pot, reduce the heat to a simmer, and cook for 15 to 20 minutes, or until the water has been absorbed and the grain is translucent and tender. If necessary, return to low heat and cook until all the water is absorbed. Let sit for 5 minutes and fluff with a fork.
3. Transfer to a large bowl and let cool for an additional 5 minutes.
4. Add the cucumber, mango, onion, parsley, and pepper. Divide into 5 storage containers.

Nutrition: Calories: 170; Fat: 3g; Carbohydrates: 32g; Protein: 6g; Sodium: 48mg

398. Cilantro Rice

Preparation: 5 minutes   **Cooking: 45 minutes**   **Serves 4**

Ingredients:

- 1 tablespoon extra-virgin olive oil
- 1 cup brown rice
- Zest and juice of 1 large lime
- 1 and 1/2 cups water
- 2 tablespoons chopped fresh cilantro

Directions:

1. In a medium pot, heat the oil over medium heat until warm. Add the rice and lime zest and cook, stirring occasionally, for 3 to 5 minutes, or until toasted.
2. Add the water and bring to a boil. Cover, reduce the heat to low, and simmer for about 45 minutes, or until the rice has absorbed all the water.
3. Stir in the lime juice and cilantro. Divide into 4 storage containers.

Nutrition: Calories: 202; Fat: 5g; Carbohydrates: 36g; Protein: 4g; Sodium: 33mg

399. Jasmine Rice with Lemongrass, Garlic, And Ginger

Preparation: 5 minutes   **Cooking: 25 to 30 minutes**   **Serves 4**

Ingredients:

- 2 teaspoons extra-virgin olive oil
- 1/2 lemongrass stalk, halved lengthwise and pounded
- 1-inch piece fresh ginger, peeled
- 1 garlic clove, minced
- 1 cup jasmine rice
- 1 cup water
- 1 scallion, thinly sliced (optional)

Directions:

1. In a small saucepan, heat the oil over medium heat. Add the lemongrass and ginger and cook for 1 minute. Toss in the garlic and cook for another minute.
2. Pour in the rice and water and bring to a boil. Reduce the heat to a simmer, cover, and cook for 25 to 30 minutes, or until all the water is absorbed and the rice is tender. Let rest for 5 minutes.
3. Fluff with a fork. Discard the lemongrass and ginger. Let cool, then divide into 4 storage containers. Top each with sliced scallion (if using).

Nutrition: Calories: 181; Fat: 2g; Carbohydrates: 36g; Protein: 3g; Sodium: 30mg

400. Mashed Sweet Potatoes

Preparation: 15 minutes   **Cooking: 25 minutes**   **Serves 4**

Ingredients:

- 6 medium sweet potatoes, peeled and cubed
- 2 tablespoons unsalted butter
- 1/4 cup nonfat plain Greek yogurt
- 1 teaspoon freshly ground black pepper
- 1/4 teaspoon salt
- 1/3 cup 1% milk
- 1/4 cup thinly sliced scallions
- 1/4 cup finely chopped fresh parsley
- 1 garlic clove, minced

Directions:

1. In a large saucepan, combine the sweet potatoes and enough water to cover them by 1 inch. Bring to a boil, then reduce the heat to a simmer and cook for 10 to 15 minutes, or until the sweet potatoes are tender.
2. Drain well and return the sweet potatoes to the saucepan. Add the butter, yogurt, pepper, and salt. With a hand mixer, a potato masher, or a fork, blend while slowly adding the milk, until the ingredients are mixed. Add the scallions, parsley, and garlic and mix until well combined. Let cool, then divide into 4 storage containers.

Nutrition: Calories: 242; Fat: 6g; Carbohydrates: 42g; Protein: 6g; Sodium: 271mg

401. Summer Rainbow Pasta Salad

Preparation: 10 minutes   **Cooking: 15 minutes**   **Serves 8**

Ingredients:

- *1 and 1/2 cups frozen peas*
- *8 ounces rainbow rotini pasta*
- *1/4 cup extra-virgin olive oil*
- *Zest and juice of 2 lemons*
- *1 garlic clove, minced*
- *1/2 cup grated Parmesan cheese*
- *1/4 cup chopped fresh mint*

Directions:

1. Bring a large pot of water to a boil. Add the peas and cook for about 3 minutes, or until tender. With a slotted spoon, transfer the peas to a large bowl and set aside.
2. Add the pasta to the boiling water and cook until al dente according to the package directions. Drain the pasta and let cool to room temperature.
3. Meanwhile, to the bowl of peas, add the oil, lemon zest, lemon juice, garlic, Parmesan cheese, and mint.
4. Add the pasta to the bowl and combine well. Divide into 8 storage containers.

Nutrition: Calories: 205; Fat: 9g; Carbohydrates: 26g; Fiber: 2g; Protein: 7g; Sodium: 116mg

402. Sweet Potatoes with Chopped Pistachios

Preparation: 10 minutes   **Cooking: 45 minutes**   **Serves 4**

Ingredients:

- *Nonstick cooking spray (optional)*
- *4 large sweet potatoes, peeled and cut into 1-inch cubes*
- *4 tablespoons extra-virgin olive oil, divided*
- *1/4 teaspoon freshly ground black pepper*
- *1/4 cup finely chopped pistachios*
- *1/2 teaspoon ground cumin*
- *1/2 teaspoon ground turmeric*
- *Pinch ground cinnamon*
- *Pinch red pepper flakes (optional)*
- *1 cup nonfat plain Greek yogurt*

Directions:

1. Preheat the oven to 375°F. Line a sheet pan with aluminum foil or coat with nonstick cooking spray.
2. In a large bowl, toss the sweet potatoes with 2 tablespoons of oil and the pepper. Spread onto the prepared sheet pan and roast for 30 to 35 minutes, or until crispy. Remove from the oven.
3. In a large skillet, heat the remaining 2 tablespoons of oil until warm. Add the pistachios, cumin, turmeric, cinnamon, and pepper flakes (if using) and stir until well combined. Add the roasted sweet potatoes, stir to coat, and remove from the heat.
4. Divide the sweet potato and pistachio mixture into 4 storage containers. Store the yogurt separately. When ready to serve, spread the yogurt out onto a serving platter. Top with the sweet potato and pistachio mixture.

Nutrition: Calories: 328; Fat: 17g; Carbohydrates: 34g; Protein: 10g; Sodium: 137mg

403. Stuffed Zucchini

Preparation: 10 minutes   **Cooking: 35 minutes**   **Serves 6**

Ingredients:

- *3 large zucchinis*
- *Nonstick cooking spray*
- *8 ounces ground chicken*
- *1 medium onion, diced*
- *2 garlic cloves, minced*
- *6 ounces mushrooms, coarsely chopped*
- *2 cups Simple Tomato Sauce or store-bought no-salt-added pasta sauce*
- *1 large tomato, diced*
- *1 medium red bell pepper, diced*
- *1 teaspoon dried oregano*
- *1/4 teaspoon salt*
- *1/2 teaspoon freshly ground black pepper*
- *3/4 cup shredded part-skim low-moisture mozzarella cheese*

Directions:
1. Preheat the oven to 375°F.
2. Halve the zucchini lengthwise and scoop out the seeds and some of the flesh to turn them into "boats" and make room for the stuffing. Place the zucchini, cut-side up, in a large baking dish.
3. Coat a large skillet with cooking spray and heat over medium-high heat. Add the chicken, onion, and garlic and cook and stir for 2 to 3 minutes. Add the mushrooms and continue to stir until the mushrooms have stopped releasing liquid and the chicken has browned.
4. Stir in the tomato sauce, diced tomato, bell pepper, oregano, salt, and black pepper. Reduce the heat to a simmer and cook for 5 to 8 minutes to thicken slightly and blend the flavors. Remove from the heat.
5. Distribute the mixture evenly among the zucchini boats. Top each zucchini boat with 2 tablespoons of mozzarella cheese.
6. Bake for 20 to 25 minutes, or until the zucchini has softened and the cheese is starting to brown. Let cool, then divide the zucchini boats among 6 storage containers.

Nutrition: Calories: 266; Fat: 7g; Carbohydrates: 21g; Protein: 15g; Sodium: 147mg

404. Pesto Mushrooms

Preparation: 5 Minutes   **Cooking: 20 minutes**   **Servings: 10**

Ingredients:
- *20 Cremini Mushrooms, Washed & Stemmed*

Toppings:
- *1 and 1/2 Cups Panko Breadcrumbs*
- *1/4 Cup Butter, Melted*
- *3 Tablespoons Parsley, Fresh & Chopped*

Filling:
- *2 Cups Basil Leaves, Fresh & Chopped*
- *1/4 Cup Parmesan Cheese, Grated Fresh*
- *2 Tablespoons Pumpkin Seeds*
- *1 Tablespoon Garlic, Fresh*
- *1 Tablespoon Olive Oil*
- *2 Teaspoons Lemon Juice, Fresh*
- *1/2 Teaspoon Sea Salt, Fine*

Directions:
1. Turn your oven to 350, and then arrange your mushrooms on a baking sheet with the caps up.
2. Prepare the topping by getting out a bowl and mixing your parsley, panko and butter.
3. Mix your pumpkin seeds, cheese, garlic, oil, basil, lemon juice and salt in a blender, blending until well combined.
4. Stuff the mushrooms with the basil paste before topping with the panko mixture.
5. Press this into the caps and bake for fifteen minutes. They should turn golden brown before serving warm.

Nutrition: Calories: 159 Protein: 2g Fat: 3g Carbohydrates: 4g Sodium: 363 mg

405. Lemon Green Beans with Almonds

Preparation: 10 Minutes   **Cooking: 20 minutes**   **Servings: 4**

Ingredients:
- *1/4 Cup Parmesan Cheese, Grated Fine*
- *1/4 Cup Almonds, Sliced*
- *1/4 Teaspoon Black Pepper*
- *1/8 Teaspoon Sea Salt, Fine*
- *1 Lemon, Juiced & Zested*
- *2 Tablespoons Olive Oil*
- *1 lb. Green Beans, Trimmed*

Directions:
1. Bring a pot of water to a boil and blanch your green beans for three minutes. Submerge them in a bowl of ice water for three minutes to stop the cooking and drain.
2. Heat your olive oil in a skillet using medium heat. Add in your green beans and sauté for five minutes or until browned lightly.
3. Add in your lemon juice and allow it to cook for two more minutes. Season with salt and pepper.

4.   Transfer it to a serving dish and top with lemon zest, parmesan, and almonds.
Nutrition: Calories: 162 Protein: 6g Fat: 11g Carbohydrates: 10g Sodium: 132 mg

406. Sweet & Savory Brussel Sprouts

Preparation: 10 Minutes   **Cooking: 20 minutes**   **Servings: 6**
Ingredients:

- 1/4 Cup Walnuts, Chopped
- 2 Tablespoons Olive Oil
- 2 lbs. Brussel Sprouts, Trimmed & Halved
- 1/4 Teaspoon Black Pepper
- 1/4 Teaspoon Sea Salt, Fine
- 1/8 Teaspoon Crushed Red Pepper Flakes
- 1 Tablespoon Maple Syrup, Pure
- 2 Tablespoons Dijon Mustard

Directions:

1. Heat a dry skillet over medium heat, and then toast your walnuts for two minutes. They should be lightly toasted, and then place them in a small bowl.
2. Heat your olive oil over a skillet over medium heat and add in the Brussel sprouts. Cook for ten minutes and stir occasionally. They should be browned and fork tender. Season with salt, pepper and red pepper.
3. Get out a bowl and whisk your Dijon mustard and maple syrup, and then pour in the pan. Stir until well combined and bring to a light simmer.
4. Transfer this to a dish and top with your toasted walnuts.

Nutrition: Calories: 151 Protein: 6g Fat: 8g Carbohydrates: 16g Sodium: 255 mg

407. Caramelized Sweet Potatoes

Preparation: 15 Minutes   **Cooking: 40 minutes**   **Servings: 4**
Ingredients:

- 2 Sweet potatoes, Cut into 1/2 Inch Wedges
- 2 Tablespoons Canola Oil
- 1/4 Teaspoon Black Pepper
- 1/4 Teaspoon Sea Salt, Fine

Directions:

1. Preheat your oven to 450, and then line a baking sheet with a with a wire rack. Spray your wire rack down with cooking spray.
2. Coat your sweet potatoes in oil before seasoning with salt and pepper, and then place them an inch apart on the rack. Bake for thirty to thirty-five minutes.
3. Turn the oven to a low broil, cooking for four minutes more. The edges should be browned. Serve warm.

Nutrition: Calories: 111 Protein: 1g Fat: 7g Carbohydrates: 12g Sodium: 166 mg

408. Vegetable & Polenta Dish

Preparation: 10 minutes   **Cooking: 50 minutes**   **Servings: 4**
Ingredients:

- 2 Tablespoons Parmesan Cheese, Grated
- 1 Cup Zucchini, Sliced
- 1 Cup Broccoli Florets, Chopped
- 1 Cup Onions, Sliced
- 1 Cup Mushrooms, Fresh & Sliced
- 1/2 Teaspoon Oregano, Fresh & Chopped
- 1 Teaspoon Basil, Fresh & Chopped
- 1/2 Teaspoon Rosemary, Fresh & Chopped
- 1 Cup Polenta, Ground Coarsely
- 4 Cups water
- 1 Teaspoon Garlic, Chopped

Directions:

1. Heat the oven to 350, and then grease a three-quart baking dish with cooking spray. Mix the polenta, garlic and water. Bake for forty minutes, and then heat a skillet that's been greased over medium heat.
2. Add in your mushrooms and onions, cooking for five minutes.
3. Boil the water in a pot and then add in the steamer basket.
4. Put your zucchini and broccoli in the basket, steaming for three minutes while covered.

5. Bake your polenta with the steamed vegetable, and garnish with cheese and herbs. Serve warm.
Nutrition: Calories: 178 Protein: 6g Fat: 1g Carbohydrates: 22g Sodium: 326 mg

409. Rosemary Potato Skins

Preparation: 10 Minutes   **Cooking: 1 hour 5 minutes**   **Servings: 2**
Ingredients:

- *2 Russet Potatoes*
- *Butter Flavored Cooking Spray*
- *1 Tablespoon Rosemary, Fresh & Minced*
- *1/8 Teaspoon Black Pepper*

Directions:
1. Heat your oven to 375, and then pierce your potatoes with a fork. Place them on a baking sheet and bake for an hour until crispy.
2. Allow them to cool and then cut them in half lengthwise.
3. Scoop the pulp out and leave 1/8 inch of a shell.
4. Brush the shells with melted butter and season with rosemary and pepper. Reserve the flesh for another recipe or time.
5. Bake for another five minutes before serving.

Nutrition: Calories: 167 Protein: 7.6g Fat: 1g Carbohydrates: 27g Sodium: 119 mg

410. Squash Fries

Preparation: 10 Minutes   **Cooking: 20 minutes**   **Servings: 4**
Ingredients:

- *1 Tablespoons Rosemary, Fresh & Chopped*
- *1 Tablespoon Thyme, Fresh & Chopped*
- *1 Tablespoon Olive Oil*
- *1 Butternut Squash*
- *1/2 Teaspoon Sea Salt, Fine*

Directions:
1. Turn the oven to 425 degrees, and then get out a baking sheet. Grease it.
2. Peel your squash and slice it into 1/2 inch wide and three-inch-long pieces.
3. Put the pieces in a bowl and toss with salt, thyme, oil and rosemary.
4. Spread your squash on the baking sheet, baking for ten minutes.
5. Toss, and bake for five minutes more. They should be golden brown.

Nutrition: Calories: 262 Protein: 11g   Fat: 7g Carbohydrates: 11g Sodium: 380 mg

411. Vegetable Kebabs

Preparation: 15 Minutes   **Cooking: 40 minutes**   **Servings: 2**
Ingredients:

- *1 Zucchini, Sliced into pieces*
- *1 Red Onion, Quartered*
- *1 Green bell Pepper, Cut into 4 Pieces*
- *8 Button Mushrooms*
- *8 Cherry Tomatoes*
- *1/2 Cup Italian Dressing, Fat Free*
- *1 Red Bell Pepper, Cut into 4 Pieces*
- *1/2 Cup Brown Rice*
- *1 Cup Water*

Directions:
1. Toss the zucchini, mushrooms, onion, peppers, and tomatoes with your Italian dressing in a bowl, allowing them to marinate for ten minutes. Make sure they're well coated.
2. Boil the water with rice in a saucepan, reducing it to simmer. Cook covered for a half hour or until your rice is done.
3. Prepare your grill by preheating it too medium.
4. Grease the grilling rack with cooking spray and position it four inches from heat.
5. Thread two tomatoes, two mushrooms, two zucchini slices, 1 onion wedge, one green pepper and one red pepper slice per skewer. Grill for five minutes per side and serve.

Nutrition: Calories: 335 Protein: 8.8g Fat: 8.2g Carbohydrates: 67g Sodium: 516 mg

412. Pistachio Mint Pesto Pasta

Preparation: 10 minutes   **Cooking: 10 minutes**   **Serves 4**

Ingredients:

- *8 ounces whole-wheat pasta*
- *1 cup fresh mint*
- *1/2 cup fresh basil*
- *1/3 cup unsalted pistachios, shelled*
- *1 garlic clove, peeled*
- *1/2 teaspoon kosher salt*
- *Juice of 1/2 lime*
- *1/3 cup extra-virgin olive oil*

Directions:

1. Cook the pasta according to the package directions. Drain, reserving 1/2 cup of the pasta water, and set aside.
2. In a food processor, add the mint, basil, pistachios, garlic, salt, and lime juice. Process until the pistachios are coarsely ground. Add the olive oil in a slow, steady stream and process until incorporated.
3. In a large bowl, mix the pasta with the pistachio pesto; toss well to incorporate. If a thinner, more saucy consistency is desired, add some of the reserved pasta water and combine

Nutrition: Calories 420, Carbohydrates 48g, Protein 11g, Fat 3g, Sodium 112mg

413. Burst Cherry Tomato Sauce with Angel Hair Pasta

Preparation: 10 minutes   **Cooking: 20 minutes**   **Serves 4**

Ingredients:

- *8 ounces angel hair pasta*
- *2 tablespoons extra-virgin olive oil*
- *3 garlic cloves, minced*
- *3 pints cherry tomatoes*
- *1/2 teaspoon kosher salt*
- *1/4 teaspoon red pepper flakes*
- *3/4 cup fresh basil, chopped*
- *1 tablespoon white balsamic vinegar (optional)*
- *1/4 cup grated Vegan Parmesan cheese (optional)*

Directions:

1. Cook the pasta according to the package directions. Drain and set aside.
2. Heat the olive oil in a skillet or large sauté pan over medium-high heat. Add the garlic and sauté for 30 seconds. Add the tomatoes, salt, and red pepper flakes and cook, stirring occasionally, until the tomatoes burst, about 15 minutes.
3. Remove from the heat and add the pasta and basil. Toss together well. (For out-of-season tomatoes, add the vinegar, if desired)
4. Serve with the grated Parmesan cheese, if desired.

Nutrition Calories: 305; Fat:8g; Carbohydrates: 53g; Protein: 11g; Sodium: 102mg

414. Balsamic Marinated Tofu with Basil and Oregano

Preparation: 30 minutes   **Cooking: 30 minutes**   **Serves 4**

Ingredients:

- *1/4 cup extra-virgin olive oil*
- *1/4 cup balsamic vinegar*
- *2 tablespoons low-sodium soy sauce or gluten-free tamari*
- *3 garlic cloves, grated*
- *2 teaspoons pure maple syrup*
- *Zest of 1 lemon*
- *1 teaspoon dried basil*
- *1 teaspoon dried oregano*
- *1/2 teaspoon dried thyme*
- *1/2 teaspoon dried sage*
- *1/4 teaspoon kosher salt*
- *1/4 teaspoon freshly ground black pepper*
- *1/4 teaspoon red pepper flakes (optional)*
- *1 (16-ounce) block extra firm tofu, drained and patted dry, cut into 1/2-inch or 1-inch cubes*

Directions:
1. 1 In a bowl or gallon zip-top bag, mix together the olive oil, vinegar, soy sauce, garlic, maple syrup, lemon zest, basil, oregano, thyme, sage, salt, black pepper, and red pepper flakes, if desired. Add the tofu and mix gently. Put in the refrigerator and marinate for 30 minutes, or up to overnight if you desire.
2. 2 Preheat the oven to 425°F. Line a baking sheet with parchment paper or foil. Arrange the marinated tofu in a single layer on the prepared baking sheet. Bake for 20 to 30 minutes, turning over halfway through, until slightly crispy on the outside and tender on the inside.

Nutrition Calories: 225; Fat: 16g; Carbohydrates: 9g; Protein: 13g; Sodium: 92mg

415. Vegan Cheese, Basil, and Pistachio–Stuffed Zucchini

Preparation: 15 minutes   **Cooking: 25 minutes**   **Serves 4**

Ingredients:

- *2 medium zucchinis, halved lengthwise*
- *1 tablespoon extra-virgin olive oil*
- *1 onion, diced*
- *1 teaspoon kosher salt*
- *2 garlic cloves, minced*

- *3/4 cup Vegan cheese*
- *1/4 cup unsalted pistachios, shelled and chopped*
- *1/4 cup fresh basil, chopped*
- *1/4 teaspoon freshly ground black pepper*

Directions:
1. 1 Preheat the oven to 425°F. Line a baking sheet with parchment paper or foil.
2. 2 Scoop out the seeds/pulp from the zucchini, leaving 1/4-inch flesh around the edges. Transfer the pulp to a cutting board and chop the pulp.
3. 3 Heat the olive oil in a large skillet or sauté pan over medium heat. Add the onion, pulp, and salt and sauté about 5 minutes. Add the garlic and sauté 30 seconds.
4. 4 In a medium bowl, combine the vegan cheese, pistachios, basil, and black pepper. Add the onion mixture and mix well.
5. 5 Place the 4 zucchini halves on the prepared baking sheet. Fill the zucchini halves with the ricotta mixture. Bake for 20 minutes, or until golden brown.

Nutrition Calories: 200; Fat: 12g; Carbohydrates: 14g; Protein: 11g; Sodium: 102mg

416. Baked Orzo with Eggplant, Swiss Chard, and Vegan Mozzarella

Preparation: 20 minutes   **Cooking: 1 hour**   **Servings: 4**

Ingredients:

- *2 tablespoons extra-virgin olive oil*
- *1 large (1-pound) eggplant, diced small*
- *2 carrots, peeled and diced small*
- *2 celery stalks, diced small*
- *1 onion, diced small*
- *1 teaspoon no-salt-added tomato paste*
- *1 1/2 cups no-salt-added vegetable stock*
- *1 cup Swiss chard, stemmed and chopped small*
- *2 tablespoons fresh oregano, chopped*

- *1/2 teaspoon kosher salt*
- *3 garlic cloves, minced*
- *1/4 teaspoon freshly ground black pepper*
- *1 cup whole-wheat orzo*
- *Zest of 1 lemon*
- *4 ounces Vegan mozzarella cheese, diced small*
- *1/4 cup grated Vegan Parmesan cheese*
- *2 tomatoes, sliced 1/2-inch-thick*

Directions:
1. 1 Preheat the oven to 400°F.
2. 2 Heat the olive oil in a large oven-safe sauté pan over medium heat. Add the eggplant, carrots, celery, onion, and salt and sauté about 10 minutes. Add the garlic and black pepper and sauté about 30 seconds. Add the orzo and tomato paste and sauté 1 minute. Add the vegetable stock and deglaze the pan, scraping up the brown bits. Add the Swiss chard, oregano, and lemon zest and stir until the chard wilts.

3. 3 Remove from the heat and mix in the mozzarella cheese. Smooth the top of the orzo mixture flat. Sprinkle the Parmesan cheese over the top. Arrange the tomatoes in a single layer on top of the Parmesan cheese. Bake for 45 minutes.

Nutrition Calories: 470; Fat: 17g;; Carbohydrates: 65g; Protein: 18g; Sodium: 272mg

417. Barley Risotto with Tomatoes

Preparation: 20 minutes   **Cooking: 45 minutes**   **Serves 4**
Ingredients:

- *2 tablespoons extra-virgin olive oil*
- *2 celery stalks, diced*
- *1/2 cup shallots, diced*
- *4 garlic cloves, minced*
- *3 cups no-salt-added vegetable stock*
- *1 (14-ounce) can no-salt-added diced tomatoes*
- *1 (14-ounce) can no-salt-added crushed tomatoes*
- *1 cup pearl barley*
- *Zest of 1 lemon*

- *1 teaspoon kosher salt*
- *1/2 teaspoon smoked paprika*
- *1/4 teaspoon red pepper flakes*
- *1/4 teaspoon freshly ground black pepper*
- *4 thyme sprigs*
- *1 dried bay leaf*
- *2 cups baby spinach*
- *1/2 cup crumbled vegan cheese*
- *1 tablespoon fresh oregano, chopped*
- *1 tablespoon fennel seeds, toasted (optional)*

Directions:

1. 1 Heat the olive oil in a large saucepan over medium heat. Add the celery and shallots and sauté, about 4 to 5 minutes. Add the garlic and sauté 30 seconds. Add the vegetable stock, diced tomatoes, crushed tomatoes, barley, lemon zest, salt, paprika, red pepper flakes, black pepper, thyme, and the bay leaf, and mix well. Bring to a boil, then lower to low, and simmer. Cook, stirring occasionally, for 40 minutes.
2. 2 Remove the bay leaf and thyme sprigs. Stir in the spinach.
3. 3 In a small bowl, combine the cheese, oregano, and fennel seeds. Serve the barley risotto in bowls topped with the feta mixture.

Nutrition Calories: 375; Fat: 12g; Carbohydrates: 57g; Protein: 11g Sodium: 102mg

418. Roasted Feta with Kale and Lemon Yogurt

Preparation: 15 minutes   **Cooking: 20 minutes**   **Serves 4**
Ingredients:

- *1 tablespoon extra-virgin olive oil*
- *1 onion, julienned*
- *1/4 teaspoon kosher salt*
- *1 teaspoon ground turmeric*
- *1/2 teaspoon ground cumin*
- *1/2 teaspoon ground coriander*

- *1/4 teaspoon freshly ground black pepper*
- *1 bunch kale, stemmed and chopped*
- *7-ounce block vegan cheese, cut into 1/4-inch-thick slices*
- *1/2 cup plain vegan yogurt*
- *1 tablespoon lemon juice*

Directions:

1. Preheat the oven to 400°F.
2. Heat the olive oil in a large ovenproof skillet or sauté pan over medium heat. Add the onion and salt; sauté until lightly golden brown, about 5 minutes. Add the turmeric, cumin, coriander, and black pepper; sauté for 30 seconds. Add the kale and sauté about 2 minutes. Add 1/2 cup water and continue to cook down the kale, about 3 minutes.
3. Remove from the heat and place the feta cheese slices on top of the kale mixture. Place in the oven and bake until the vegan cheese softens, 10 to 12 minutes.
4. In a small bowl, combine the vegan yogurt and lemon juice.
5. Serve the kale and feta cheese topped with the lemon yogurt.

Nutrition: Calories: 210; Fat: 14g; Carbohydrates: 11g Protein: 11g Sodium: 112mg

419. <u>Roasted Eggplant and Chickpeas with Tomato Sauce</u>

Preparation: 15 minutes   **Cooking: 1 hour**   **Serves 4**
Ingredients:

- *Olive oil cooking spray*
- *1 large (about 1 pound) eggplant, sliced into 1/4-inch-thick rounds*
- *1 teaspoon kosher salt, divided*
- *1 tablespoon extra-virgin olive oil*
- *3 garlic cloves, minced*
- *1 (28-ounce) can no-salt-added crushed tomatoes*
- *1/2 teaspoon honey*
- *1/4 teaspoon freshly ground black pepper*
- *2 tablespoons fresh basil, chopped*
- *1 (15-ounce) can no-salt-added or low-sodium chickpeas, drained and rinsed*
- *3/4 cup crumbled vegan cheese*
- *1 tablespoon fresh oregano, chopped*

Directions:
1. Preheat the oven to 425°F. Line two baking sheets with foil and lightly spray with olive oil cooking spray. Arrange the eggplant in a single layer and sprinkle with 1/2 teaspoon of the salt. Bake for 20 minutes, turning once halfway, until lightly golden brown.
2. Meanwhile, heat the olive oil in a large saucepan over medium heat. Add the garlic and sauté for 30 seconds. Add the crushed tomatoes, honey, the remaining 1/2 teaspoon salt, and black pepper. Simmer about 20 minutes, until the sauce reduces a bit and thickens. Stir in the basil.
3. After removing the eggplant from the oven, reduce the oven temperature to 375°F. In a large rectangular or oval baking dish, ladle in the chickpeas and 1 cup sauce. Layer the eggplant slices on top, overlapping as necessary to cover the chickpeas. Spread the remaining sauce on top of the eggplant. Sprinkle the vegan cheese and oregano on top.
4. Cover the baking dish with foil and bake for 15 minutes. Remove the foil and bake an additional 15 minutes.

Nutrition Calories: 320; Fat: 11g; Carbohydrates: 40g; Protein: 14g Sodium: 102mg

420. <u>Baked Falafel Sliders</u>

Preparation: 10 minutes   **Cooking: 30 minutes**   **Makes 6 sliders**

Ingredients:

- Olive oil cooking spray
- 1 (15-ounce) can no-salt-added or low-sodium chickpeas, drained and rinsed
- 1 onion, roughly chopped
- 2 garlic cloves, peeled
- 2 tablespoons fresh parsley, chopped
- 2 tablespoons whole-wheat flour
- 1/2 teaspoon ground coriander
- 1/2 teaspoon ground cumin
- 1/2 teaspoon baking powder
- 1/2 teaspoon kosher salt
- 1/4 teaspoon freshly ground black pepper

Direction:
1. Preheat the oven to 350°F. Line a baking sheet with parchment paper or foil and lightly spray with olive oil cooking spray.
2. In a food processor, add the chickpeas, onion, garlic, parsley, flour, coriander, cumin, baking powder, salt, and black pepper. Process until smooth, stopping to scrape down the sides of the bowl.
3. Make 6 slider patties, each with a heaping 1/4 cup of mixture, and arrange on the prepared baking sheet. Bake for 30 minutes, turning over halfway through.

Nutrition: Calories: 90; Fat: 1g; Carbohydrates: 17g; Protein: 4g Sodium: 278mg

421. <u>Moroccan-Inspired Tagine with Chickpeas & Vegetables</u>

Preparation: 15 minutes   **Cooking: 45 minutes**   **Servings: 3**
Ingredients:

- *2 teaspoons olive oil*
- *1 cup chopped carrots*
- *1/2 cup finely chopped onion*
- *1 sweet potato, diced*
- *1 cup low-sodium vegetable broth*
- *1/4 teaspoon ground cinnamon*

- *1/8 teaspoon salt*
- *1 1/2 cups chopped bell peppers, any color*
- *3 ripe plum tomatoes, chopped*
- *1 tablespoon tomato paste*
- *1 garlic clove, pressed or minced*
- *1 (15-oz.) can chickpeas, drained and rinsed*
- *1/2 cup chopped dried apricots*
- *1 teaspoon curry powder*
- *1/2 teaspoon paprika*
- *1/2 teaspoon turmeric*

Directions:

1. Warm-up oil over medium heat in a large Dutch oven or saucepan. Add the carrots and onion and cook until the onion is translucent about 4 minutes. Add the sweet potato, broth, cinnamon, and salt and cook for 5 to 6 minutes until the broth is slightly reduced.
2. Add the peppers, tomatoes, tomato paste, and garlic. Stir and cook for another 5 minutes. Add the chickpeas, apricots, curry powder, paprika, and turmeric to the pot. Bring all to a boil, then reduce the heat to low, cover, simmer for about 30 minutes, and serve.

Nutrition: Calories: 469 Fat: 9g Carbohydrates: 88g Protein: 16g Sodium: 256 mg

422. Stuffed Tex-Mex Baked Potatoes

Preparation: 15 minutes   **Cooking: 45 minutes**   **Servings: 2**

Ingredients:

- *2 large Idaho potatoes*
- *1/2 cup black beans, rinsed and drained*
- *1/4 cup store-bought salsa*
- *1 avocado, diced*
- *1 teaspoon freshly squeezed lime juice*
- *1/2 cup vegan Greek yogurt*
- *1/4 teaspoon reduced sodium: taco seasoning*

Directions:

1. Preheat the oven to 400° F. Scrub the potatoes, then slice an "X" into the top of each using a paring knife. Put the potatoes on the oven rack, then bake for 45 minutes until they are tender.
2. In a small bowl, stir the beans and salsa and set aside. In another small bowl, mix the avocado and lime juice and set aside. In a third small bowl, stir the yogurt and the taco seasoning until well blended.
3. When the potatoes are baked, carefully open them up. Top each potato with the bean and salsa mixture, avocado, seasoned yogurt, evenly dividing each component, and serve.

Nutrition: Calories: 624 Fat: 21 g Carbohydrates: 91g Protein: 24 g Sodium 204mg

423. Baked Eggplant Parmesan

Preparation: 15 minutes   **Cooking: 35 minutes**   **Servings: 4**

Ingredients:

- *1 small to medium eggplant, cut into 1/4-inch slices*
- *1/2 teaspoon salt-free Italian seasoning blend*
- *1 tablespoon olive oil*
- *1/4 cup diced onion*
- *1/2 cup diced yellow or red bell pepper*
- *2 garlic cloves, pressed or minced*
- *1 (8-oz.) can tomato sauce*
- *3 oz. fresh mozzarella, cut into 6 pieces*
- *5 to 6 fresh basil leaves, chopped*

Directions:

1. Preheat an oven-style air fryer to 400° F.
2. Working in two batches, place the eggplant slices onto the air-fryer tray and sprinkle them with Italian seasoning. Bake for 7 minutes. Repeat with the remaining slices, then set them aside on a plate.
3. In a medium skillet, heat the oil over medium heat and sauté the onion and peppers until softened for about 5 minutes. Add the garlic and sauté for 1 to 2 more minutes. Add the tomato sauce and stir to combine. Remove the sauce from the heat.
4. Spray a 9-by-6-inch casserole dish with cooking spray. Spread one-third of the sauce into the bottom of the dish. Layer eggplant slices onto the sauce.

5. Continue layering the sauce and eggplant, ending with the sauce. Place the mozzarella pieces on the top. Sprinkle the remaining Parmesan evenly over the entire dish. Bake in the oven for 20 minutes. Garnish with fresh basil, cut into four servings, and serve.

Nutrition: Calories: 196 Fat: 12 g Carbohydrates: 20 g Protein: 10 g Sodium: 222 mg

424. Vegetable Red Curry

Preparation: 15 minutes   **Cooking: 25 minutes**   **Servings: 2**

Ingredients:

- *2 teaspoons olive oil*
- *1 cup sliced carrots*
- *1/2 cup chopped onion*
- *1 garlic clove, pressed or minced*
- *2 bell peppers, seeded and thinly sliced*
- *1 cup chopped cauliflower*
- *2/3 cup light coconut milk*
- *1/2 cup low-Sodium: vegetable broth*

- *1 tablespoon tomato paste*
- *1 teaspoon curry powder*
- *1/2 teaspoon ground cumin*
- *1/2 teaspoon ground coriander*
- *1/4 teaspoon turmeric*
- *2 cups fresh baby spinach*
- *1 cup quick-cooking brown rice*

Directions:

1. Heat-up oil in a large nonstick skillet over medium heat. Add the carrots, onion, and garlic and cook for 2 to 3 minutes. Reduce the heat to medium-low, add the peppers and cauliflower to the skillet, cover, and cook within 5 minutes.
2. Add the coconut milk, broth, tomato paste, curry powder, cumin, coriander, and turmeric, stirring to combine. Simmer, cover (vent the lid slightly) for 10 to 15 minutes until the curry is slightly reduced and thickened.
3. Uncover, add the spinach, and stir for 2 minutes until it is wilted and mixed into the vegetables. Remove from the heat. Cook the rice as stated in the package instructions. Serve the curry over the rice.

Nutrition: Calories: 584 kcal Fat: 16 g Carbohydrates: 101 g Protein: 13g Sodium: 102 mg

425. Black Bean Burgers

Preparation: 15 minutes   **Cooking: 20 minutes**   **Servings: 4**

Ingredients:

- *1/2 cup quick-cooking brown rice*
- *2 teaspoons canola oil, divided*
- *1/2 cup finely chopped carrots*
- *1/4 cup finely chopped onion*

- *1 can black beans, drained*
- *1 tablespoon salt-free mesquite seasoning blend*
- *4 small, hard rolls*

Directions:

1. Cook the rice as stated in the package directions and set aside. Heat-up 1 teaspoon of oil in a large nonstick skillet over medium heat. Add the carrots and onions and cook until the onions are translucent about 4 minutes. Adjust the heat to low, and cook again for 5 to 6 minutes, until the carrots are tender.
2. Add the beans and seasoning to the skillet and continue cooking for 2 to 3 more minutes. Blend the bean mixture in a food processor within 3 to 4 times or until the mixture is coarsely blended.
3. Put the batter in a medium bowl and fold in the brown rice until well combined.
4. Divide the mixture evenly and form it into 4 patties with your hands. Heat the remaining oil in the skillet. Cook the patties within 4 to 5 minutes per side, turning once.
5. Serve the burgers on the rolls with your choice of toppings.

Nutrition: Calories: 368 kcal Fat: 6 g Carbohydrates: 66 g Protein: 13g Sodium: 322 mg Potassium: 413 mg

426. Summer Barley Pilaf with Yogurt Dill Sauce

Preparation: 15 minutes   **Cooking: 30 minutes**   **Servings: 3**

Ingredients:

- *2 2/3 cups low-Sodium: vegetable broth*
- *2 teaspoons avocado oil*
- *1 small zucchini, diced*
- *1/3 cup slivered almonds*
- *2 scallions, sliced*
- *1 cup barley*
- *1/2 cup vegan Greek yogurt*
- *2 teaspoons grated lemon zest*
- *1/4 teaspoon dried dill*

Directions:

1. Boil the broth in a large saucepan. Heat-up the oil in a skillet. Add the zucchini and sauté for 3 to 4 minutes. Add the almonds and the white parts of the scallions and sauté for 2 minutes. Remove, and transfer it to a small bowl.
2. Add the barley to the skillet and sauté for 2 to 3 minutes to toast. Transfer the barley to the boiling broth and reduce the heat to low, cover, and simmer for 25 minutes or until tender.
3. Remove, and let stand within 10 minutes or until the liquid is absorbed.
4. Simultaneously, mix the yogurt, lemon zest, and dill in a small bowl and set aside. Fluff the barley with a fork. Add the zucchini, almond, and onion mixture and mix gently
5. To serve, divide the pilaf between two bowls and drizzle the yogurt over each bowl.

Nutrition: Calories: 345 Fat: 15g Carbohydrates: 87g Protein: 21g Sodium: 237 mg

427. Brown Rice Casserole

Preparation: 15 minutes   **Cooking: 45 minutes**   **Servings: 3**

Ingredients:

- *Nonstick cooking spray*
- *1 cup quick-cooking brown rice*
- *1 teaspoon olive oil*
- *1/2 cup diced sweet onion*
- *1 (10-oz.) bag fresh spinach*
- *1/4 cup sunflower seed kernels*

Directions:

1. Preheat the oven to 375° F. Spray a small 11/2-quart casserole dish with cooking spray. Cook the rice, as stated in the package directions. Set aside.
2. Warm-up oil in a large nonstick skillet over medium-low heat. Add the onion and sauté for 3 to 4 minutes. Add the spinach and cover the skillet, cooking for 1 to 2 minutes until the spinach wilts. Remove the skillet from the heat.
3. In a medium bowl, mix the rice and spinach mixture. Transfer the mixture to the prepared casserole dish. Top with the sunflower seeds, bake for 25 minutes until lightly browned, and serve.

Nutrition: Calories: 334 Fat: 9g Carbohydrates: 47g Protein: 19 g Sodium: 425 mg

428. Greek Flatbread with Spinach, Tomatoes & Feta

Preparation: 15 minutes   **Cooking: 9 minutes**   **Servings: 2**

Ingredients:

- *2 cups fresh baby spinach, coarsely chopped*
- *2 teaspoons olive oil*
- *2 slices Naan, or another flatbread*
- 1/4 cup sliced black olives
- 2 plum tomatoes, thinly sliced
- 1 teaspoon salt-free Italian seasoning blend
- 1/4 cup crumbled feta

Directions:

1. Preheat the oven to 400° F. Heat 3 tablespoons of water in a small skillet over medium heat. Add the spinach, cover, and steam until wilted, about 2 minutes. Drain off any excess water, then put it aside.
2. Drizzle the oil evenly onto both flatbreads. Top each evenly with the spinach, olives, tomatoes, seasoning, and feta. Bake the flatbreads within 5 to 7 minutes, or until lightly browned.
3. Cut each into four pieces and serve hot.

Nutrition: Calories: 411 Fat: 15 g Carbohydrates: 53g Protein: 15 g Sodium: 321 mg

429. Vegan Meatloaf

Preparation: 10 minutes   **Cooking: 30 minutes**   **Servings: 2**

Ingredients:

- 1 cup chickpeas, cooked
- 1 onion, diced
- 1 tablespoon ground flax seeds
- 1/2 teaspoon chili flakes
- 1 tablespoon coconut oil
- 1/2 cup carrot, diced
- 1/2 cup celery stalk, chopped
- 1 tablespoon tomato paste

Directions:

1. Heat up coconut oil in the saucepan.
2. Add carrot, onion, and celery stalk. Cook the vegetables for 8 minutes or until they are soft.
3. Then add chickpeas, chili flakes, and ground flax seeds.
4. Blend the mixture until smooth with the help of the immersion blender.
5. Then line the loaf mold with baking paper and transfer the blended mixture inside.
6. Flatten it well and spread with tomato paste.
7. Bake the meatloaf in the preheated to 365F oven for 20 minutes.

Nutrition: Calories 162, Carbohydrates 5g, Protein 24g, Fat 7g, Sodium 125mg

430. Loaded Potato Skins

Preparation: 15 minutes   **Cooking: 45 minutes**   **Servings: 2**

Ingredients:

- 6 potatoes
- 1 teaspoon ground black pepper
- 2 tablespoons olive oil
- 1/2 teaspoon minced garlic
- 1/4 cup of soy milk

Directions:

1. Preheat the oven to 400F.
2. Pierce the potatoes with the help of the knife 2-3 times and bake in the oven for 30 minutes or until the vegetables are tender.
3. After this, cut the baked potatoes into halves and scoop out the potato meat in the bowl.
4. Sprinkle the scooped potato halves with olive oil and ground black pepper and return them back to the oven. Bake them for 15 minutes or until they are light brown.
5. Meanwhile, mash the scooped potato meat and mix it up with soy milk and minced garlic.
6. Fill the cooked potato halves with the mashed potato mixture.

Nutrition: Calories 194, Carbohydrates 5g, Protein 34g, Fat 5g, Sodium 118mg

431. Vegan Shepherd Pie

Preparation: 15 minutes   **Cooking: 35 minutes**   **Servings: 2**

Ingredients:

- 1/2 cup quinoa, cooked
- 1/2 cup tomato puree
- 1/2 cup carrot, diced
- 1 shallot, chopped
- 1 tablespoon coconut oil
- 1/2 cup potato, cooked, mashed
- 1 teaspoon chili powder
- 1/2 cup mushrooms, sliced

Directions:

1. Put carrot, shallot, and mushrooms in the saucepan.
2. Add coconut oil and cook the vegetables for 10 minutes or until they are tender but not soft.
3. Then mix up cooked vegetables with chili powder and tomato puree.
4. Transfer the mixture to the casserole mold and flatten well.
5. After this, top the vegetables with mashed potatoes. Cover the shepherd pie with foil and bake in the preheated to 375F oven for 25 minutes.

Nutrition: Calories 136, Carbohydrates 5g, Protein 20g, Fat 3g, Sodium 127mg

432. Cauliflower Steaks

Preparation: 15 minutes   **Cooking: 25 minutes**   **Servings: 2**

Ingredients:

- *1-pound cauliflower head*
- *1 teaspoon ground turmeric*
- *1/2 teaspoon cayenne pepper*
- *2 tablespoons olive oil*
- *1/2 teaspoon garlic powder*

Directions:

1. Slice the cauliflower head into the steaks and rub with ground turmeric, cayenne pepper, and garlic powder.
2. Then line the baking tray with baking paper and put the cauliflower steaks inside.
3. Sprinkle them with olive oil and bake at 375F for 25 minutes or until the vegetable steaks are tender.

Nutrition:92 calories 2.4g protein 6.8g carbohydrates 7.2g fat 3.1g fiber 0mg cholesterol 34mg sodium

433. Quinoa Burger

Preparation: 15 minutes   **Cooking: 20 minutes**   **Servings: 2**

Ingredients:

- *1/3 cup chickpeas, cooked*
- *1/2 cup quinoa, cooked*
- *1 teaspoon Italian seasonings*
- *1 teaspoon olive oil*
- *1/2 onion, minced*

Directions:

1. Blend the chickpeas until they are smooth.
2. Then mix them up with quinoa, Italian seasonings, and minced onion. Stir the ingredients until homogenous.
3. After this, make the burgers from the mixture and place them in the lined baking tray.
4. Sprinkle the quinoa burgers with olive oil and bake them at 275F for 20 minutes.

Nutrition: Calories 158, Carbohydrates 4g, Protein 6g, Fat 5g, Sodium 51mg

434. Cauliflower Tots

Preparation: 15 minutes   **Cooking: 20 minutes**   **Servings: 1**

Ingredients:

- *1 cup cauliflower, shredded*
- *3 oz vegan Parmesan, grated*
- *1/3 cup flax seeds meal*
- *1 teaspoon Italian seasonings*
- *1 teaspoon olive oil*

Directions:

1. In the bowl mix up shredded cauliflower, vegan Parmesan, flax seeds, and Italian seasonings.
2. Knead the cauliflower mixture. Add water if needed.
3. After this, make the cauliflower tots from the mixture.
4. Line the baking tray with baking paper and place the cauliflower tots inside.
5. Sprinkle them with the olive oil and transfer in the preheated to 375F oven.
6. Bake the meal for 15-20 minutes or until golden brown.

Nutrition: Calories 109, Carbohydrates 7g, Protein 6g, Fat 4g, Sodium 72mg

435. Zucchini Soufflé

Preparation: 10 minutes   **Cooking: 60 minutes**   **Servings: 2**

Ingredients:

- *2 cups zucchini, grated*
- *1/2 teaspoon baking powder*
- *1/2 cup oatmeal, grinded*
- *1 onion, diced*
- *3 tablespoons water*
- *1 teaspoon cayenne pepper*
- *1 teaspoon dried thyme*

Directions:
1. Mix up all ingredients together in the casserole mold.
2. Flatten well the zucchini mixture and cover with foil.
3. Bake the soufflé at 365F for 60 minutes.

Nutrition: Calories 41, Carbohydrates 16g, Protein 10g, Fat 4g, Sodium 66mg

436. Honey Sweet Potato Bake

Preparation: 20 minutes   **Cooking: 20 minutes**   **Servings: 2**

Ingredients:
- *4 sweet potatoes, baked*
- *1 tablespoon honey*
- *1 teaspoon ground cinnamon*
- *1/4 teaspoon ground cardamom*
- *1/3 cup soy milk*

Directions:
1. Peel the sweet potatoes and mash them.
2. Then mix mashed potato with ground cinnamon, cardamom, and soy milk. Stir it well.
3. Transfer the mixture to the baking pan and flatten well.
4. Sprinkle the mixture with honey and cover with foil.
5. Bake the meal at 375F for 20 minutes.

Nutrition:30 calories 0.7g protein 61/2g carbohydrates 0.4g fat 01/2g fiber 0mg cholesterol 11mg sodium

437. Lentil Quiche

Preparation: 15 minutes   **Cooking: 35 minutes**   **Servings: 2**

Ingredients:
- *1 cup green lentils, boiled*
- *1/2 cup carrot, grated*
- *1 onion, diced*
- *1 tablespoon olive oil*
- *1/4 cup flax seeds meal*
- *1 teaspoon ground black pepper*
- *1/4 cup of soy milk*

Directions:
1. Cook the onion with olive oil in the skillet until light brown.
2. Then mix up cooked onion, lentils, and carrot.
3. Add flax seeds meal, ground black pepper, and soy milk. Stir the mixture until homogenous.
4. After this, transfer it to the baking pan and flatten it.
5. Bake the quiche for 35 minutes at 375F.

Nutrition: Calories 351, Carbohydrates 13g, Protein 41g, Fat 23g, Sodium 129mg

438. Corn Patties

Preparation: 15 minutes   **Cooking: 10 minutes**   **Servings: 1**

Ingredients:
- *1/2 cup chickpeas, cooked*
- *1 cup corn kernels, cooked*
- *1 tablespoon fresh parsley, chopped*
- *1 teaspoon chili powder*
- *1/2 teaspoon ground coriander*
- *1 tablespoon tomato paste*
- *1 tablespoon almond meal*
- *1 tablespoon olive oil*

Directions:
1. Mash the cooked chickpeas and combine them with corn kernels, parsley, chili powder, ground coriander, tomato paste, and almond meal.
2. Stir the mixture until homogenous.
3. Make the small patties.
4. After this, heat up olive oil in the skillet.
5. Put the prepared patties in the hot oil and cook them for 3 minutes per side or until they are golden brown.
6. Dry the cooked patties with the help of paper towel if needed.

Nutrition: Calories 168 , Carbohydrates 6g, Protein 24g, Fat 6g, Sodium 23mg

439. Mac Stuffed Sweet Potatoes

Preparation: 20 minutes   **Cooking: 25 minutes**   **Servings: 2**

Ingredients:
- *1 sweet potato*
- *1/4 cup whole-grain penne pasta*
- *1 teaspoon tomato paste*
- *1 teaspoon olive oil*
- *1/4 teaspoon minced garlic*
- *1 tablespoon soy milk*

Directions:
1. Cut the sweet potato in half and pierce it 3-4 times with the help of the fork.
2. Sprinkle the sweet potato halves with olive oil and bake in the preheated to 375F oven for 25-30 minutes or until the vegetables are tender.
3. Meanwhile, mix up penne pasta, tomato paste, minced garlic, and soy milk.
4. When the sweet potatoes are cooked, scoop out the vegetable meat and mix it up with a penne pasta mixture.
5. Fill the sweet potatoes with the pasta mixture.

Nutrition: Calories 105, Carbohydrates 2.8g, Protein 18g, Fat 3g, Sodium 28mg

440. Tofu Tikka Masala

Preparation: 10 minutes   **Cooking: 25 minutes**   **Servings: 2**

Ingredients:
- *8 oz tofu, chopped*
- *1/2 cup of soy milk*
- *1 teaspoon garam masala*
- *1 teaspoon olive oil*
- *1 teaspoon ground paprika*
- *1/2 cup tomatoes, chopped*
- *1/2 onion, diced*

Directions:
1. Heat up olive oil in the saucepan.
2. Add diced onion and cook it until light brown.
3. Then add tomatoes, ground paprika, and garam masala. Bring the mixture to a boil.
4. Add soy milk and stir well. Simmer it for 5 minutes.
5. Then add chopped tofu and cook the meal for 3 minutes.
6. Leave the cooked meal for 10 minutes to rest.

Nutrition: Calories 155, Carbohydrates 8g, Protein 20.7g, Fat 2.9g, Sodium 51mg

441. Spicy Bean Chili

Preparation: 15 Minutes   **Cooking: 20 Minutes**   **Serving: 4**

Ingredients:
- *2 teaspoons olive oil*
- *1 medium red onion, thinly sliced*
- *2 garlic cloves, minced*
- *2 (15-ounce) cans kidney beans, drained and rinsed*
- *1 (8-ounce) can no-salt crushed tomatoes*
- *1 cup low-sodium vegetable broth*
- *1/2 cup water*
- *2 teaspoons chili powder*
- *1/4 teaspoon ground cinnamon*

Description:
1. Heat the olive oil in a large saucepan over medium-high heat. Add the onion and sauté until the onion is lightly caramelized, about 5 minutes. Add the garlic and sauté until fragrant, about 30 seconds.
2. Stir in the remaining ingredients and bring to a boil on high for 1 minute. Cover, reduce heat to low, and simmer until flavors are well combined, about 10 minutes and enjoy!

Nutrition: Calories 223, Carbohydrates 37g, Protein 12g, Fat 4g, Sodium237 mg

442. Garlic Lovers Hummus

Preparation: 2 minutes   **Serving: 12**
Ingredients:

- 3 tbsps. Freshly squeezed lemon juice
- All-purpose salt-free seasoning
- 3 tbsps. Sesame tahini
- 4 garlic cloves
- 15 oz. no-salt-added garbanzo beans
- 2 tbsps. Olive oil

Directions:

1. Drain garbanzo beans and rinse well.
2. Place all the ingredients in a food processor and pulse until smooth.
3. Serve immediately or cover and refrigerate until serving.

Nutrition: Calories: 103, Fat:5 g, Carbohydrates:11 g, Protein:4 g, Sodium:88 mg

443. Thyme Mushrooms

Preparation: 10 minutes   **Cooking: 30 minutes**   **Serving: 4**
Ingredients:

- 1 tbsp. chopped thyme
- 2 tbsps. olive oil
- 2 tbsps. chopped parsley
- 4 minced garlic cloves
- Black pepper
- 2 lbs. halved white mushrooms

Directions:

1. In a baking pan, combine the mushrooms with the garlic and the other ingredients, toss, introduce in the oven and cook at 400 0F for 30 minutes.
2. Divide between plates and serve.

Nutrition: Calories 251, Fat 9g, Carbohydrates 13g, Protein:6 g, Sodium:37 mg

444. Herbed Mushroom Rice

Preparation: 10 Minutes   **Cooking: 15 Minutes**   **Serving: 4**
Ingredients:

- 2 teaspoons olive oil
- 12 ounces sliced mushrooms
- 3 scallion stalks, thinly sliced and separated
- 3/4 teaspoon freshly ground black pepper
- 2 cups water
- 1 teaspoon dried rosemary
- 1 cup dry instant brown rice
- 2 cups frozen lima beans

Direction:

1. Heat the olive oil in a large saucepan over medium-high heat. Add the mushrooms, the white parts of the scallions, and the black pepper and sauté until the mushrooms are just cooked through, about 5 minutes.
2. Add the water and rosemary and bring to a boil over high heat. Stir in the rice, lima beans, and half of the green parts of the scallions, and reduce the heat to medium. Cook, stirring occasionally, for 6 to 8 minutes, or until the rice is cooked and the lima beans are tender.
3. Sprinkle each serving with the remaining green parts of the **Nutrition**: Calories 220, Carbohydrates 40g, Protein 10g, Fat 4g, Sodium 111mg

445. White Bean and Roasted Red Pepper Soup

Preparation: 10 Minutes   **Cooking: 45 Minutes**   **Serving: 4**
Ingredients:

- 3 large red bell peppers
- 1 tablespoon olive oil
- 1 small onion, chopped
- 1/8 teaspoon crushed red pepper
- 2 cups low-sodium vegetable broth
- 2 cups water
- 1 (15-ounce) can cannellini (white kidney) beans, drained and rinsed

Direction:

1. Preheat the broiler to high. Place the bell peppers on a baking sheet. Broil, turning peppers frequently, until sides are blistered and charred. Remove from broiler.
2. Carefully place peppers in a plastic or paper bag; let stand 20 minutes. Peel off the layer of skin and remove core and seeds.
3. Heat the olive oil in a large skillet over medium-high heat. Add the onion. Cook, stirring occasionally, for 3 to 5 minutes, or until the onions are tender.
4. Add the roasted peppers and crushed red pepper and cook for 1 minute.
5. Stir in the broth, water, and beans. Bring to a boil. Reduce the heat to low and cook for 5 minutes.
6. Serve immediately.

Nutrition: Calories: 169; Fat: 5g;; Carbohydrates: 26g; Protein: 7g Sodium: 180mg

446. Red Lentil Stew

Preparation: 5 Minutes   **Cooking: 40 Minutes**   **Serving: 4**

Ingredients:

- *1 yellow onion, chopped*
- *2 garlic cloves, minced*
- *1 small bell pepper, chopped*
- *3 medium carrots, peeled and chopped*
- *1 (14-ounce) can no-salt diced tomatoes in juice*
- *1 cup dried red lentils, rinsed*
- *5 cups low-sodium vegetable broth*

Directions:

1. Spray a large pot with nonstick cooking spray and heat over medium heat. Add the onions and garlic and sauté until translucent, about 5 minutes.
2. Add the pepper and carrots, and sauté for 2 to 3 minutes.
3. Add the tomatoes and their juice, lentils, and vegetable broth and bring to a boil.
4. Reduce the heat to low. Cover the pot and simmer for about 30 minutes, until the lentils are tender.
5. Ladle the stew into soup bowls and serve.

Nutrition: Calories 197, Carbohydrates 34g, Protein 11g, Fat 1g, Sodium 222mg

447. Chickpea Burgers

Preparation: 5 Minutes   **Cooking: 30 Minutes**   **Serving: 4**

Ingredients:

- *2 teaspoons olive oil*
- *1 small yellow onion, diced*
- *2 cups rolled oats (not instant)*
- *1/2 cup ground walnuts*
- *1 (15-ounce) can chickpeas, drained and rinsed*
- *3/4 cup nonfat or low-fat milk*
- *1/2 teaspoon garlic powder*
- *1/2 teaspoon onion powder*
- *1/2 teaspoon dried sage*

Directions:

1. In a large skillet, heat the olive oil. Add the onions and cook for about 10 minutes, until very tender and golden brown. Set aside.
2. In a large bowl, toss together the oats and ground walnuts. Set aside.
3. In a blender, combine the chickpeas, milk, garlic powder, onion powder, and dried sage, and process until smooth and creamy.
4. Pour the chickpea mixture into the bowl with the oats and walnuts. Add the browned onions and mix well.
5. Allow the mixture to rest for 5 to 10 minutes, so the oats can absorb the liquid.
6. Form the mixture into eight thin, flat patties. Using the same skillet, brown the burgers over medium-low heat for 5 to 7 minutes on each side.
7. Serve with your favorite toppings.

Nutrition: Calories:375; Fat:16g; Carbohydrates: 48g; Protein: 14g Sodium: 112mg

448. Tofu Scramble with Potatoes and Mushrooms

Preparation: 10 Minutes   **Cooking: 15 Minutes**   **Serving: 4**

Ingredients:

- *1 large Yukon gold potato, peeled and cut into 1/2-inch pieces*
- *1 tablespoon olive oil*
- *1 bunch scallions, thinly sliced*
- *2 garlic cloves*
- *1 teaspoon chili powder*
- *1 teaspoon cumin*
- *2 cups sliced mushrooms*
- *1 (14-ounce) block firm tofu, drained and crumbled*
- *1 large tomato, sliced or diced (optional)*

Directions:

1. Place the potato pieces in a large skillet and cover with water. Bring to a boil, then reduce the heat to medium and simmer for 3 minutes. Pour out all but 1 tablespoon of the water.
2. Add the olive oil, scallions, garlic, chili powder, and cumin to the skillet, and cook, stirring, for 2 minutes. Add the mushrooms and cook, stirring occasionally, for 5 to 7 minutes, or until the potatoes are tender and mushrooms are browned.
3. Add the tofu and 2 tablespoons of cooking water and cook until the tofu is heated through, about 3 more minutes.
4. Divide the scramble among four plates and serve with tomato slices (if using).

Nutrition: Calories 186, Carbohydrates 14g, Protein 15g, Fat 10g, Sodium 133mg

449. Asparagus and Wild Garlic Risotto

Preparation: 10 Minutes   **Cooking: 40 Minutes**   **Serving: 4**

Ingredients:

- *8 cups no-salt vegetable broth*
- *2 tablespoons olive oil*
- *4 garlic cloves, minced*
- *1 cup Arborio rice*
- *1 cup white wine*
- *Zest and juice of 1 lemon*
- *1 bunch asparagus, trimmed and thinly sliced*
- *1/4 chopped fresh sage*

Directions:

1. In a large pot, bring the broth just to a simmer.
2. Meanwhile, heat a large skillet over medium heat. Add the olive oil and heat for 30 to 60 seconds, until shimmering. Add the garlic and cook for 30 seconds.
3. Add the rice. Cook, stirring constantly for about 1 minute, and then add the wine. Continue to stir and cook, allowing the wine to absorb into the rice. Add the lemon zest and juice, and stir.
4. Reduce the heat to medium-low, and ladle about 1 cup of the warm broth into the skillet. Cook, stirring constantly, allowing the liquid to be absorbed completely.
5. Add another cup of broth and continue to stir, once again allowing the liquid to be absorbed completely. Repeat with additional broth until the rice is creamy and cooked through for an al dente (or slightly firm) consistency.
6. Remove the skillet from the heat and stir in the uncooked asparagus and sage. Serve immediately.

Nutrition: Calories: 288; Fat: 7g; Carbohydrates: 42g; Protein: 6g Sodium: 106mg

450. Vegan Rice Pudding

Preparation: 5 Minutes   **Cooking: 20 Minutes**   **Serving: 8**

Ingredients:

- *1/2 tsp. ground cinnamon*
- *1 c. rinsed basmati*
- *1/8 tsp. ground cardamom*
- *1/4 c. sugar*
- *1/8 tsp. pure almond extract*
- *1-quart vanilla nondairy milk*
- *1 tsp. pure vanilla extract*

Directions:
1. Measure all of the ingredients into a saucepan and stir well to combine. Bring to a boil over medium-high heat.
2. Once boiling, reduce heat to low and simmer, stirring very frequently, about 15–20 minutes.
3. Remove from heat and cool. Serve sprinkled with additional ground cinnamon if desired.

Nutrition: Calories: 148, Fat:2 g, Carbohydrates:26 g, Protein:4 g, Sodium:150 mg

451. Cinnamon-Scented Quinoa

Preparation: 5 Minutes   **Cooking: 6 Minutes**   **Serving: 4**

Ingredients:
- *Chopped walnuts*
- *1 1/2 c. water*
- *Maple syrup*
- *2 cinnamon sticks*
- *1 c. quinoa*

Directions:
1. Add the quinoa to a bowl and wash it in several changes of water until the water is clear. When washing quinoa, rub grains and allow them to settle before you pour off the water.
2. Use a large fine-mesh sieve to drain the quinoa. Prepare your pressure cooker with a trivet and steaming basket. Place the quinoa and the cinnamon sticks in the basket and pour the water.
3. Close and lock the lid. Cook at high pressure for 6 minutes. When the cooking time is up, release the pressure using the quick release method.
4. Fluff the quinoa with a fork and remove the cinnamon sticks. Divide the cooked quinoa among serving bowls and top with maple syrup and chopped walnuts.

Nutrition: Calories 160, Carbohydrates 28g, Protein 6g, Fat 3g, Sodium 40mg

452. Green Vegetable Smoothie

Preparation: 5 Minutes   **Serving: 4**

Ingredients:
- *1 c. cold water*
- *1/2 c. strawberries*
- *2 oz. baby spinach*
- *1 lemon juice*
- *1 tbsp. fresh mint*
- *1 banana*
- *1/2 c. blueberries*

Directions:
1. Put all the ingredients in a juicer or blender and puree.

Nutrition: Calories: 52, Fat:2 g, Carbohydrates:12 g, Protein:1 g, Sugars:18 g, Sodium:36 mg

453. Penne with White Beans and Roasted Tomato Sauce

Preparation: 5 Minutes   **Cooking: 25 Minutes**   **Serving: 4**

Ingredients:
- *2 pints cherry tomatoes, halved*
- *2 tablespoons chopped fresh basil*
- *2 tablespoons olive oil, divided*
- *8 ounces whole-wheat penne*
- *2 garlic cloves, minced*
- *1 (15-ounce) can white beans (navy or great northern), drained and rinsed*
- *1 tablespoon balsamic vinegar*

Directions:
1. On a large sheet pan, toss the tomatoes with the basil and 1 tablespoon of the olive oil. Place the pan in the oven and roast until wilted and beginning to brown, about 20 minutes.
2. Meanwhile, cook the penne according to the package directions. Reserve 1/4 cup of the cooking water, and drain. Add the pasta, beans, tomato mixture, garlic, balsamic vinegar, and the cooking water to a medium pot and simmer for 2 minutes.
3. Drizzle the pasta with the remaining 1 tablespoon of olive oil and serve.

Nutrition: Calories 370, Carbohydrates 66g, Protein 13g, Fat 1g, Sodium 121mg

454. Tomato-Avocado Soup

Preparation: 5 Minutes **Cooking: 12 Minutes** **Serving: 4**

Ingredients:

- *1/2 tablespoon olive oil*
- *1 cup chopped onion*
- *1 clove garlic, minced*
- *1 (14-ounce) can no-salt diced tomatoes in juice*
- *1 cup low-sodium vegetable broth*
- *1 cup water*
- *1/2 teaspoon freshly ground black pepper*
- *1 cup low-fat buttermilk*
- *1 large ripe avocado, halved, pitted, peeled, and sliced*

Directions:

1. Heat the olive oil in a large pot over medium heat. Add the onion, and cook, stirring frequently, about 5 minutes, or until translucent. Add the garlic and cook for 1 minute.
2. Transfer the onion-and-garlic mixture to a blender. Add the tomatoes and their juice, broth, water, and black pepper, and purée until smooth.
3. Transfer the purée back to the pot and heat the soup mixture over medium-low heat for 5 minutes, or until heated through. Add the buttermilk and stir to combine.
4. Garnish each serving with a quarter of the avocado slices.

Nutrition: Calories: 155; Fat: 9g; Carbohydrates: 17g; Protein: 5g Sodium: 116mg

455. Mexican Beans and Rice

Preparation: 5 Minutes **Cooking: 35 Minutes** **Serving: 4**

Ingredients:

- *1 cup uncooked medium-grain brown rice*
- *2 cups cold water*
- *1 (14 1/2 ounce) can no-salt diced tomatoes in juice*
- *2 tablespoons olive oil*
- *6 garlic cloves, finely chopped*
- *1 medium jalapeño pepper, cored, seeded, and finely chopped*
- *1 (15-ounce) can black beans, drained and rinsed*
- *2 teaspoons cumin*
- *1 teaspoon chili powder*
- *1/4 cup finely chopped fresh oregano*
- *1/4 cup finely chopped fresh cilantro*

Directions:

1. In a 1-quart saucepan, combine the rice with the cold water. Bring to a boil over medium-high heat. Cover, reduce heat to low, and simmer for 20 minutes.
2. Remove the pan from the heat and let stand, covered, another 5 minutes.
3. While the rice steams, set a fine colander or sieve in a bowl and drain the can of tomatoes. Pour the tomato juices into a 1-cup liquid measure. Add enough water to the tomato juice to equal 1 cup. Set the tomatoes aside.
4. Heat the olive oil in a medium skillet over medium-high heat. Add the garlic and jalapeño, and stir-fry until the garlic browns and the jalapeño smells pungent, about 1 minute.
5. Add the black beans, cumin, and chili powder; stir two to three times to incorporate the mixture and cook the spices, about 30 seconds.
6. Stir in the tomato liquid and bring to a boil. Adjust the heat to maintain a gentle boil and cook, stirring occasionally, for 5 to 7 minutes, or until the beans absorb much of the liquid.
7. Add the tomatoes, oregano, cilantro, and cooked rice. Continue cooking, stirring occasionally, for 1 to 2 minutes, or until the rice is warm.
8. Serve immediately.

Nutrition: Calories 356, Carbohydrates 59g, Protein 11g, Fat 10g, Sodium 128mg

456. Sweet Potato and Black Bean Wraps

Preparation: 10 Minutes   **Cooking: 20 Minutes**   **Serving: 4**

Ingredients:

- *1 large, sweet potato, cubed*
- *2 teaspoons olive oil*
- *1/2 small onion, finely chopped*
- *1 bell pepper, chopped*
- *2 garlic cloves, minced*

TOPPINGS

- *1 to 2 slices avocado (optional)*
- *1 to 2 slices tomato (optional)*

- *2 teaspoons cumin*
- *1 (15-ounce) can black beans, drained and rinsed*
- *1 cup cooked brown rice*
- *8 small corn tortillas*

- *1/4 cup shredded lettuce (optional)*

Directions:

1. Preheat the oven to 425°F and line a baking sheet with foil. Spread the sweet potato evenly over the baking sheet, spray with nonstick cooking spray, and roast for 15 to 20 minutes, or until tender.
2. Meanwhile, in a large skillet over medium heat, add the olive oil, onion, bell pepper, and minced garlic. Sauté for 5 to 10 minutes, stirring frequently. Add the cumin and stir well.
3. Add the beans and cooked rice, and sauté for another 5 minutes over medium heat.
4. Add the roasted sweet potato to the rice mixture and stir well, mashing some of the larger pieces of sweet potato if desired.
5. Add the filling to the tortillas along with your desired toppings and serve immediately.

Nutrition: Calories 301, Carbohydrates 55g, Protein 11g, Fat 6g, Sodium 157mg

457. Asparagus and Mushroom Crustless Quiche

Preparation: 5 Minutes   **Cooking: 45 Minutes**   **Serving: 4**

Ingredients:

- *1 tablespoon olive oil*
- *1 large yellow or white onion, sliced into half-moons*
- *1/2 teaspoon freshly ground black pepper*

- *2 cups chopped mushrooms*
- *2 cups chopped asparagus*
- *1 cup nonfat or low-fat milk*

Direction:

1. Preheat the oven to 350°F.
2. Heat the olive oil in a cast iron or ovenproof skillet over medium heat. Add the onion slices and sprinkle with the black pepper. Cook the onions until they are golden brown and starting to caramelize, about 10 minutes.
3. Remove the skillet from the heat and spread the onions evenly across the bottom. Spread the mushrooms and asparagus evenly over the onions.
4. In a medium bowl, add the milk, , and black pepper. Stir with a fork, beating just enough to break up the yolks and white. Pour the custard over the vegetables and onions.
5. Transfer the skillet to the oven, and bake for 45 minutes to 1 hour, until fully cooked and lightly browned across the top. Let the quiche cool for 20 minutes, and then slice into four wedges.

Nutrition: Calories 213, Carbohydrates 12g, Protein 19g, Fat 11g, Sodium mg

458. Enchiladas with Bean Medley

Preparation: 15 Minutes   **Cooking: 35 Minutes**   **Serving: 4**

Ingredients:

- *2 tablespoons olive oil*
- *1-pound green beans, washed and ends snipped*
- *1 teaspoon cumin*

- *1 (15-ounce) can black beans, drained and rinsed*
- *1 (14-ounce) can red enchilada sauce*
- *Freshly ground black pepper*
- *8 corn tortillas*

Directions:

1. Preheat the oven to 400°F with one rack in the middle of the oven and one in the upper third. Lightly grease a 9-by-13-inch baking pan with nonstick cooking spray.
2. In a large skillet over medium heat, heat the olive oil until shimmering. Add the green beans and cook, stirring occasionally, for 5 to 7 minutes, or until the green beans are brighter green. Add the cumin to the skillet, and cook until fragrant, about 30 seconds.
3. Transfer the contents of the pan to a medium-size mixing bowl. Add the black beans, and about 2 tablespoons of the enchilada sauce. Season with black pepper.
4. Assemble the enchiladas: Pour 1/4 cup of the enchilada sauce into the prepared pan and tilt it from side to side until the bottom of the pan is evenly coated.
5. To assemble the enchiladas, spread 1/4 cup of the filling mixture down the middle of a tortilla, and then snugly wrap the left side over and then the right to make a wrap. Place it in the pan and repeat with the remaining tortillas and filling
6. Drizzle the remaining enchilada sauce evenly over the enchiladas, leaving the ends of the enchiladas bare.
7. Bake, uncovered, on the middle rack, for 20 minutes, carefully transfer the enchiladas to the upper rack and bake for an additional 3 to 6 minutes, or until golden and bubbly. Serve.

Nutrition: Calories 368, Carbohydrates 40g, Protein 18g, Fat 1g, Sodium 316mg

459. Pasta Primavera

Preparation: 10 Minutes   **Cooking: 15 Minutes**   **Servings: 4**

Ingredients:

- *2 cups broccoli florets*
- *1 cup sliced mushrooms*
- *1 cup sliced zucchini or yellow squash*
- *1 tablespoon olive oil, plus 1 teaspoon*
- *2 garlic cloves, minced*
- *3/4 cup fat-free evaporated milk*
- *8 ounces whole-wheat angel-hair or spaghetti pasta*
- *1/3 cup chopped fresh parsley (optional)*

Directions:

1. In a large pot fitted with a steamer basket, bring about 1 inch of water to a boil. Add the broccoli, mushrooms, and zucchini. Cover and steam until tender-crisp, about 10 minutes. Remove from the pot.
2. In a large saucepan, heat 1 tablespoon of the olive oil over medium heat. Add the garlic and sauté over medium heat for 2 to 3 minutes. Add the steamed vegetables and stir or shake to coat the vegetables with the garlic. Remove the saucepan from the heat but keep warm.
3. In another large saucepan, heat the remaining 1 teaspoon of olive oil, evaporated milk, Stir continuously over medium heat until somewhat thickened and heated through without scalding. Remove the saucepan from the heat but keep warm.
4. Fill a large pot three-quarters full of water and bring to a boil. Put the pasta and cook according to the package directions, until the desired doneness. Drain the pasta.
5. Divide the pasta evenly among four plates. Top each serving with a quarter of the vegetables and Parmesan sauce. Garnish with fresh parsley (if using) and serve immediately.

Nutrition: Calories 350, Carbohydrates 53g, Protein 17g, Fat 9g, Sodium 317mg

DESSERTS

460. Banana Bread

Preparation: 15 minutes **Cooking: 60 minutes** **Servings: 14**

Ingredients:

- *Vegetable oil cooking spray*
- *2 cups whole wheat flour*
- *1/2 cup quinoa flour*
- *1/2 cup of raw sugar*
- *3/4 cup egg whites*
- *1/8 teaspoon iodized salt*
- *1 teaspoon baking soda*
- *2 tablespoons grapeseed oil*
- *2 pieces of mashed banana*

Directions:

1. Preheat oven to 350 °F. Coat a loaf pan with a vegetable oil cooking spray, dust evenly with a bit of flour, and set aside. In a bowl, mix all the flour, and baking soda.
2. Coat a separate bowl with vegetable oil, then mix eggs, sugar, and mashed bananas. Pour the bowl of wet fixing into the bowl of dry fixing and mix thoroughly. Scoop the mixture into the loaf pan. Bake within an hour.
3. To check the doneness, insert a toothpick in the center of the loaf pan; if you remove the toothpick and it has no batter sticking to it, remove the bread from the oven. Slice and serve immediately and store the remaining banana bread in a refrigerator to prolong shelf life.

Nutrition: Calories 150, Carbohydrates 12g, Protein 4g, Fat 3g, Sodium 178mg

461. Milk Chocolate Pudding

Preparation: 15 minutes **Cooking: 15 minutes** **Servings: 4**

Ingredients:

- *1/2 teaspoon vanilla extract*
- *1/3 cup chocolate chips*
- *1/8 teaspoon salt*
- *2 cups nonfat milk*
- *2 tablespoons cocoa powder*
- *2 tablespoons sugar*
- *3 tablespoons cornstarch*

Directions:

1. Mix cocoa powder, cornstarch, sugar, and salt in a saucepan and whisk in milk; frequently stir over medium heat.
2. Remove, put the chocolate chips and vanilla extract, stir until the chocolate chips and vanilla melt into the pudding. Pour contents into serving bowls and store in a chiller. Serve chilled.

Nutrition: Calories 197 Fats 5g Carbohydrates 9g Proteins 5g Sodium 105mg

462. Minty Lime and Grapefruit Yogurt Parfait

Preparation: 15 minutes **Servings: 6**

Ingredients:

- *A handful of torn mint leaves*
- *2 teaspoons grated lime zest*
- *2 tablespoons lime juice extract*
- *3 tablespoons raw honey*
- *4 large red grapefruits*
- *4 cups reduced-fat plain yogurt*

Directions:

1. Cut the top and lower part of the red grapefruits and stand the fruit upright on a cutting board. Discard the peel with a knife and slice along the membrane of each segment to remove the skin.
2. Mix yogurt, lime juice extract, and lime zest in a bowl. Layer half of the grapefruit and yogurt mixture into 6 parfait glasses; add another layer until the glass is filled and then drizzle with honey and top with mint leaves. Serve immediately.

Nutrition: Calories 207 Fats 3g Carbohydrates 39g Protein 4g Sodium 115mg

463. Peach Tarts

Preparation: 15 minutes   **Cooking: 55 minutes**   **Servings: 8**
Ingredients:
Tart Ingredients:
- 1/4 cup softened butter
- 1/4 teaspoon ground nutmeg

Filling Ingredients:
- 1/4 teaspoon ground cinnamon
- 1/4 cup coarsely chopped almonds
- 1/8 teaspoon almond extract

- 1 cup all-purpose flour
- 3 tablespoons sugar

- 1/3 cup sugar
- 2 pounds peaches medium, peeled, thinly sliced

Directions:
1. Preheat oven to 375 °F. Mix butter, nutmeg, and sugar in a bowl until light and fluffy. Add and beat in flour until well-blended. Place the batter on an ungreased fluted tart baking pan and press firmly on the bottom and topsides.
2. Put it in the medium rack of the preheated oven and bake for about 10 minutes until it turns to a crust. In a bowl, coat peaches with sugar, flour, cinnamon, almond extract, and almonds.
3. Open the oven, put the tart crust on the lower rack of the oven, and pour in the peach filling; bake for about 40-45 minutes. Remove, cool, and serve; or cover with a cling wrap and refrigerate to serve chilled.

Nutrition: Calories 222 Fats 8 g Carbohydrates 36 g Proteins 4 g Sodium: 78mg

464. Raspberry Nuts Parfait

Preparation: 15 minutes   **Cooking: 10 minutes**   **Servings: 1**
Ingredients:
- 1/4 cup frozen raspberries
- 1/4 cup frozen blueberries
- 1/4 cup toasted, thinly sliced almonds

- 1 cup nonfat, plain Greek yogurt
- 2 teaspoons raw honey

Directions:
1. First, layer Greek yogurt in a parfait glass; add berries; layer yogurt again, top with almonds and more berries; drizzle with honey. Serve chilled.

Nutrition: Calories 378 Fats 15 g Carbohydrates 35 g Proteins 30g Sodium 83 mg

465. Strawberry Bruschetta

Preparation: 15 minutes   **Servings: 12**
Ingredients:
- 1 loaf sliced Ciabatta bread
- 8 ounces goat cheese
- 1 cup basil leaves

- 2 containers of strawberries, sliced
- 5 tablespoons balsamic glaze

Directions:
1. Wash and slice strawberries; set aside. Wash and chop the basil leaves; set aside. Slice the ciabatta bread and spread some goat cheese evenly on each slice; add strawberries, balsamic glaze, and top with basil leaves. Serve on a platter.

Nutrition: Calories 80 Fats 2 g Carbohydrates 12 g Proteins 3 g Sodium: 78mg

466. Chocolate Chip Banana Muffin Top Cookies

Preparation: 15 minutes   **Cooking: 15 minutes**   **Servings: 16**
Ingredients:
- 1 cup quick oats
- 1 cup white whole-wheat flour
- 1/4 cup sugar

- 1 tablespoon sodium-free baking powder
- 1 teaspoon ground cinnamon
- 3 ripe medium bananas, mashed

- 4 tablespoons canola oil
- 1 tablespoon pure vanilla extract
- 3/4 cup chocolate chips

Directions:
1. Preheat oven to 350°F. Put aside a baking sheet with parchment paper. Measure the oats, flour, sugar, baking powder, and cinnamon into a mixing bowl and whisk. Put the rest of the fixing and stir just until combined.
2. Using a medium-sized ice cream scoop, scoop the batter onto the prepared baking sheet, leaving an inch or two between cookies. Bake within 15 minutes. Remove, then put on a wire rack to cool. Serve immediately.

Nutrition: Calories: 150 Fat: 6 g Protein: 2 g Carbohydrates: 23 g Sodium: 56mg

467. Lemon Cookies

Preparation: 15 minutes　　　**Cooking: 10 minutes**　　　**Servings: 36**

Ingredients:
- 2 1/2 cups white whole-wheat flour
- 1 1/2 cups sugar
- 1 tablespoon sodium-free baking powder
- 3/4 cup canola oil
- 2 large lemons, juice, and grated zest
- 1 tablespoon pure vanilla extract

Directions:
1. Preheat oven to 350°F. Mix the flour, sugar, plus baking powder into a mixing bowl. Put the rest of the fixing and stir to form a stiff dough.
2. Drop by rounded tablespoons onto an ungreased baking sheet. Bake within 10 minutes. Remove, then let cool on sheet for a few minutes before transferring to a wire rack to cool fully. Serve immediately.

Nutrition: Calories: 106 Fat: 5 g Protein: 1 g Carbohydrates: 15 g Sodium: 58mg

468. Easy Apple Crisp

Preparation: 15 minutes　　　**Cooking: 25 minutes**　　　**Servings: 8**

Ingredients:
- 6 medium apples
- 1 tablespoon lemon juice
- 1/3 cup sugar
- 1/2 cup rolled or quick oats
- 1/2 cup white whole-wheat flour
- 1/2 cup light brown sugar
- 1 tablespoon pure vanilla extract
- 1 teaspoon ground cinnamon
- 1/2 teaspoon ground ginger
- 3 tablespoons unsalted butter

Directions:
1. Preheat oven to 425°F. Take out a 2-quart baking pan and set aside. Slice each apple into 16 wedges. Put into a mixing bowl, place the lemon juice and sugar, and toss well to coat.
2. Turn batter out into the baking pan, then set aside. Place the oats, flour, sugar, vanilla, and spices into a mixing bowl and stir to combine.
3. Slice the butter into the mixture using your hands and process until a wet crumb has formed. Sprinkle mixture over the fruit. Bake within 25 minutes. Remove, then let it cool and serve.

Nutrition: Calories: 232 Fat:5 g Protein: 2g Carbohydrates: 46g Sodium: 68mg

469. Mango Crumble

Preparation: 15 minutes　　　**Cooking: 25 minutes**　　　**Servings: 8**

Ingredients:
- 2 barely ripe mangoes
- 2 tablespoons light brown sugar
- 1 tablespoon cornstarch
- 1 1/2 teaspoons minced fresh ginger
- 1/2 cup unbleached all-purpose flour
- 1/2 cup white whole-wheat flour
- 1/2 cup sugar
- 1 teaspoon ground cinnamon
- 1/4 teaspoon ground ginger
- 3 tablespoons unsalted butter

Directions:

1. Preheat oven to 375°F. Take out an 8-inch square baking pan and set aside. Peel mangoes and cut into 1-inch chunks. Place in a mixing bowl.
2. Add the brown sugar, cornstarch, and minced ginger and toss to coat. Put the batter out into the baking pan and spread to even. In another bowl, whisk the flours, sugar, cinnamon, and ginger.
3. Slice the butter into pieces and put it in the bowl. Work the butter into the mixture using your hands until it resembles damp sand and sticks when squeezed. Sprinkle mixture evenly over the fruit.
4. Bake within 25 minutes, until fruit is tender. Remove, and put on a wire rack to cool. Serve warm or cool.

Nutrition: Calories: 190 Fat:5g Protein: 3g Carbohydrates: 37g Sodium: 83 mg

470. Grilled Apricots with Cinnamon

Preparation: 5minutes   **Cooking: 10 minutes**   **Serving 4**

Ingredients

- *4 large apricots, halved and pitted*
- *1 tablespoon extra-virgin olive oil*
- *1/4 teaspoon ground cinnamon*

Directions

1. Brush with oil on both sides of each apricot half, and put flat
2. On the hot grill or grill pan, side down. Grill for around 4 minutes, turn over the apricot halves and grill until soft for a few more minutes. Sprinkle with cinnamon and cut the apricots from the grill. Enjoy being wet or cold.

Nutrition: Calories: 245, Fat: 7g, Carbohydrates:6g, Protein: 20g. Sodium: 18mg

471. Grilled Peaches with Ricotta Stuffing and Balsamic Glaze

Preparation: 5minutes   **Cooking: 10 minutes**   **Serving 4**

Ingredients

- *4 large peaches, halved and pitted*
- *1 tablespoon extra-virgin olive oil*
- *1 cup low-fat ricotta cheese*
- *1/4 teaspoon ground cinnamon*
- *1/8 teaspoon ground nutmeg*
- *2 tablespoons low-fat milk*
- *2 tablespoons Balsamic Glaze*

Directions

1. Brush the two sides of each half of the peach with oil and put them down. On the hot grill or grill pan, side down. Grill for about 4 minutes, turn over the peach halves and grill until soft for a few more minutes.
2. When the peaches are grilling, in a small bowl, mix the ricotta, milk, cinnamon, and nutmeg, stirring evenly to combine flavors.
3. Take the peaches from the grill and add 1/4 cup of the mixture of ricotta to the middle of each half of the peach. Drizzle and serve the balsamic glaze on each one.

Nutrition: Calories: 276, Fat: 3g, Carbohydrates: 14g, Protein: 20g. Sodium: 43mg

472. Grilled Pineapple

Preparation: 5minutes   **Cooking: 5 minutes**   **Serving 6**

Ingredients

- *1 large pineapple, sliced into rounds and cored*

Directions

1. By laying it on its side and chopping off the pineapple, cut the pineapple bottom and top. On its freshly flat frame, stand it up. Cut the skin off in a downward motion, beginning from the top and moving to the root, operating in a circular direction.
2. Be careful not to take too much of the skin off the fruit. Cut out any brown stains until the skin has been removed. Then lay it again lengthwise and split the rounds to the thickness you like. Cut out the inedible heart at the middle of each round with a cookie cutter or knife.

3. Place the rings directly on a hot grill with the pineapple. Grill for roughly three minutes, or before char marks emerge. Switch the rings over, then barbecue for an extra 2 to 3 minutes. Serve chilled or hot.

Nutrition: Calories: 300, Fat: 1g Carbohydrates: 18g, Protein:16g. Sodium: 34mg

473. Red Sangria

Preparation: 5minutes   **Serving 8**

Ingredients

- *1 (750 mL) bottle Spanish red table wine*
- *1/4 cup brandy*
- *1/4 cup Cointreau*
- *1/2 cup orange juice*
- *1 cup pomegranate juice*
- *2 oranges, thinly sliced*
- *2 Granny Smith apples, thinly sliced*
- *1 1/2 cups seltzer, mineral water, or club soda*

Directions

1. Stir together the champagne, brandy, Cointreau, and the fruit juices in a big pitcher.
2. Add the sliced fruit and chill for at least 30 minutes in the refrigerator before eating. Just prior to serving, add the seltzer, sparkling water, or club soda.

Nutrition: Calories: 186, Fat: 3g, Carbohydrates: 8g, Protein: 12g, Sodium: 28mg

474. Baked Apples Stuffed with Cranberries and Walnuts

Preparation: 10 minutes   **Cooking: 25 minutes**   **Serving 4**

Ingredients

- *Four baking apples, such as Braeburn or Rome1/2 lemon*
- *1/3 cup dried cranberries*
- *1/3 cup chopped walnuts*
- *6 tablespoons grade B maple syrup*
- *1/4 teaspoon ground cinnamon*
- *1/4 teaspoon freshly grated nutmeg*
- *4 teaspoons unsalted butter*
- *1 cup boiling water*

Directions

1. Preheat the oven to 350°F.
2. Break off the top inch of an apple one at a time to make a "lid." With a melon baller, scoop out the heart, stopping about half an inch from the bottom of the apple. Pick out the top half of the apple skin using a vegetable peeler. Rub the raw flesh with half of the lemon all over it.
3. Combine the cranberries, walnuts, 2 teaspoons of maple syrup, cinnamon, and nutmeg in a medium cup. Stuff the mixture into the apples. Top each one with 1 butter teaspoon. Replace the' lids of the fruit.'
4. In order to keep the apples, move to a baking dish only big enough. Squeeze half of the lemon juice from the lemon over the apples. Pour the boiling water in and securely cover it with aluminum foil. 20 minutes of baking. Uncover and baste with the liquid in the baking dish. Continue to bake until the apples are tender, 20 to 30 minutes longer, depending on the size of the apples when pierced with the tip of a small, sharp knife. Take it out of the oven and let it stand for 5 minutes.
5. Move each apple to a dessert bowl and add 1 tablespoon of maple syrup each to drizzle. Serve it sweet.

Nutrition: Calories: 290, Fat: 6g, Carbohydrates: 17g, Protein: 10g. Sodium: 34mg

475. Buttermilk Panna Cotta with Fresh Berries

Preparation: 30 Minutes **Cooking: 10 minutes** **Serving 4**

Ingredients

- 3 teaspoons unflavored gelatin powder
- 1/4 cup plus 2 tablespoons low-fat (1%) milk
- 23/4 cups buttermilk
- 1/2 cup amber agave nectar or honey
- 1/2 teaspoon vanilla extract
- Canola oil in a pump sprayer
- 1/2 cup fresh blueberries
- 1/2 cup fresh raspberries

Directions

1. Sprinkle the gelatin in a small heatproof bowl over the milk and let stand until the milk is absorbed by the gelatin, for about 5 minutes. To get 1/2 inch up the sides, add enough water to a small skillet and bring it to a simmer over low heat. Put the bowl in the water with the gelatin mixture and constantly stir with a small heatproof spatula until the gelatin melts and dissolves completely around 2 minutes.
2. Meanwhile, over medium-low heat, heat the buttermilk in a medium saucepan, stirring continuously, only until it is warm to the touch. Do not overheat, or maybe it will curdle. Remove yourself from the sun. Attach the mixture of the gelatin and whisk until mixed. Agave and vanilla whisk. Transfer to a large measuring cup or pitcher of liquid.
3. Oil six 6-ounce custard cups or ramekins. Pour the buttermilk mixture into the ramekins in equal quantities. Cover with plastic wrap for each one. Refrigerate for at least 4 hours, or up to 2 days, until chilled and set.
4. Run a dinner knife around each ramekin's inside, making sure you hit bottom to crack the air seal. Place a plate over the top of the ramekin when working with one panna cotta at a time. Offer them a firm shake by holding the ramekin and plate together to unmold the panna cotta on the plate. Dip the ramekin (right side up) in a bowl of hot water if it is soilborne and keep it for 10 seconds, dry the ramekin, invert, and try again to unmold. The blueberries and raspberries are sprinkled and served chilled.

Nutrition: Calories 245, Carbohydrates 6g, Protein 20g, Fat 7g, Sodium 212mg

476. Cantaloupe and Mint Ice Pops

Preparation: 30 Minutes **Serving 4**

Ingredients

- 3 cups peeled, seeded, and cubed ripe cantaloupe
- 1/2 cup amber agave nectar
- 2 tablespoons fresh lemon juice
- 1 tablespoon finely chopped fresh mint

Directions

1. Have eight ice pop molds ready. In a food processor or blender, purée 2 1/2 cups of the cantaloupe cubes. Transfer to a bowl. Pulse in the food processor or blender (or slice by hand) the remaining 1/2 cup of cantaloupe cubes until finely chopped and add to the puree. Apply the agave, lemon juice, and mint to the whisk.
2. Divide the puree between the ice pop molds and cover the lid of each mold. Freeze for at least 4 hours, until the pops are strong. (The pops can be kept in the freezer for up to 1 week.)
3. Rinse the pop mold under lukewarm water to serve, then remove the pop from the mold. Frozen serve.
4. Cantaloupe and Mint Granita: In the freezer, put a metal baking dish or cake pan and a metal fork until very cold, approximately 15 minutes. The whole cantaloupe purée. To combine well, add the agave and the lemon juice and pulse. Only to mix, add the mint and pulse. Pour into the metal dish and freeze for around 1 hour until the mixture is icy along the sides of the bowl. Stir the ice crystals into the middle using the cold fork. Freeze again, around 1 hour more, until icy, and stir again; the mixture becomes more solid. Freeze for about 1 hour more, until the consistency is slushy. Freeze for up to 4 hours before serving. Using the fork's tines to scrape the mixture into frozen slush just before serving. Serve in chilled bowls immediately.

Nutrition: Calories 244, Carbohydrates 25g, Protein 12g, Fat 4g, Sodium 149mg

477. Peach and Granola Parfaits

Preparation: 30 Minutes   **Serving 4**

Ingredients

- *1 cup plain low-fat Greek yogurt*
- *2 tablespoons amber agave nectar, honey, or grade B maple syrup*
- *1/4 teaspoon vanilla extract*
- *8 tablespoons Make It Your Way Granola*
- *4 ripe peaches or nectarines, pitted and cut into 1/2-inch dice*

Directions

1. Stir the yogurt, agave, and vanilla in a small cup.
2. Layer 1 tablespoon of granola, 2 tablespoons of yogurt, and one-eighth of the diced peaches in a large parfait glass or wineglass for each serving, then repeat again. Immediately serve.

Nutrition: Calories:300, Fat: 14g, Carbohydrates:18g, Protein:16g Sodium: 254mg

478. Easy Pear Crisp

Preparation: 10 Minutes   **Cooking: 40 minutes**   **Serving 4**

Ingredients

- *Canola oil in a pump sprayer*
- *5 ripe, juicy pears, such as Comic or Anjou, peeled, cored, and cut into 1/2-inch pieces*
- *2 tablespoons amber agave nectar or grade B maple syrup*
- *1 tablespoon fresh lemon juice*
- *2 teaspoons cornstarch*
- *1/2 teaspoon freshly grated nutmeg1 cup Make It Your Way Granola.*

Directions

1. Preheat the oven to 350°F. Lightly spray the oil on an 11 8 1/2-inch baking dish.
2. In the baking dish, mix the pears, agave, lemon juice, cornstarch, and nutmeg. Bake for about 30 minutes, stirring every 15 minutes, until the pears are tender and have released their juices. Sprinkle the granola over the pear mixture and extract it from the oven. Go back to the oven and bake for about 5 minutes just to heat the granola. Remove from the oven and leave to stand at room temperature for 5 to 10 minutes.
3. Spoon into bowls for dessert and serve warm.

Nutrition: Calories: 242, Fat: 9g, Carbohydrates: 20g, Protein:31g Sodium: 128mg

479. Roasted Pineapple with Maple Glaze

Preparation: 10 Minutes   **Cooking: 20 minutes**   **Serving 4**

Ingredients

- *1 ripe pineapple*
- *Canola oil in a pump spray*
- *1/4 cup grade B maple syrup*
- *1 tablespoon unsalted butter, melted*

Directions

1. Preheat the oven to 425 F.
2. Cut the pineapple lengthwise into quarters using a big, sharp knife. To yield 8 wedges, cut each quarter lengthwise. For another use, reserve 4 of the wedges.
3. Using a paring knife to cut the flesh from the rind into one piece while dealing with 1 pineapple wedge at a time. Break the flesh into 5 large chunks vertically, holding them nestled in the rind.
4. Arrange the pineapple wedges in a baking dish and brush lightly with oil. Roast for about 15 minutes before it just begins to brown. In a small cup, whisk the maple syrup and butter together. Brush the mixture over the pineapple and bake for about 5 more minutes until the pineapple is glazed. Transfer to four large plates, drizzle with the baking dish liquid and serve warm.

Nutrition: Calories: 290, Fat:6g, Carbohydrates: 17g, Protein:10g, Sodium: 112mg

480. Fresh Strawberries with Chocolate Dip

Preparation: 30 Minutes   **Cooking:** 15 minutes   **Serving** 4

Ingredients

- *1/2 cup low-fat (2%) canned evaporated milk*
- *5 ounces bittersweet chocolate (about 60% cacao content), finely chopped*
- *24 strawberries, unpulled*

Directions

1. In a tiny saucepan, carry the evaporated milk to a boil over medium heat. Remove from the heat and add the chocolate. Let it stand for about 3 minutes before the chocolate softens. Until smooth, whisk.
2. Divide the mixture of chocolate into four tiny ramekins. To dip, serve the strawberries with the chocolate mixture.

Nutrition: Calories 245, Carbohydrates 6g, Protein 20g, Fat 7g, Sodium 154mg

481. Raspberry Swirl Brownie Bites

Preparation: 12minutes   **Cooking:** 30 minutes   **Serving** 6

Ingredients

- *1 (19.9-oz) box Duncan Hines Chewy Fudge Brownie Mix*
- *1 (3.13-oz) package chocolate pudding mix*
- *3 eggs*
- *1/4 cup water*
- *1/2 cup vegetable oil*
- *1 cup raspberry jam*
- *Confectioners' sugar*
- *1/2-pint fresh raspberries*

Directions:

1. Preheat oven to 350°F.
2. Coat a 9-by-13-inch baking pan with cooking spray.
3. In a large bowl, combine brownie mix, pudding mix, eggs, water, and oil. Beat well. Transfer to baking pan. Drop jam 1-spoonful at a time onto the batter. Swirl using a table knife.
4. Bake for 28 minutes or until done. Cool in pan. Cut into 24 brownies. Top with raspberries.

Nutrition: Calories 200, Carbohydrates 10g, Protein 5g, Fat 4g, Sodium 112mg

482. Carrot Cake Cookies

Preparation: 15 minutes   **Cooking:** 12 minutes   **Servings:** 36

Ingredients:

- *3 medium carrots, shredded*
- *1 and 1/2 cups white whole-wheat flour*
- *3/4 cup oat flour*
- *3/4 cup light brown sugar*
- *1 egg white*
- *1/3 cup canola oil*
- *1 tablespoon pure vanilla extract*
- *1 teaspoon sodium-free baking powder*
- *1 and 1/2 teaspoons ground cinnamon*
- *1/2 teaspoon ground nutmeg*
- *1/4 teaspoon ground ginger*
- *1/8 teaspoon ground cloves*

Directions:

1. Preheat oven to 375°F. Prepare and line a baking sheet with parchment paper and set aside. Place all the ingredients into a mixing bowl and stir well to combine. The dough will be quite sticky.
2. Put onto a lined baking sheet. Bake for 12 minutes. Remove, then transfer cookies to a wire rack to cool. Store in an airtight container.

Nutrition: Calories 167, Carbohydrates 22g, Protein 1g, Fat 12g, Sodium 207mg

483. Grilled Pineapple Strips

Preparation: 15 minutes   **Cooking:** 5 minutes   **Servings:** 6

Ingredients:

- *Vegetable oil*
- *Dash of iodized salt*
- *1 pineapple*
- *1 tablespoon lime juice extract*

- 1 tablespoon olive oil
- 1 tablespoon raw honey
- 3 tablespoons brown sugar

Directions:
1. Peel the pineapple, remove the eyes of the fruit, and discard the core. Slice lengthwise, forming six wedges. Mix the rest of the ingredients in a bowl until blended.
2. Brush the coating mixture on the pineapple (reserve some for basting). Grease an oven or outdoor grill rack with vegetable oil.
3. Place the pineapple wedges on the grill rack and heat for a few minutes per side until golden brownish, basting it frequently with a reserved glaze. Serve on a platter.

Nutrition: Calories 197, Carbohydrates 20g, Protein 1g, Fat 2g, Sodium 102mg

484. Raspberry Peach Pancake

Preparation: 15 minutes   **Cooking: 30 minutes**   **Servings: 4**

Ingredients:
- 1/2 teaspoon sugar
- 1/2 cup raspberries
- 1/2 cup fat-free milk
- 1/2 cup all-purpose flour
- 1/4 cup vanilla yogurt
- 1/8 teaspoon iodized salt
- 1 tablespoon butter
- 2 medium peeled, thinly sliced peaches
- 3 lightly beaten organic eggs

Directions:
1. Preheat oven to 400 °F. Toss peaches and raspberries with sugar in a bowl. Melt butter on a 9-inch round baking plate. Mix eggs, milk, plus salt in a small bowl until blended, whisk in the flour.
2. Remove the round baking plate from the oven, tilt to coat the bottom and sides with the melted butter; pour in the flour mixture.
3. Put it in the oven until it becomes brownish and puffed. Remove the pancake from the oven. Serve immediately with more raspberries and vanilla yogurt.

Nutrition: Calories 199, Carbohydrates 25g, Protein 9g, Fat 7g, Sodium 173mg

485. Berries Marinated in Balsamic Vinegar

Preparation: 10 minutes   **Servings: 2**

Ingredients:
- 1/4 cup balsamic vinegar
- 2 tablespoons brown sugar
- 1 teaspoon vanilla extract
- 1/2 cup sliced strawberries
- 1/2 cup blueberries
- 1/2 cup raspberries
- 2 shortbread biscuits

Directions:
1. Combine balsamic vinegar, vanilla, and brown sugar in a small bowl. Toss strawberries with raspberries and blueberries in a bowl. Pour the vinegar mixture on top and marinate them for 15 minutes. Serve immediately.

Nutrition: Calories 176, Carbohydrates 33g, Protein 13g, Fat 12g, Sodium 179mg

486. Lemon Pudding Cakes

Preparation: 10 minutes   **Cooking: 40 minutes**   **Servings: 4**

Ingredients:
- 2 eggs
- 1/4 teaspoon salt
- 3/4 cup sugar
- 1 cup skim milk
- 1/3 cup freshly squeezed lemon juice
- 3 tablespoons all-purpose flour
- 1 tablespoon finely grated lemon peel
- 1 tablespoon melted butter

Directions:
1. Warm oven at 350 degrees F. Grease the custard cups with cooking oil. Whisk egg whites with salt and 1/4 cup sugar in a mixer until it forms stiff peaks. Beat egg yolks with 1/2 cup sugar until mixed.
2. Stir in lemon juice, milk, butter, flour, and lemon peel. Mix it until smooth. Fold in the egg white mixture. Divide the batter into the custard cups. Bake them for 40 minutes until golden from the top. Serve.

Nutrition: Calories 174, Carbohydrates 19g, Protein 13g, Fat 10g, Sodium 176mg

487. Strawberries and Cream Cheese Crepes

Preparation: 10 minutes **Cooking: 10 minutes** **Servings: 2**

Ingredients:
- *4 tbsp cream cheese, softened*
- *2 tbsp powdered sugar, sifted*
- *2 tsp vanilla extract*
- *2 pre-packaged crepes, each about 8 inches in diameter*
- *8 strawberries, hulled and sliced*

Directions:
1. Set the oven to heat at 325 degrees F. Grease a baking dish with cooking spray. Mix cream cheese with vanilla plus powdered sugar in a mixer. Spread the cream cheese mixture on each crepe and top it with 2 tablespoons of strawberries.
2. Roll the crepes and place them in the baking dish. Bake them for 10 minutes until golden brown. Garnish as desired. Serve.

Nutrition: Calories 144, Carbohydrates 19g, Protein 4g, Fat 5g, Sodium 113mg

488. Chocolate Cake in A Mug

Preparation: 5 minutes **Cooking: 1 minute** **Servings: 1**

Ingredients:
- *3 tablespoons white whole-wheat flour*
- *2 tablespoons unsweetened cocoa powder*
- *2 teaspoons sugar*
- *1/8 teaspoon baking powder*
- *1 egg white*
- *1/2 teaspoon olive oil*
- *3 tablespoons nonfat or low-fat milk*
- *1/2 teaspoon vanilla extract*
- *Cooking spray*

Directions:
1. Place the flour, cocoa, sugar, and baking powder in a small bowl and whisk until combined. Then add in the egg white, olive oil, milk, and vanilla extract, and mix to combine.
2. Oiled a mug with cooking spray and pour batter into the mug. Microwave on high for 60 seconds or until set. Serve.

Nutrition: Calories 217, Carbohydrates 35g, Protein 11g, Fat 4g, Sodium 139mg

489. Peanut Butter Banana "Ice Cream"

Preparation: 10 minutes **Servings: 4**

Ingredients:
- *2 tablespoons peanut butter*
- *4 bananas, very ripe, peeled, and sliced into 1/2-inch rings*

Directions:
1. On a large baking sheet or plate, spread the banana slices in an even layer. Freeze for 1 to 2 hours. Puree the frozen banana until it forms a smooth and creamy mixture in a food processor or blender, scraping down the bowl as needed.
2. Add the peanut butter, pureeing until just combined. For a soft-serve ice cream consistency, serve immediately. For a harder consistency, place the ice cream in the freezer for a few hours before serving.

Nutrition: Calories 153, Carbohydrates 29g, Protein 3g, Fat 4g, Sodium 106mg

490. Banana-Cashew Cream Mousse

Preparation: 55 minutes   **Servings:** 2
Ingredients:

- *1/2 cup cashews, presoaked*
- *1 tablespoon honey*
- *1 teaspoon vanilla extract*
- *1 cup plain nonfat Greek yogurt*
- *1 large banana, sliced (reserve 4 slices for garnish)*

Directions:

1. Put the cashews in your small bowl, then cover with 1 cup of water. Dip at room temperature for 2 to 3 hours. Drain, rinse and set aside. Place honey, vanilla extract, cashews, and bananas in a blender or food processor.
2. Blend until smooth. Place mixture in a medium bowl. Fold in yogurt, mix well. Cover, then chill for 45 minutes. Portion mousse into 2 serving bowls. Garnish each with 2 banana slices.

Nutrition: Calories 329, Carbohydrates 21g, Protein 16g, Fat 18g, Sodium 166mg

491. Grilled Plums with Vanilla Bean Frozen Yogurt

Preparation: 10 minutes   **Cooking:** 15 minutes   **Servings:** 4
Ingredients:

- *4 large plums, sliced in half and pitted*
- *1 tablespoon olive oil*
- *1 tablespoon honey*
- *1 teaspoon ground cinnamon*
- *2 cups vanilla bean frozen yogurt*

Directions:

1. Preheat the grill to medium heat. Brush the plum halves with olive oil. Grill, flesh-side down, for 4 to 5 minutes, then flip and cook for another 4 to 5 minutes, until just tender.
2. Mix the honey plus cinnamon in a small bowl. Scoop the frozen yogurt into 4 bowls. Place 2 plum halves in each bowl and drizzle each with the cinnamon-honey mixture.

Nutrition: Calories 192, Carbohydrates 13g, Protein 12g, Fat 18g, Sodium 158mg

492. Key Lime Cherry "Nice" Cream

Preparation: 10 minutes   **Cooking:** 15 minutes   **Servings:** 4
Ingredients:

- *4 frozen bananas, peeled*
- *1 cup frozen dark sweet cherries*
- *Zest and juice of 1 lime, divided*
- *1/2 teaspoon vanilla extract*
- *1/4 teaspoon kosher or sea salt*

Directions:

1. Blend the ingredients in a food processor and enjoy a frozen treat. Place the bananas, cherries, lime juice, vanilla extract, and salt in a food processor and purée until smooth, scraping the sides as needed.
2. Transfer the "nice" cream to bowls and top with the lime zest. For leftovers, place the "nice" cream in airtight containers and store them in the freezer for up to 1 month. Let thaw for 30 minutes until it reaches a soft-serve ice cream texture.

Nutrition: Calories 231, Carbohydrates 10g, Protein 12g, Fat 15g, Sodium 107mg

493. Oatmeal Dark Chocolate Chip Peanut Butter Cookies

Preparation: 15 minutes   **Cooking:** 10 minutes   **Servings:** 24
Ingredients:

- *1 and 1/2 cups natural creamy peanut butter*
- *1/2 cup dark brown sugar*
- *2 large eggs*
- *1 cup old-fashioned rolled oats*
- *1 teaspoon baking soda*
- *1/2 teaspoon kosher or sea salt*
- *1/2 cup dark chocolate chips*

Directions:
1. Preheat the oven to 350°F. Line a baking sheet with parchment paper. Whip the peanut butter in the bowl of a stand mixer until very smooth. Continue beating and add the brown sugar, then one egg at a time, until fluffy.
2. Beat in the oats, baking soda, and salt until combined. Fold in the dark chocolate chips. Put the cookie dough on the baking sheet, about 2 inches apart. Bake for 8 to 10 minutes, depending on your preferred level of doneness.

Nutrition: Calories 152, Carbohydrates 28g, Protein 5g, Fat 14g, Sodium 175mg

494. Grapefruit Compote

Preparation: 5 minutes   **Cooking: 8 minutes**   **Servings: 4**

Ingredients:
- *1 cup palm sugar*
- *64 oz. Sugar-free red grapefruit juice*
- *1/2 cup chopped mint*
- *2 peeled and cubed grapefruits*

Directions:
1. Take all ingredients and combine them into an instant pot.
2. Cook on low for 8 minutes, then divide into bowls and serve!

Nutrition: Calories 131, Carbohydrates 12g, Protein 2g, Fat 4g, Sodium 116mg

495. Instant Applesauce

Preparation: 10 minutes   **Cooking: 10 minutes**   **Servings: 8**

Ingredients:
- *3 pounds of apples*
- *1/2 cup water*

Directions:
1. Core and peel the apples and then put them at the bottom of the instant pot and then secure the lid and seal the vent. Let it cook for 10 minutes, then natural pressure release.
2. From there, when it's safe to remove the lid, take the apples and juices and blend this till smooth.
3. Stores these in jars or serve immediately.

Nutrition: Calories 166, Carbohydrates 18g, Protein 4g, Fat 1g, Sodium 56mg

496. Cocoa Banana Dessert Smoothie

Preparation: 5 minutes   **Servings: 2**

Ingredients:
- *2 medium bananas, peeled*
- *2 teaspoons cocoa powder*
- *1/2 big avocado, pitted, peeled, and mashed*
- *3/4 cup almond milk*

Directions:
1. In your blender, combine the bananas with the cocoa, avocado, and milk, pulse well, divide into 2 glasses and serve.

Nutrition: Calories 155, Carbohydrates 16g, Protein 10g, Fat 2g, Sodium 98mg

497. Kiwi Bars

Preparation: 30 minutes   **Servings: 4**

Ingredients:
- *1 cup olive oil*
- *1 and 1/2 bananas, peeled and chopped*
- *1/3 cup coconut sugar*
- *1/4 cup lemon juice*
- *1 teaspoon lemon zest, grated*
- *3 kiwis, peeled and chopped*

Directions:
1. In your food processor, mix bananas with kiwis, almost all the oil, sugar, lemon juice, and lemon zest, and pulse well.

2. Grease a pan with the remaining oil, pour the kiwi mix, spread, keep in the fridge for 30 minutes, slice and serve,

Nutrition: Calories 206, Carbohydrates 20g, Protein 10g, Fat 4g, Sodium 112mg

498. Black Tea Bars

Preparation: 10 minutes   **Cooking: 35 minutes**   **Servings: 12**

Ingredients:

- *6 tablespoons black tea powder*
- *2 cups almond milk*
- *1/2 cup low-fat butter*
- *2 cups coconut sugar*
- *4 eggs*
- *2 teaspoons vanilla extract*
- *1/2 cup olive oil*
- *3 and 1/2 cups whole wheat flour*
- *1 teaspoon baking soda*
- *3 teaspoons baking powder*

Directions:

1. Put the milk in a pot, heat it up over medium heat, add tea, stir, take off the heat and cool down.
2. Add butter, sugar, eggs, vanilla, oil, flour, baking soda, and baking powder, stir well, pour into a square pan, spread, introduce in the oven, bake at 350°F for 35 minutes, cool down, slice, and serve.

Nutrition: Calories 120, Carbohydrates 21g, Protein 9g, Fat 2g, Sodium 105mg

499. Green Pudding

Preparation: 2 hours   **Cooking: 5 minutes**   **Servings: 6**

Ingredients:

- *14 ounces almond milk*
- *2 tablespoons green tea powder*
- *14 ounces coconut cream*
- *3 tablespoons coconut sugar*
- *1 teaspoon gelatin powder*

Directions:

1. Put the milk in a pan, add sugar, gelatin, coconut cream, and green tea powder, stir, bring to a simmer, cook for 5 minutes, divide into cups and keep in the fridge for 2 hours before serving.

Nutrition: Calories 166, Carbohydrates 26g, Protein 13g, Fat 6g, Sodium 156mg

500. Lemony Plum Cake

Preparation: 80 minutes   **Cooking: 40 minutes**   **Servings: 8**

Ingredients:

- *7 ounces whole wheat flour*
- *1 teaspoon baking powder*
- *1-ounce low-fat butter, soft*
- *1 egg, whisked*
- *5 tablespoons coconut sugar*
- *3 ounces warm almond milk*
- *1- and 3/4-pounds plums, pitted and cut into quarters*
- *Zest of 1 lemon, grated*
- *1-ounce almond flakes*

Directions:

1. In a bowl, combine the flour with baking powder, butter, egg, sugar, milk, and lemon zest, stir well, transfer the dough to a lined cake pan, spread plums and almond flakes all over, introduce in the oven and bake at 350°F for 40 minutes.
2. Slice and serve cold.

Nutrition: Calories 197, Carbohydrates 41g, Protein 17g, Fat 9g, Sodium 201mg

501. Lentils Sweet Bars

Preparation: 10 minutes   **Cooking: 25 minutes**   **Servings: 14**

Ingredients:

- *1 cup lentils, cooked, drained, and rinsed*
- *1 teaspoon cinnamon powder*
- *2 cups whole wheat flour*
- *1 teaspoon baking powder*
- *1/2 teaspoon nutmeg, ground*
- *1 cup low-fat butter*

- 1 cup coconut sugar
- 1 egg
- 2 teaspoons almond extract
- 1 cup raisins
- 2 cups coconut, unsweetened and shredded

Directions:
1. Put the lentils in a bowl, mash them well using a fork, add cinnamon, flour, baking powder, nutmeg, butter, sugar, egg, almond extract, raisins, and coconut, stir, spread on a lined baking sheet, introduce in the oven, bake at 350°F for 25 minutes, cut into bars and serve cold.

Nutrition: Calories 214, Carbohydrates 25g, Protein 11g, Fat 12g, Sodium 114mg

502. Lentils and Dates Brownies

Preparation: 10 minutes   **Cooking: 15 minutes**   **Servings: 8**

Ingredients:
- 28 ounces canned lentils, no-salt-added, rinsed and drained
- 12 dates
- 1 tablespoon coconut sugar
- 1 banana, peeled and chopped
- 1/2 teaspoon baking soda
- 4 tablespoons almond butter
- 2 tablespoons cocoa powder

Directions:
1. Put lentils in your food processor, pulse, add dates, sugar, banana, baking soda, almond butter, and cocoa powder, pulse well, pour into a lined pan, spread, bake in the oven at 375°F for 15 minutes, leave the mix aside to cool down a bit, cut into medium pieces and serve.

Nutrition: Calories 198, Carbohydrates 33g, Protein 12g, Fat 16g, Sodium 147mg

503. Rose Lentils Ice Cream

Preparation: 30 minutes   **Cooking: 80 minutes**   **Servings: 4**

Ingredients:
- 1/2 cup red lentils, rinsed
- Juice of 1/2 lemon
- 1 cup coconut sugar
- 1 and 1/2 cups water
- 3 cups almond milk
- Juice of 2 limes
- 2 teaspoons cardamom powder
- 1 teaspoon rose water

Directions:
1. Heat up a pan over medium-high heat with the water, half of the sugar, and lemon juice, stir, bring to a boil, add lentils, stir, reduce heat to medium-low and cook for 1 hour and 20 minutes.
2. Drain lentils, transfer them to a bowl, add coconut milk, the rest of the sugar, lime juice, cardamom, and rose water, whisk everything, transfer to your ice cream machine, process for 30 minutes and serve.

Nutrition: Calories 194, Carbohydrates 21g, Protein 14g, Fat 13g, Sodium 116mg

504. Mandarin Pudding

Preparation: 10 minutes   **Cooking: 30 minutes**   **Servings: 8**

Ingredients:
- 1 mandarin, peeled and sliced
- Juice of 2 mandarins
- 4 ounces low-fat butter, soft
- 2 eggs, whisked
- 3/4 cup coconut sugar + 2 tablespoons
- 3/4 cup whole wheat flour
- 3/4 cup almonds, ground

Directions:
1. Grease a loaf pan with some of the butter, sprinkle 2 tablespoons of sugar on the bottom, and arrange mandarin slices inside.
2. In a bowl, combine the butter with the rest of the sugar, eggs, almonds, flour, and mandarin juice and whisk using a mixer.
3. Spoon mix over mandarin slices, introduce in the oven, bake at 350°F for

4. 30 minutes, divide into bowls, and serve
5. Enjoy!

Nutrition: Calories 133, Carbohydrates 28g, Protein 5g, Fat 4g, Sodium 109mg

505. Cauliflower Cinnamon Pudding

Preparation: 10 minutes　　**Cooking: 20 minutes**　　**Servings: 6**

Ingredients:
- *1 tablespoon coconut oil, melted*
- *7 ounces cauliflower rice*
- *4 ounces water*
- *16 ounces coconut milk*
- *3 ounces coconut sugar*
- *1 egg*
- *1 teaspoon cinnamon powder*
- *1 teaspoon vanilla extract*

Directions:
1. In a pan, combine the oil with the rice, water, milk, sugar, egg, cinnamon and vanilla, whisk well, bring to a simmer, cook for 20 minutes over medium heat, divide into bowls and serve cold.

Nutrition: Calories 202, Carbohydrates 31g, Protein 9g, Fat 6g, Sodium 154mg

506. Pumpkin Pudding

Preparation: 1 hour　　**Servings: 4**

Ingredients:
- *1 and 1/2 cups almond milk*
- *1/2 cup pumpkin puree*
- *2 tablespoons coconut sugar*
- *1/2 teaspoon cinnamon powder*
- *1/4 teaspoon ginger, grated*
- *1/4 cup chia seeds*

Directions:
1. In a bowl, combine the milk with pumpkin, sugar, cinnamon, ginger and chia seeds, toss well, divide into small cups and keep them in the fridge for 1 hour before serving.

Nutrition: Calories 236, Carbohydrates 45g, Protein 12g, Fat 16g, Sodium 100mg

507. Cashew Lemon Fudge

Preparation: 2 hours　　**Servings: 4**

Ingredients:
- *1/3 cup natural cashew butter*
- *1 and 1/2 tablespoons coconut oil, melted*
- *2 tablespoons coconut butter*
- *5 tablespoons lemon juice*
- *1/2 teaspoon lemon zest*
- *1 tablespoons coconut sugar*

Directions:
1. In a bowl, mix cashew butter with coconut butter, oil, lemon juice, lemon zest and sugar and stir well
2. Line a muffin tray with some parchment paper, scoop 1 tablespoon of lemon fudge mix in a lined muffin tray, keep in the fridge for 2 hours and serve

Nutrition: Calories 201, Carbohydrates 29g, Protein 6g, Fat 16g, Sodium 114mg

508. Brown Cake

Preparation: 10 minutes　　**Cooking: 2 hours 30min**　　**Servings: 8**

Ingredients:
- *1 cup flour*
- *1 and 1/2 cup stevia*
- *1/2 cup chocolate almond milk*
- *2 teaspoons baking powder*
- *1 and 1/2 cups hot water*
- *1/4 cup cocoa powder+ 2 tablespoons*
- *2 tablespoons canola oil*
- *1 teaspoon vanilla extract*
- *Cooking spray*

Directions:
1. In a bowl, mix flour with 1/4-cup cocoa, baking powder, almond milk, oil and vanilla extract, whisk well and spread on the bottom of the slow cooker greased with cooking spray.

2. In a separate bowl, mix stevia with the water and the rest of the cocoa, whisk well, spread over the batter, cover, and cook your cake on High for 2 hours and 30 minutes.
3. Leave the cake to cool down, slice and serve.

Nutrition: Calories 150, Carbohydrates 57g, Protein 3g, Fat 8g, Sodium 117mg

509. Delicious Berry Pie

Preparation: 10 minutes   **Cooking: 1 hour**   **Servings: 6**

Ingredients:
- *1/2 cup whole wheat flour*
- *Cooking spray*
- *1/3 cup almond milk*
- *1/4 teaspoon baking powder*
- *1/4 teaspoon stevia*
- *1/4 cup blueberries*
- *1 teaspoon olive oil*
- *1 teaspoon vanilla extract*
- *1/2 teaspoon lemon zest, grated*

Directions:
1. In a bowl, mix flour with baking powder, stevia, blueberries, milk, oil, lemon zest and vanilla extract, whisk, pour into your slow cooker lined with parchment paper and greased with the cooking spray, cover and cook on High for 1 hour.
2. Leave the pie to cool down, slice and serve.

Nutrition: Calories 82, Carbohydrates 10g, Protein 2g, Fat 5g, Sodium 95mg

510. Cinnamon Peach Cobbler

Preparation: 10 minutes   **Cooking: 4 hours**   **Servings: 4**

Ingredients:
- *4 cups peaches, peeled and sliced*
- *Cooking spray*
- *1/4 cup coconut sugar*
- *1 and 1/2 cups whole wheat sweet crackers, crushed*
- *1/2 cup almond milk*
- *1/2 teaspoon cinnamon powder*
- *1/4 cup stevia*
- *1 teaspoon vanilla extract*
- *1/4 teaspoon nutmeg, ground*

Directions:
1. In a bowl, mix peaches with sugar, cinnamon, and stir.
2. In a separate bowl, mix crackers with stevia, nutmeg, almond milk and vanilla extract and stir.
3. Spray your slow cooker with cooking spray, spread peaches on the bottom, and add the crackers mix, spread, cover and cook on Low for 4 hours.
4. Divide into bowls and serve.

Nutrition: Calories 249, Carbohydrates 43g, Protein 4g, Fat 12g, Sodium 179mg

511. Resilient Chocolate Cream

Preparation: 10 minutes   **Cooking: 1hour 30 min**   **Servings: 4**

Ingredients:
- *1 cup dark and unsweetened chocolate, chopped*
- *1/2-pound cherries, pitted and halved*
- *1 teaspoon vanilla extract*
- *1/2 cup coconut cream*
- *3 tablespoons coconut sugar*
- *2 teaspoons gelatin*

Directions:
1. In the slow cooker, combine the chocolate with the cherries and the other ingredients, toss, put the lid on and cook on Low for 1 hour and 30 minutes.
2. Stir the cream well, divide into bowls and serve.

Nutrition: Calories 526, Carbohydrates 47g, Protein 14g, Fat 40g, Sodium 157mg

512. _Vanilla Poached Strawberries_

Preparation: 10 minutes   **Cooking: 3 hours**   **Servings: 10**

Ingredients:

- _4 cups coconut sugar_
- _2 tablespoons lemon juice_
- _2 pounds strawberries_
- _1 cup water_
- _1 teaspoon vanilla extract_
- _1 teaspoon cinnamon powder_

Directions:

1. In your slow cooker, mix strawberries with water, coconut sugar, lemon juice, cinnamon and vanilla, stir, cover, cook on Low for 3 hours, divide into bowls and serve cold.

Nutrition: Calories 169, Carbohydrates 15g, Protein 1g, Fat 1g, Sodium 71mg

21-DAY MEAL PLAN

This meal plan is made to give you less than 2000mg Sodium per day. However, it is important to understand that sometimes hunger may be insidious and the best way to help your body to defeat it, is to add raw, fresh and healthy fruit or vegetables.
Working in this way will give your body good vitamins and energy without extremely increase the amount of sodium consumed during the day. Anyway, it is important to count also sodium contained in fresh fruit and veggie to be able to have a more precise approach to this diet as possible.

DAY	BREAKFAST	FRUIT	LUNCH	SNACK	DINNER
1	Apple Oats (2) **44mg Sodium**	1 medium apple	Shepherd's Pie (69) **89mg Sodium**	Acorn Squash with Apple (364) **246mg Sodium**	Oregano Chicken Thighs (225) **730mg Sodium**
2	Banana Almond Yogurt (6) **65mg Sodium**	¼ cup of dried Apricots	Veggie Sushi (75) **116mg Sodium**	Baby Minted Carrots (366) **51mg Sodium**	Currant Pork Chops (298) **120mg Sodium**
3	Basil and Tomato Baked Eggs (11) **126mg Sodium**	1 medium banana	Spinach Salad with Walnuts and Strawberry (72) **120mg Sodium**	Cilantro Brown Rice (376) **300mg Sodium**	Lemony Parmesan Shrimps (321) **344mg Sodium**
4	Fresh Fruit Smoothie (21) **87mg Sodium**	½ cup peaches	Salmon and Edamame Cakes (70) **206mg Sodium**	Tomatoes Side Salad (377) **67mg Sodium**	Chicken Tortillas (228) **300mg Sodium**
5	Chocolate Berry Dash Smoothie (19) **105mg Sodium**	1 medium orange	Baked Macaroni (67) **99mg Sodium**	Buttermilk Mashed Potatoes (372) **353mg Sodium**	Hoisin Pork (282) **130mg Sodium**
6	Asparagus Omelet Tortilla Wrap (30) **444 mg Sodium**	1 medium Nectarine	Juicy and Peppery Tenderloin (78) **130mg Sodium**	Squash Salsa (378) **201mg Sodium**	Simple One-Pot Mussels (330) **302mg Sodium**
7	Green Smoothie (41)	Sliced Kiwi	Almond Butternut Chicken (80)	Cauliflower Risotto (386)	Ginger Tuna Kabobs (339)

	48mg Sodium		96mg Sodium	112mg Sodium	214mg Sodium
8	Spiced Scramble (44) **30 mg Sodium**	1 medium Pear	Zucchini Zoodles with Chicken (81) **180mg Sodium**	Bell Pepper Mix (389) **76mg Sodium**	Lemon-Dill Tilapia (344) **194mg Sodium**
9	Strawberry Buckwheat Pancakes (45) **79mg Sodium**	½ cup Mango	Spicy Chili Crackers (83) **70mg Sodium**	Carrot Slaw (382) **282mg Sodium**	Honey Spiced Cajun Chicken (230) **158mg Sodium**
10	Spinach and Avocado Smoothie (27) **238mg Sodium**	½ cup Pineapples	Golden Eggplant Fries (84) **120mg Sodium**	Roasted Carrots and Beets (395) **151mg Sodium**	Spiced Beef (280) **316mg Sodium**
11	Blueberry Pancakes (15) **152mg Sodium**	½ cup Melon	Stuffed Eggplant (88) **116mg Sodium**	Lima Bean Dish (391) **255mg Sodium**	Spicy Ginger Seabass (354) **123mg Sodium**
12	Berries Deluxe Oatmeal (12) **115mg Sodium**	1 medium apple	Spinach Mushroom Frittata (92) **124mg Sodium**	Sweet and Savory Brussel Sprouts (406) **255mg Sodium**	The Delish Turkey Wrap (240) **121 mg Sodium**
13	Orange Juice Smoothie (25) **70mg Sodium**	¼ cup of dried Apricots	Lovely Faux Mac and Cheese (79) **150mg Sodium**	Squash Fries (410) **680mg Sodium**	Cheesy Shrimp Mix (360) **112mg Sodium**
14	At-Home Cappuccino (5) **112mg Sodium**	1 medium banana	Chicken, Bamboo and Chestnuts (97) **125mg Sodium**	Vegetable & Polenta Dish (408) **326mg Sodium**	Tender Pork Medallions (276) **338mg Sodium**
15	Apple and Spice Oatmeal (1) **52mg Sodium**	1 medium apple	Rice with Chicken (99) **105mg Sodium**	Caramelized Sweet Potatoes (407) **166mg Sodium**	Pistachio-Crusted Tilapia (349) **348mg Sodium**
16	Banana Steel Oats (8) **48mg Sodium**	¼ cup of dried Apricots	Cod Soup (101) **334mg Sodium**	Soy Sauce Green Beans (392) **290mg Sodium**	Beef Stroganoff (265) **193mg Sodium**

17	Barley Porridge (10) **110mg Sodium**	1 medium banana	Leeks Soup (105) **152mg Sodium**	Apples and Fennel Mix (379) **112mg Sodium**	White Wine Garlic Chicken (248) **381mg Sodium**
18	High-Protein Strawberry Smoothie (24) **141mg Sodium**	½ cup peaches	Fish Stew (107) **151mg Sodium**	Braised Kale (368) **133mg Sodium**	Garlic Pork Meatballs (277) **362mg Sodium**
19	Egg White and Vegetable Omelet (35) **77mg Sodium**	1 medium orange	Salmon and Cabbage Mix (110) **345mg Sodium**	Brown Rice Pilaf (370) **222mg Sodium**	Pork Chili (305) **301mg Sodium**
20	Cheesy Baked Eggs (42) **45mg Sodium**	1 medium Nectarine	Lime Shrimp Kale (112) **250mg Sodium**	Cabbage Slaw (385) **206mg Sodium**	Lemon Chicken Mix (263) **180mg Sodium**
21	Sweet Potatoes and Apples Mix (51) **214mg Sodium**	Sliced Kiwi	Parsley Cod Mix (113) **380mg Sodium**	Black Bean Cakes (367) **156mg Sodium**	Chicken, Tomato and Green Beans (227) **168mg Sodium**
22	Chickpeas Breakfast Salad (52) **196mg Sodium**	1 medium Pear	Brown Rice and Chicken Soup (168) **167mg Sodium**	Broccoli with Garlic and Lemon (369) **153mg Sodium**	White Steamed Fish (336) **90mg Sodium**
23	Apple Oats (2) **44mg Sodium**	1 medium apple	Shepherd's Pie (69) **89mg Sodium**	Acorn Squash with Apple (364) **246mg Sodium**	Oregano Chicken Thighs (225) **730mg Sodium**
24	Banana Almond Yogurt (6) **65mg Sodium**	¼ cup of dried Apricots	Veggie Sushi (75) **116mg Sodium**	Baby Minted Carrots (366) **51mg Sodium**	Currant Pork Chops (298) **120mg Sodium**
25	Basil and Tomato Baked Eggs (11) **126mg Sodium**	1 medium banana	Spinach Salad with Walnuts and Strawberry (72) **120mg Sodium**	Cilantro Brown Rice (376) **300mg Sodium**	Lemony Parmesan Shrimps (321) **344mg Sodium**

26	Fresh Fruit Smoothie (21) **87mg Sodium**	½ cup peaches	Salmon and Edamame Cakes (70) **206mg Sodium**	Tomatoes Side Salad (377) **67mg Sodium**	Chicken Tortillas (228) **300mg Sodium**
27	Chocolate Berry Dash Smoothie (19) **105mg Sodium**	1 medium orange	Baked Macaroni (67) **99mg Sodium**	Buttermilk Mashed Potatoes (372) **353mg Sodium**	Hoisin Pork (282) **130mg Sodium**
28	Asparagus Omelet Tortilla Wrap (30) **444 mg Sodium**	1 medium Nectarine	Juicy and Peppery Tenderloin (78) **130mg Sodium**	Squash Salsa (378) **201mg Sodium**	Simple One-Pot Mussels (330) **302mg Sodium**
29	Green Smoothie (41) **48mg Sodium**	1 Sliced Kiwi	Almond Butternut Chicken (80) **96mg Sodium**	Cauliflower Risotto (386) **112mg Sodium**	Ginger Tuna Kabobs (339) **214mg Sodium**
30	Spiced Scramble (44) **30 mg Sodium**	1 medium Pear	Zucchini Zoodles with Chicken (81) **180mg Sodium**	Bell Pepper Mix (389) **76mg Sodium**	Lemon-Dill Tilapia (344) **194mg Sodium**
31	Strawberry Buckwheat Pancakes (45) **79mg Sodium**	½ cup Mango	Spicy Chili Crackers (83) **70mg Sodium**	Carrot Slaw (382) **282mg Sodium**	Honey Spiced Cajun Chicken (230) **158mg Sodium**
32	Spinach and Avocado Smoothie (27) **238mg Sodium**	½ cup Pineapples	Golden Eggplant Fries (84) **120mg Sodium**	Roasted Carrots and Beets (395) **151mg Sodium**	Spiced Beef (280) **316mg Sodium**
33	Blueberry Pancakes (15) **152mg Sodium**	½ cup Melon	Stuffed Eggplant (88) **116mg Sodium**	Lima Bean Dish (391) **255mg Sodium**	Spicy Ginger Seabass (354) **123mg Sodium**
34	Berries Deluxe Oatmeal (12) **115mg Sodium**	1 medium apple	Spinach Mushroom Frittata (92) **124mg Sodium**	Sweet and Savory Brussel Sprouts (406) **255mg Sodium**	The Delish Turkey Wrap (240) **121 mg Sodium**

35	Orange Juice Smoothie (25) **70mg Sodium**	¼ cup of dried Apricots	Lovely Faux Mac and Cheese (79) **150mg Sodium**	Squash Fries (410) **680mg Sodium**	Cheesy Shrimp Mix (360) **112mg Sodium**
36	At-Home Cappuccino (5) **112mg Sodium**	1 medium banana	Chicken, Bamboo and Chestnuts (97) **125mg Sodium**	Vegetable & Polenta Dish (408) **326mg Sodium**	Tender Pork Medallions (276) **338mg Sodium**
37	Apple and Spice Oatmeal (1) **52mg Sodium**	½ cup peaches	Rice with Chicken (99) **105mg Sodium**	Caramelized Sweet Potatoes (407) **166mg Sodium**	Pistachio-Crusted Tilapia (349) **348mg Sodium**
38	Banana Steel Oats (8) **48mg Sodium**	1 medium orange	Cod Soup (101) **334mg Sodium**	Soy Sauce Green Beans (392) **290mg Sodium**	Beef Stroganoff (265) **193mg Sodium**
39	Barley Porridge (10) **110mg Sodium**	1 medium Nectarine	Leeks Soup (105) **152mg Sodium**	Apples and Fennel Mix (379) **112mg Sodium**	White Wine Garlic Chicken (248) **381mg Sodium**
40	High-Protein Strawberry Smoothie (24) **141mg Sodium**	Sliced Kiwi	Fish Stew (107) **151mg Sodium**	Braised Kale (368) **133mg Sodium**	Garlic Pork Meatballs (277) **362mg Sodium**
41	Egg White and Vegetable Omelet (35) **77mg Sodium**	1 medium Pear	Salmon and Cabbage Mix (110) **345mg Sodium**	Brown Rice Pilaf (370) **222mg Sodium**	Pork Chili (305) **301mg Sodium**
42	Cheesy Baked Eggs (42) **45mg Sodium**	½ cup Mango	Lime Shrimp Kale (112) **250mg Sodium**	Cabbage Slaw (385) **206mg Sodium**	Lemon Chicken Mix (263) **180mg Sodium**
43	Sweet Potatoes and Apples Mix (51) **214mg Sodium**	½ cup Pineapples	Parsley Cod Mix (113) **380mg Sodium**	Black Bean Cakes (367) **156mg Sodium**	Chicken, Tomato and Green Beans (227) **168mg Sodium**

44	Basil and Tomato Baked Eggs (11) **126mg Sodium**	1 medium banana	Spinach Salad with Walnuts and Strawberry (72) **120mg Sodium**	Cilantro Brown Rice (376) **300mg Sodium**	Lemony Parmesan Shrimps (321) **344mg Sodium**
45	Fresh Fruit Smoothie (21) **87mg Sodium**	½ cup peaches	Salmon and Edamame Cakes (70) **206mg Sodium**	Tomatoes Side Salad (377) **67mg Sodium**	Chicken Tortillas (228) **300mg Sodium**
46	Chocolate Berry Dash Smoothie (19) **105mg Sodium**	1 medium orange	Baked Macaroni (67) **99mg Sodium**	Buttermilk Mashed Potatoes (372) **353mg Sodium**	Hoisin Pork (282) **130mg Sodium**
47	Asparagus Omelet Tortilla Wrap (30) **444 mg Sodium**	1 medium Nectarine	Juicy and Peppery Tenderloin (78) **130mg Sodium**	Squash Salsa (378) **201mg Sodium**	Simple One-Pot Mussels (330) **302mg Sodium**
48	Green Smoothie (41) **48mg Sodium**	Sliced Kiwi	Almond Butternut Chicken (80) **96mg Sodium**	Cauliflower Risotto (386) **112mg Sodium**	Ginger Tuna Kabobs (339) **214mg Sodium**
49	Spiced Scramble (44) **30 mg Sodium**	1 medium Pear	Zucchini Zoodles with Chicken (81) **180mg Sodium**	Bell Pepper Mix (389) **76mg Sodium**	Lemon-Dill Tilapia (344) **194mg Sodium**

CONCLUSION

The Dash Diet is a weight-loss and blood-pressure control program for everyone. This cookbook contains many helpful hints and simple recipes to help you better understand the Diet and make good food choices.

This cookbook can help you make a well-made, delicious dinner even if you aren't following the Diet. Starting with a good quality diet is the first thing to have a great life change.

The Dash Diet Cookbook will have you hacking away at your cutlery in no time, allowing you to finally become a healthy person! It's all about staying healthy and rediscovering how to love your food once more. We've come to the conclusion that this diet is a fantastic approach to lose weight and eat a healthy, balanced diet. Our editors and staff are hard at work on another terrific Cookbook, which will be released in December. The Diet Cookbook is a collection of easy-to-follow recipes that are also delicious. There are many various cooking methods represented, so you can find something that suits you. This Cookbook is ideal for anyone looking to improve their diet and feel better while saving money and time.

The Cookbook is here to assist you if you're ready to get started. This cookbook has something for everyone, from oatmeal and French toast for breakfast to zucchini noodles and ranch dressing for dinner. With the Dash Diet Cookbook, you can feel good about what you eat!

will appreciate the information in this guide if you have been following the diet for any length of time. To guarantee that you succeed on a diet, make use of the materials provided in this handbook.

Some people appear to be concerned by the lack of a portion size indicated in the diet. While the plan does not specify any food requirements, it does instruct you on how to prepare nutritious meals and snacks using the ingredients given in the recipes. Anyone with the necessary supplies may make a healthy and delicious supper after learning how to prepare Dash dishes. The Dash Diet Cookbook shows you how to plan ahead of time, so you don't have to worry about dinner preparation when you get home from work.

The majority of food selections in the normal American diet are unhealthy. Therefore, you might be at risk for lifestyle illnesses. Consider adopting the DASH diet if you're concerned about your health. The DASH diet is your ticket to better health and a healthier lifestyle.